More Praise for *Building the Future*

"City building may be the most important challenge of the 21st century, and it is a challenge that needs entrepreneurial brilliance as much as engineering. Edmondson and Reynolds provide an engaging glimpse at innovators—such as Living PlanIT and Quintain—who are changing our urban world. This thoughtful book is full of managerial wisdom and urban insight."

—**Edward Glaeser, Glimp Professor of Economics, Harvard University, and author of *Triumph of the City***

"*Building the Future* is a remarkable book. It introduces readers to the cross-industry teaming that's needed to build the cities of tomorrow and offers an urgent reminder that technology alone can't solve global problems—cooperation, ingenuity, and empathy are needed to innovate on a grand stage. A must-read for anyone interested in the future of business or the future of the planet."

—**Douglas Stone, Lecturer on Law, Harvard Law School, and coauthor of *Difficult Conversations* and *Thanks for the Feedback***

"Every start-up wants to change the world and disrupt an industry or two along the way. But what happens when you don't? Edmondson and Reynolds glean important lessons from the story of one such company grappling with the biggest challenge of our time: building more sustainable cities. Their inside account of setbacks and brushes with failure has more to teach us than any just-so stories of success."

—**Greg Lindsay, coauthor of *Aerotropolis* and Senior Fellow, New Cities Foundation**

"What we witness in this thoughtful and compelling study is one of the heroic battles that are being enacted across the globe as visionary, fleet-footed technology start-ups collide with big business and the politics of government. As the urbanization of the planet gathers pace and governments grapple with the fateful consequences, can technology support a better future for our cities? *Building the Future* follows a small start-up business that believes it can and examines the leadership demands of ambition on this scale."

—**Andrew Comer, Partner and Director of the Cities Group, BuroHappold Engineering**

"Get ready. What you are about to read is unlike anything you've read before on innovation, teams, the built environment, or even leadership. Edmondson and Reynolds—a world-class academic and journalist—have joined forces to explore, document, and understand how complex innovation actually unfolds and the leadership required for its success. Based on multiyear observations of an entrepreneurial effort to build a smart, green city, *Building the Future* brings the challenges of the future into the present so we can see what it will take to create a world that works for all of us."

—**Diana McLain Smith, author of *The Elephant in the Room***

Building the
FUTURE

Other Books by Amy C. Edmondson:

A Fuller Explanation: The Synergetic Geometry of R. Buckminster Fuller

Teaming: How Organizations Learn, Innovate, and Compete in the Knowledge Economy

Teaming to Innovate

Building the
FUTURE

Big Teaming for

Audacious Innovation

Amy C. Edmondson

Susan Salter Reynolds

BK

Berrett–Koehler Publishers, Inc.
a BK Business book

Berrett-Koehler Publishers, Inc.
1333 Broadway, Suite 1000, Oakland, CA 94612-1921
Tel: (510) 817-2277   Fax: (510) 817-2278   www.bkconnection.com

Ordering Information

Quantity sales. Special discounts are available on quantity purchases by corporations, associations, and others. For details, contact the "Special Sales Department" at the Berrett-Koehler address above.

Individual sales. Berrett-Koehler publications are available through most bookstores. They can also be ordered directly from Berrett-Koehler:

Tel: (800) 929-2929; Fax: (802) 864-7626; www.bkconnection.com.

Orders for college textbook/course adoption use. Please contact Berrett-Koehler:

Tel: (800) 929-2929; Fax: (802) 864-7626.

Orders by U.S. trade bookstores and wholesalers. Please contact Ingram Publisher Services, Tel: (800) 509-4887; Fax: (800) 838-1149; E-mail: customer.service@ ingrampublisherservices.com; or visit www.ingrampublisherservices.com/Ordering for details about electronic ordering.

Berrett-Koehler and the BK logo are registered trademarks of Berrett-Koehler Publishers, Inc.

Printed in the United States of America

Berrett-Koehler books are printed on long-lasting acid-free paper. When it is available, we choose paper that has been manufactured by environmentally responsible processes. These may include using trees grown in sustainable forests, incorporating recycled paper, minimizing chlorine in bleaching, or recycling the energy produced at the paper mill.

Library of Congress Cataloging-in-Publication Data
Names: Edmondson, Amy C., author.
Title: Building the future : big teaming for audacious innovation / Amy C. Edmondson, Susan Salter Reynolds.
Description: First Edition. | Oakland : Berrett-Koehler Publishers, 2016. | Includes bibliographical references and index.
Identifiers: LCCN 2015048077 | ISBN 9781626564190 (hardcover)
Subjects: LCSH: Diversity in the workplace. | Teams in the workplace. | Organizational learning. | Industries—Technological innovations. | Urban renewal.
Classification: LCC HD66 .E326 2016 | DDC 658.4/022—dc23
LC record available at http://lccn.loc.gov/2015048077

20   19   18   17   16   10   9   8   7   6   5   4   3   2   1

Cover design by Kirk DouPonce, DogEared Design. Cover illustration by iStock/Hakkiarslan. Interior design and composition by Gary Palmatier, Ideas to Images. Elizabeth von Radics, copyeditor; Mike Mollett, proofreader; Rachel Rice, indexer.

To future-builders everywhere

Contents

Preface

CURIOUS ABOUT INNOVATION IN THE BUILT ENVIRONMENT, WE JUMPED at the chance to study a startup with the audacious goal of transforming the urban landscape with technology. Wherever you work, the demand for innovation is likely intense. After all, developing great new products that delight customers is a surefire way to win in a competitive marketplace. But this book tackles a different kind of innovation challenge—the kind that involves introducing not a new product but an entire new system.

Consider two history-shaping innovations found in the kitchen of most modern households. One, the refrigerator, transformed how we eat by enabling the preservation of perishable foods for days and even weeks. The other, the telephone, a smaller object with far greater physical reach, puts us in instant contact with distant friends and colleagues. Today both are taken-for-granted household objects.

A crucial difference between these familiar innovations is that one is a stand-alone product and the other functions as part of a complex system. That difference motivates this book. The refrigerator can be purchased, delivered, and used—like hundreds of other products we might find in the home. The telephone, in contrast, does little on its own. To have practical use, an entire system of components, wires, poles, regulations, services, and customers had to be developed around it, involving players from multiple industry sectors. Putting Alexander Graham Bell's 1876 patent for a device to transmit the human voice through an electric current into world-changing use required, in short, the cooperative action of technologists, service personnel, government regulators, real estate owners, designers, builders, electricians, lumber companies, operators, and more. When the first telephone exchange—with 21 subscribers—was built in 1877 in New

Haven, Connecticut, a few of these players had come together to present a first, small-scale demonstration of a telecommunications system.

It would be many years before thousands of people participated in the telecommunications system, even more years (and more technological innovation) before the first transcontinental call in 1915, and another decade still before the first transatlantic call in 1926. Although continued innovation in telecommunications has occurred in every decade since, the massive world-changing innovation lay in the creation of that first telephone exchange system. Interestingly, that innovation was inspired by a lecture given by Bell but was not created by him. Its lead creator, George Coy, not a household name like the famous Bell, nonetheless played an essential a role in building the future of telecommunications.[1]

Just as a telecommunications system could not be developed by a single individual or a single product development team, or even by a single company, the innovation journey we highlight in this book also involves players from multiple industries. And as we argue in this book, introducing system innovations, no matter how audacious, starts small, with a pilot of some kind from which people can learn—the equivalent of that New Haven exchange.

Because it is hard for most of us to imagine a world before telephony, we rarely step back to consider *What does it take for determined visionaries to mobilize people and technologies to build the future?* That is the question we tackle in this book. Certain kinds of audacious, world-changing innovations—like smart, green, livable, human-scale cities—are difficult to bring into being because there are simply too many things that have to change in a coordinated manner. These are the very real challenges of building the future, of bringing desired new and complex possibilities into existence, on purpose. They are considerable and at times overwhelming to contemplate, but they *are* surmountable, as human history has shown.

To bring to life the human story that underlies multisector collaboration and future-building, we decided to take a deep dive into a single case study of audacious innovation.[2] We followed the journey of a smart-city startup and found that it offered a fascinating and intimate glimpse of the people—their ideas and their interactions—behind audacious innovation.

One of us (Amy) is a management professor and expert in leadership, teaming, and innovation; the other (Susan) is a seasoned journalist who has written countless pieces in the popular press that bring engaging human stories to a wide audience. We hope you will find that the combination of our backgrounds brings timely leadership lessons to life in a new and compelling way.

As is true for all startups, the odds were stacked against the young company you'll get to know in the pages ahead. Most startups fail—90 percent, according to *Fortune* magazine[3]—yet most entrepreneurs are confident that *their* new enterprises will defy the odds. The inherently overconfident (some might say delusional) nature of the entrepreneur is part of the phenomenon we encounter when we study future-building. But most books about startups look back through hindsight-tinted glasses to describe the fortuitous beginnings of iconic companies like Apple or Google. Instead we took the risky path of following a startup in real time, from its initial coalescing around a big vision through its next few years. Without knowing the ultimate fate of the company, much can be learned about building the future from studying its journey. We are grateful for the privileged access the founders gave us, and of course we agreed not to disclose information they wished to keep confidential. At times that agreement limits our narrative, but it does not hamper the development of broadly applicable leadership lessons from our research.

The context we chose for studying audacious innovation is the smart-city industry. This new and fast-growing domain is focused on transforming the potential of cities to be green and livable by integrating the latest information technologies into the urban built environment. Few arenas offer more potential to transform the future—nor more hurdles to doing so.

One hurdle in particular emerged early in our research and became the central thread throughout this book: the need for what we now call *Big Teaming* to design and deliver transformational change in the built environment. Big Teaming takes cross-disciplinary teamwork to the next level, to a larger stage than prior books on this topic. We show why cross-sector teaming is so hard, and we offer research-based ideas for how to do it well in the pursuit of audacious innovation. In so doing we hope that this book contributes a small piece of a complex, adaptive blueprint for building the future.

Amy C. Edmondson and Susan Salter Reynolds
October 2015

PROLOGUE

A Citizen of the World

He ALMOST MISSED CLASS.

Steve Lewis arrived on the Harvard campus on a clear, cold February morning in 2010, minutes before the start of class, just slightly out of breath. Second-year business school students were already in their seats—talking, opening laptops, reviewing their notes—as Lewis came in hurriedly and sat down to observe. The class would be discussing a brand-new case study written about his young company, a startup with the lofty goal of building a state-of-the-art smart city in Portugal.

Toward the end of the class, Lewis took his place in front of the room with a noticeable lack of notes, papers, briefcase, or burden of any kind. He placed his iPhone next to the water glass and began to tell his story—the story of founding a company called Living PlanIT.

It had been an ordinary week for Lewis—five countries in two days— that included meetings with government officials and business executives, panels, interviews, and keynote speeches, followed by a quick hop to the United States to give several talks, including at Harvard Business School. Lewis had been giving lectures for years, especially when he was a senior executive at Microsoft, so why was he out of breath?

"I call myself a 'world citizen,'" he says with a chuckle, "which means I don't always carry the correct papers." Lewis, actually a citizen of the United Kingdom, was on his way through immigration at New York's JFK Airport when he was told he didn't have the correct visa. Some years earlier he had applied to renew his green card, but he missed the deadline for reapplication. By the time a judge issued a summary deportation notice, Lewis had left the country, so immigration officials on the ground in February

2010 would not let him enter the United States. They drove him around the perimeter of the airport to a holding room. Asked if he had any relatives in the country, Lewis supplied two names. Immigration officials first called his son, Christian Lewis, who thought the call was a prank. "I have no idea who he is," Christian retorted and hung up. They then called his stepdaughter, a US Marine, but she was on a base in San Diego and could not be reached. At that point, Lewis admits, "it was looking a bit dodgy."

Here's where his story takes a bizarre turn—and reveals much about the founder of the future-building company at the center of this book. Lewis had been held for so long that the airport office was closing. As a detainee, he now had certain rights: a shower, some food, and a rest at a not-so-nearby detention center in New Jersey. Apologetic staff shackled Lewis in handcuffs and leg braces and put him in the back of a van with his luggage, which fortunately held a cell phone. Once in the van, Lewis was able to send texts to friends and thereby contact an acquaintance at the US State Department, who told him they would send a lawyer.

At the detention center, Lewis was strip-searched, and his personal possessions were confiscated. The young official checking him in admitted he had been on the job for only two weeks and did not really know how to enter Lewis's information in the computer or print out the necessary labels for his possessions. "So I had to check myself in," Lewis recalls with irony.

He was put in a large shared cell with long-term immigration detainees, a coin-operated phone box, and a toilet in full view. Some of the guys had been in there for months. Fights broke out over toothbrushes. "They were scary guys," he says. "And there I was, an ex-executive from Microsoft. But I grew up in a rough neighborhood," Lewis explains. "I knew how to handle them."

After many hours a guard announced that they would be deporting Lewis from the United States. Lewis was escorted back to the terminal by four policemen. Then one of the immigration officials who had been helpful the day before came in on his day off to deliver good news: Lewis's papers had come through from the State Department. To bypass immigration regulations, Lewis was admitted to the United States on humanitarian grounds. (His passport, Lewis notes, stills bears that stamp on the last page: Admitted for Humanitarian Reasons.) "It was," he says, "my 36 hours in hell."

Did Lewis lose his temper at any point during this humiliating process? Apparently not. In telling the story, he seems to not even consider outrage as a response. His stance is more bemused than shocked. Lewis does not seem to remember the bad guys from the episode—those who were rude or insensitive—but he remembers the ones who were polite and kind.

What really gets him, he explains, is the galling inefficiency of the bureaucracies involved—the poor communication, the splintered data, the siloed agencies (not unlike most modern cities). What drives Lewis forward, we began to realize, is the opportunity to use technology to solve problems that originate between silos. He wants to fix the system. Sometimes, in his desire to problem-solve into the future, he forgets the little things that populate the present—like visas.

Lewis's talk about Living PlanIT in the Harvard Business School class ended, abruptly, like a car running out of gas midjourney. Students stopped typing or scribbling but remained hovered over keyboards and notebooks, unsure that he had, in fact, come to an end. Some looked puzzled; others, eager or amazed; still others, downright skeptical. Was the company viable? What was it? A tech startup? A real estate play? An office park? Was he really going to build a brand-new green city from scratch? The classroom was silent for a moment, but only a moment.

Then the hands shot up in the air.

CHAPTER 1

Building the Future

There is nothing more difficult to take in hand, more perilous to conduct, or more uncertain in its success, than to take the lead in the introduction of a new order of things.

—**Machiavelli**, *The Prince*

BUILDING THE FUTURE. TAKE A DEEP BREATH AND CONSIDER WHAT THIS means, living in the twenty-first century. It doesn't mean the next iPhone, the next electric car, or even the first molecular teletransporter (à la *Star Trek*). These could all certainly qualify as life-changing, history-shaping innovations, but building the future does not mean building isolated products. The lone innovator bathed in cathode-ray green lights in his garage late at night designing the next amazing thing is not the protagonist of our story.

We are interested instead in innovations that constitute a new order of things—interacting elements that must work together and simply aren't worth much alone. When we talk about building the future, we're talking about bringing new complex systems into being. This book explains why this is so hard and what leaders can do to make it easier.

The very phrase *building the future* has two critical parts, the verb and the noun. *Building* captures the process of constructing something, of putting pieces together into a new integrated whole. The noun, the *future,* is the target. Envisioning the future is only the first step toward building it. What's the next step? Read on.

You could say that with every step each of us takes, we are, in fact, building the future: each time we use resources carefully, each time we remember to turn out the lights, each time we choose a bicycle over a car. While it is certainly true that the future is always unfolding—arriving whether we actively pursue it or not—some pioneers glimpse techno-logical or societal possibilities before the rest of us do, and they set out to make them happen. Building the future is about bringing a desired future into being *on purpose.*

Today we have the opportunity to build the future consciously and proactively. Building the future is by its nature audacious innovation. Inherently creative, building a desired future is fueled by vision and real-ized through experimentation. Our research focused on the built envi-ronment as a particularly timely and vital arena for future-building. We studied people from organizations in several industries that contribute to innovation in the built environment, and we learned that it requires intense collaboration and a particular kind of leadership. As we will see, future-building takes time—and failure is a necessary part of the journey.

A New Order of Things

Future-building is hard. When success requires introducing what Machiavelli, in the sixteenth century, called "a new order of things," success is likely to be elusive. This is because bringing together diverse elements (technologies, plans, people, or organizations) to create a functioning whole presents countless ways for integration to break down. Teaming across disciplinary and industry boundaries is needed to respond to the spectacular challenges the world faces today, but it requires a new way of working, a new way of thinking, and a new way of being.

Future-building challenges are not limited to the built environment. The 2014 Ebola outbreak in West Africa was a terrifying example of a specific need for a novel systemic response, enacted by diverse organiza-tions working together around the world. A response had to be designed on the fly under enormous pressure, while more and more people inside and outside Africa were diagnosed with the disease. Government, health-care, university, and nonprofit organizations with varying priorities were forced to work together. President Barack Obama appointed Ron Klain as (the unfortunately titled) "Ebola czar" to help coordinate the diverse inputs of all of these groups. The idea, as reported (and hotly contested) at the time, was that the situation called for someone who could set priorities and get government agencies and private-sector organizations of all kinds to work together to innovate. Its success was also contested.

The 2010 rescue of 33 Chilean miners trapped beneath 2,000 feet of rock harder than granite was another such situation. Against all odds a magnificently coordinated and highly innovative rescue operation unfolded—knitting together the ideas and efforts of experts from multiple countries, industries, and sectors to produce a novel process and a remarkable outcome.[1] The leadership practices that allowed this success are remarkably similar to those we develop in this book.

In these examples crisis-motivated innovation required cross-boundary collaboration. Other cases of future-building involve pioneers setting the forces of complex innovation in motion. Consider the emergence of the telecommunications system a century ago. It starts, of course, with the invention of a telephone, and before that its subcomponents—the mechanical acoustic devices for transmitting speech and music over a distance greater than that of normal human interaction. But to function in its intended way, the telephone required a complex infrastructure of components—wires, poles, monitors, switches, protocols, regulations, and more, extending over vast geographies—to be developed around it.

Sometimes future-building requires little in the way of technological innovation—just system building. When Fred Smith, CEO of FedEx, wrote a college term paper on the idea of an overnight-delivery service, he could not possibly have imagined—or single-handedly developed—all the moving parts that would be required to turn that vision into the $27 billion company it is today. What he did imagine was "a completely different logistics system."[2]

Working as a charter pilot, Smith could see the extent to which air travel was used to fly packages around, primarily for big companies like IBM and Xerox. The logistics, as reported by fellow pilots, were a nightmare. Airfreight at the time, Smith noticed, relied on passenger planes. What was needed was a whole new infrastructure that would take the logistical burden off passenger airlines and centralize it. He envisioned a nationwide clearinghouse and an integrated system of cars, trucks, and planes. His system required sophisticated information technology (IT) to allow unprecedented precision and a new way of tracking items as they moved around the world. For the service to function as intended, the tracking system would need handheld computers and machine-readable, sequentially numbered bar codes. It required obtaining new radio frequencies and designing new equipment for trucks. Government deregulation of the airlines in 1978 was the final piece of the puzzle, clearing FedEx for takeoff. Smith, leading the innovation journey that put all of these parts together, thus created a whole new order of things.

What It Takes to Build the Future

Future-building is creative and iterative but not haphazard. It is interdisciplinary, and it takes leadership to bring it about. While few would advocate for rigid organizational hierarchies anymore, understanding and practicing the new forms of leadership that enable complex, team-based, whole-system innovation is—we'll say it again and again—challenging. In this book we describe two basic requirements that entrepreneurs and leaders of mature organizations alike must embrace to build a sustainable future.

The first is a new kind of collaboration that spans more (and more-diverse) groups than ever before. We call this *Big Teaming*. The second— essential to enabling the first—is leadership that blends big vision and small action to pursue *audacious innovation*. Big vision inspires, calling attention to what might be possible. But achieving big vision is never straightforward. It is essential to empower people to experiment with small action that might, with luck and skill, help bring the vision about. In the case study of a smart-city startup that runs throughout this book, the challenge of spanning industry boundaries looms large, while experimenting through small action proves both elusive and essential.

Big Teaming

Many organizations have shifted to a new way of working that makes teaming and learning part of the job.[3] Prior work on teaming includes examples of people in crisis situations working together to surmount seemingly impossible, but finite, challenges. In such situations people often team up across geographical, social, and cultural boundaries to get the job done. Building the future takes teaming to the next level. The same fundamental principles apply, but the distances between players are greater than when we encourage cross-functional teamwork within a company. The boundaries are more difficult to cross. Goals are more often at odds. And clashing professional cultures are likely to inhibit meaningful communication.

In this book we highlight both the challenges and the opportunities that lie in teaming across the cultural divides that separate people in different industries. To do this we first must explore how industry cultures differ, taking a deep dive, chapter by chapter, into five domains—information technology (chapter 3), real estate development (chapter 4), city government (chapter 5), architecture and construction (chapter 6), and the modern corporation (chapter 7). As we do so, we follow the ups and downs of a startup's efforts to span these industry boundaries. In each chapter we supplement our field research with published sources to paint fuller portraits of the industry than our case study could provide on its own. We then take a look, in chapter 8, at why it's difficult to collaborate across these worlds and what leaders can do to facilitate it. Chapter 9 updates our case study and concludes with ideas about how leaders can integrate big vision with small smart action.

Leading Audacious Innovation

Future-building leadership starts with imagination that fuels vision: ambitious, bold, creative vision informed by deep expertise in a relevant field and yet paradoxically open enough to adapt when needed. Such vision thus has three essential components; it's bold, it's meaningful, and it's open to adaptation as more is learned.

Big vision must be followed—and dynamically realized—by *small action:* small, tentative action that is deliberately framed as an experiment and that builds knowledge quickly. This iterative process of action, feedback, and learning expects and tolerates failure on the way to success. It takes a particular leadership mind-set to cope with the contradictory demands of envisioning and advocating audacious new possibilities while engaging in small imperfect action, not to mention the contradictory demands of believing in one's own vision while enrolling a host of other experts to help transform that vision.

Balancing the competing goals of influencing and innovating is thus a new and essential leadership practice for future-building. When you're doing the new-new thing, it is easy to prioritize activities that build credibility in the external world, such as giving talks and building relationships with prestigious players in varied sectors.[4] This can mean that the actual work of the organization—the day-to-day work of innovating and developing products and people—takes a backseat to selling a story and building a reputation. The charisma and excitement that swirl around a pioneer's vision are critical for drawing people into the orbit, building a solid team, generating funds, and building the ecosystem of players it takes to realize that vision. But a leader's focus must encompass the outside and the inside, influencing (vision) *and* innovating (action). Through our multicultural journey across the various industries with which we came into close contact during our study, we offer some ideas about how to manage this tension.[5]

In sum this book proposes that *building the future* requires three crucial, ongoing activities: *building a shared vision that evolves as more is learned, building meaningful cross-sector relationships,* and *building an iterative collaborative process.* The diagram *Leading Audacious Innovation through Big Teaming* depicts these activities. To explain why they matter—and how to bring them about—we use a case study that highlights both the opportunities and the challenges of Big Teaming for audacious innovation.

A Case Study of Future-Building

This book is our way of wrapping our minds around these enormous challenges by studying people who, one brick, one dollar, one sensor at a time, sit in meetings and in front of computer screens and occasionally get out to see a physical landscape in their efforts to create a new order of things. In fact, so much is new about these efforts that it can be hard for observers (and even for those involved) to know what to make of the promises, the expectations, and the progress along the way.

Our ideas are conveyed with the help of a longitudinal case study—a human story that reveals certain truths about managing complex innovations—supplemented by archival research on smart-city projects carried

Leading Audacious Innovation through Big Teaming

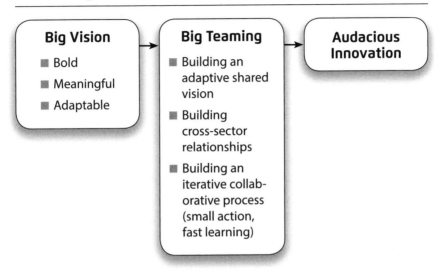

Big Vision
- Bold
- Meaningful
- Adaptable

Big Teaming
- Building an adaptive shared vision
- Building cross-sector relationships
- Building an iterative collab-orative process (small action, fast learning)

Audacious Innovation

out by other organizations and by interviews with leading thinkers and practitioners in related fields. These additional sources help us set the context that gave rise to the founding of the small company at the center of our research: Living PlanIT. We watched the company grow and change, stumble and get back up, and reinvent itself. Sometimes we thought we could see the future of Living PlanIT alongside the Apples and Googles and Facebooks of the world. Other times we wondered whether Living PlanIT could navigate the seemingly insurmountable challenges ahead.

Living PlanIT was pursuing a bold vision. When we encountered the company, its scope—building a brand-new sustainable high-tech city from scratch to lead the way to building more such cities around the world—was breathtaking. The company struggled with doing anything small, anything partway. We learned of the team's conviction that being big was integral to their strategy. It seemed, sometimes, that it had to be all or nothing. But what might the company do to test its vision, develop its strategies, and make steady progress toward the ultimate prize of building the future?

Whatever the long-term fate of Living PlanIT, we could not have chosen a better opportunity to learn what building the future truly involves. The company gave us a rare opportunity to glimpse a group of creative, hardworking people pursuing a dream. Intrigued by the promise of smart-city innovation, at times we suspended disbelief. To set the stage for our research, we start with some background on the urban built environment, drawing from the chorus of voices that has considered its challenges and opportunities.

The Built Environment

To study how pioneers introduce a new order of things, we chose to focus on the built environment because of the opportunity it affords for audacious innovation. Long a laggard in the innovation landscape, the built environment today is suddenly again a target for change. Just as Renaissance visionaries like Leonardo da Vinci and Christopher Wren combined applied mathematics and philosophy to introduce revolutionary advances that transformed the size, span, and strength of buildings, modern-day visionaries are recognizing the potential to transform what we build—and how we build it—by leveraging advances in materials and information technologies. Buildings and cities, they argue, can be smarter, greener, more efficient, and more livable. And many have begun to believe that there are business opportunities to be exploited in making them that way. Today, as we explain in chapter 2, these activities are called the *smart-city industry*.

The *built environment* refers to "the human-made surroundings that provide the setting for human activity, ranging in scale from buildings and parks or green space to neighborhoods and cities that can often include their supporting infrastructure, such as water supply or energy networks."[6] Public health experts define the built environment as "the human-made space in which people live, work, and recreate on a day-to-day basis." The term encompasses places and spaces created or modified by people, including buildings, parks, and transportation systems. In short the built environment comprises the complex systems that we inhabit and depend on in our daily lives.

Cities—collections of buildings, streets, parks, airports, offices, stores, transportation systems, and more—have become the target of future-building innovation across a surprising range of disciplines. Some innovations relate to retrofitting existing cities with smart technologies; others involve creating new cities from scratch.

What is a city? The dividing lines between cities, towns, and non-cities are difficult to draw. Wikipedia defines a city as a relatively large and permanent settlement. But how large? In Shanghai recently, a graduate student told us she was from a small town. Probing further, we learned that her hometown's population was 400,000—a large city in New England. For now we'll have to be content with understanding cities as locations, people, economic activity, and municipal entities combined. Cities today have become critical hotspots for innovation. How cities are built and managed matters far more than ever for the future of humanity.

But why hasn't the innovation happened faster?

This book shows that innovation in the built environment can be stymied by a lack of common language among the essential players. Industry expertise, jargon, values, time frames, and more form silos that make it hard to collaborate. People in real estate have their business models and priorities; people in construction have certain ways of planning and completing projects; mayors and others in city government have their priorities and time lines; and techies, long portrayed as social mavericks, have their expectations and frustrations, too.

Cities have always evolved—but gradually. The earliest cities were powered by human decisions and actions, with human and animal power the only source of energy. People transported water, grew food, built structures, and removed waste products as best they could with the help of their livestock. Later cities developed extensive mechanized supply systems—waterworks, sewer systems, power supplies, streetlights—that took over and managed critical urban inputs and outputs centrally, each with its own specialized workforce. Today more and more essential functions are digital in nature[7]—smart.

Smart cities, as defined by author Anthony Townsend, are "places where information technology is combined with infrastructure, architecture, everyday objects, and even our bodies to address social, economic, and environmental problems."[8] With novelty comes a proliferation of terms, and this arena is no exception.[9] Whether cities are problems or solutions is a matter of some debate.

Cities as Problems, Cities as Solutions

Historically, cities have gotten a bad rap. Cities are resource hogs. Higher average living standards in cities compared with rural areas translate into greater energy use and higher per capita carbon emissions. Cities are responsible for roughly 70 percent of all greenhouse gas emissions but house only half of the population.[10] The city as physical or moral cesspool is an engrained postindustrial image. Here urbanization and squalor go hand in hand. In part this notion is a true depiction of rapid, unplanned growth. Vast population increases at the edges of so-called megacities give rise to health hazards, desperate places, shantytowns replete with environmental risks, and crime, often in the shadow of affluent suburbs. The *favelas* of Brazil provide vivid examples.

As many have noted, global urbanization brings a host of challenges. The UN *World Economic and Social Survey 2013: Sustainable Development Challenges* report calls for a "transformation of the energy system," particularly in cities:

> To achieve this energy transformation together with food and nutrition security, sustainability of cities, and other development goals after 2015, large-scale investments will be needed. Such investments will require sufficient levels of supply of long-term financing, and they will have to be carried out both by public actors through increased public expenditure and by the private sector, which will depend critically on creating the right incentives for investments in sustainable development.[11]

A recent study comparing data from 100 cities in 33 nations showed that cities without well-developed public transportation had dramatically higher levels of greenhouse gas emissions.[12] Denver, for example, weighed in with twice the greenhouse gas emissions per capita (21.5 tons) of New York City and even Shanghai.[13]

In his popular albeit controversial 2010 book, *Green Metropolis*, David Owen makes the case that cities are, in fact, an ecological way to live because they boast density, which means less driving compared with suburban communities.[14] Economist Edward Glaeser makes a similar point in *Triumph of the City*.[15] Both books fairly gush about the social, economic, and environmental virtues of cities.

A growing chorus of voices conjures the city as a sparkling solution to environmental ills, with images of silent transportation gliding along, energy-producing architecture in harmony with the environment, and landscaping both beautiful and edible. Open space, places to walk and play. Café's everywhere. Green parks. Bicycles. The Emerald City.

Interest in smart sustainable cities has grown as people in different sectors investigate pieces of the urban population boom puzzle. The idea that humans are the problem, long a tenet of the environmental movement, has shifted a bit to make room for a vision of people as problem solvers.[16] Despite substantial differences in beliefs, strategies, principles, and methods, most agree that an explosion in the apparent need for cities offers a clear, if challenging, opportunity for getting it right, for building cities that are viable and dynamic, exciting and green, and hotbeds of innovation and efficiency.

Peter Calthorpe, a founder of the Congress of New Urbanism, an organization promoting sustainable, walkable, mixed-use urban communities, and the author of *Urbanism in the Age of Climate Change,* has written that "urbanism is the foundation for a low-carbon future," and the most cost-effective solution to climate change, even more so than renewable energy.[17] Urbanism allows us to do more with less. Calthorpe's eponymous urban design firm, Calthorpe Associates, was named one of the 25 "innovators on the cutting edge" by *Newsweek* for its work redefining models of growth in America. "Good urbanism," Calthorpe maintains, is defined by "three basic principles":

> One is *human scale,* which has to do with designing public spaces around the pedestrian rather than the car. Ironically, human scale can exist in incredibly dense places, like Manhattan, or in relatively low density places, like the historic centers of our rural towns. . . . *Diversity* is another key ingredient of urbanism . . . you have to have a range of uses mixed together, you can't isolate housing and shopping and employment into separate zones. . . . You [also] need a diverse population—you can't isolate age groups, income groups, and family types. . . . The third principle, which wasn't historically part of urbanism, is *conservation and restoration.*[18]

These principles—human scale, diversity, and conservation—are not at odds with smart technologies but rather are complementary strategies for improving urban livability and resource use.

Meanwhile cities are widely recognized as engines for economic growth and innovation. Today only 600 urban centers generate about 60 percent of global gross domestic product (GDP). Tokyo, with its 35 million people and nearly $1.2 trillion in economic output, ranks among the world's top 15 economies, larger than the nations of India and Mexico. Cities encompass the largest and fastest-growing concentration of natural resource consumption and are, consequently, a logical place to focus sustainability efforts.

Taken together these perspectives—viewing cities as solutions that foster livability, sustainability, and innovation—have laid a foundation for smart-city innovation.

Smart Cities, Smart Buildings

The late William J. Mitchell, professor at the Massachusetts Institute of Technology (MIT) and a leading thinker in the field of digital technology and urban studies, believed in the possibility of smart cities. Technologically networked urban environments could be superbly responsive to the needs of their inhabitants, he argued. Through information and communication technology (ICT), combining hardware (embedded sensors in buildings and infrastructure that can detect activity of various types) and software (that stores and uses data), cities could provide customized services to inhabitants on demand, enhancing efficiency and livability. In Mitchell's vision networked smart cities would generate collective intelligence in communities. It would be easy to make better decisions—without ever having to sit around a table to debate them.

This vision may slowly be turning into reality. ICT systems are starting to be used in managing energy, transportation, and waste.[19] Smart-city advocates conceive of vast systems for collecting and analyzing big data on human behavior patterns—using networks of sensors and micro-controllers (tiny computer systems that combine processing, memory, and input/output devices)—to make cities more sustainable and more livable. Sensors detect activity, and microcontrollers analyze the data against targets and deliver output to users (through some linked device, like a smartphone) to influence their behavior. For example, consider how today's access to traffic data may lead you to choose a different route home. More-sophisticated systems could eventually control the car itself, leaving driver decisions out of it.

A target for innovation far less ambitious than driverless cars is the building itself. The use of sensors for operating and maintaining buildings is a strategy to minimize environmental harm and enrich the user experience. A 2011 McKinsey study on resource productivity placed improved building energy efficiency first of 130 opportunities. The report identified potential savings of almost $700 billion by 2030, if we took advantage of new, improved, energy-efficient buildings.[20] According to the Center for Climate and Energy Solutions, buildings have been responsible for 38 percent of carbon emissions.[21] Leading experts around the world maintain that the potential to build environmentally sustainable buildings is vastly underrealized.

At nearly 3.4 percent of the US GDP, construction, already a large industry, is growing to accommodate urban growth around the world. The industry, however, is fraught with waste and inefficiency.[22] Buildings are thus not only the largest opportunity for emission reductions but also the most cost-effective. In fact, of the cost-neutral reduction opportunities across all sectors identified by the Intergovernmental Panel on Climate Change, 90 percent come from reduction measures in the building sector.[23] The potential to build and retrofit green buildings and infrastructure is thus enormous. Funding mechanisms, however, remain underdeveloped despite the promise of significant economic returns over time.[24]

In sum the need for innovation in the built environment is widely felt, and cities are a primary domain for that innovation.[25] The Internet has already transformed many businesses,[26] and today it seems only a matter of time before the physical landscape catches up.

Companies large and small have been developing technologies—including sensors, software, and data analytics—to make cities more environmentally sustainable, livable, and functional. For example, some explore systems to reduce energy consumption or manage traffic flows on city streets. Others develop integrated solutions to help city governments, like IBM Smarter Cities and Cisco Smart+Connected Communities. According to a 2011 Cisco news release, the aim was to "transform physical communities"; a smart-city approach encapsulated "a new way of thinking about how communities are designed, built, managed, and renewed to achieve social, economic, and environmental sustainability."[27] Large companies have the advantage of resources to fund the needed research and the pilot projects, but startups have the advantage of believing anything is possible. We talked to executives in both arenas and decided to focus on a startup to see how this might play out.

As we did so, every day it seemed a new innovation would enter the smart-city arena, some more outlandish than others. "The Smartest Cities Will Use People as Their Sensors: By networking individuals and their gadgets, urban apps will tell inhabitants what is happening all around them, in real time," ran a headline in *Scientific American*.[28] Many had potential. For example, Trash Track, a Seattle-based innovation, reveals how garbage flows through and out of the city's waste management system, identifying items traveling around the United States to legal and illegal dumps. The results uncovered ways to improve compliance and minimize carbon dioxide emissions by transporting waste more efficiently. Real-Time Copenhagen generates data about shifting traffic and pollution patterns, as well as where nightlife is unfolding. "As Sea Levels Rise, Dutch See Floating Cities" ran the headline to a *New York Times* story about Dutch architects investigating the possibility of a floating Holland.[29] There seemed to be no end to human inventiveness.

Sobering realities and exciting possibilities co-exist in an uneasy partnership in this space, but there is no question that assessing the earth's resources against humanity's growing needs poses an immense opportunity for audacious innovation.

A Perfect Storm

While smart-technology innovations around the globe percolate, two intertwined megatrends have laid the foundation for their eventual use. One trend is growing awareness of threats to the sustainability of the earth's natural environment. The second is the rapid rise in the number of people moving into and living in cities. Combined, these large-scale shifts create a perfect storm for urban innovation.

Megatrend One: Climate Change

News of floods, earthquakes, tsunamis, famine, chronic disease, toxic waste, nuclear winter, and species extinctions have become too frequent to count. Epic storms with human names—Katrina, Sandy, Haiyan (in the Philippines)—increasingly terrify and devastate. A 2010 article in *Scientific American,* darkly titled "How Much Is Left? The Limits of Earth's Resources," presented a long and frightening list of concerns: glacier melt (in some places more than a half meter per year); oil scarcity (by 2050 we will have used all but 10 percent of the earth's available oil); freshwater scarcity (by 2025 renewable water reserves may drop below 500 cubic meters per person per year, considered the minimum for a functioning society); and even mass extinction (biologists warn of events on par with those that killed the dinosaurs).[30] Climate change threatens to alter every-thing about our lives, from agriculture and food supplies to productivity and the frequency of extreme weather events. The *Scientific American* article also estimated that even coal, long thought inexhaustible, would dwindle to nothing by 2072, given the current rates of extraction.

Our ability to feed ourselves in the future has been increasingly revealed as precarious. Even today roughly 925 million people are hungry. And the number is growing; the United Nations' Food and Agriculture Organization (FAO) warned that by 2080, 600 million additional people could be at risk of hunger as a direct result of climate change.[31] In addition to those who face starvation, many more will be chronically malnourished. The *Scientific American* report predicted that counteracting the ill effects of climate change on nutrition would cost more than $7 billion per year by 2050, while the FAO and the Organisation for Economic Co-operation and Development warned that the direct impacts of climate disruptions on food production patterns would lead to more "extreme volatility events on international food commodities markets."[32]

Ecological footprint analysis, introduced in a 1992 University of British Columbia doctoral dissertation, compares human demand on nature with the biosphere's ability to regenerate resources and provide services.[33] It does this by assessing the biologically productive land and marine area required to produce the resources a population consumes and absorb the corresponding waste using prevailing technology. The WWF (formerly known as the World Wildlife Fund), a proponent of this approach, claims that the human footprint already has exceeded the biocapacity (the available supply of natural resources) of the planet by 20 percent.[34] Yet, as readers well know, the earth's population continues to rise. The United Nations (UN) estimates that the global population will grow from 6.5 billion in 2010 to 8.5 billion in 2050.[35] Moreover, the average standard of living across the globe, which translates into greater per capita resource consumption, has also risen steadily. Clearly, with more people consuming more, the ecological footprint problem is exacerbated.

Megatrend Two: Urbanization

We are fast becoming an urban planet. With 180,000 new people moving into cities each day, the twenty-first century is the era of urbanization. In 2008 the world reached an invisible but profound milestone: half of its population was living in cities, for the first time in history.[36] By 2050, according to UN estimates, 70 percent of the world's population will live in cities.[37]

Many of these cities have yet to be built. China's announcement in spring 2013 of plans to move 250 million people into cities over the next 15 years sent ripples through the blogosphere.[38] Some estimate a need for more than 10,000 new cities by 2050 to house an anticipated 3 billion new urban inhabitants. Such estimates represent a massive construction project.

Should this construction occur in the same way as it did in the creation of today's existing cities? Logically, given environmental challenges, technological advances, and the relative speed of the growth in urbanization, this would not be the best approach. Letting cities merely evolve, as in centuries past, is likely to lead to sprawling slums and suburbs, excessive use of personal cars, divergent economic opportunities, inadequate infrastructure, and a lack of open space. Coming up with better-designed and more coordinated alternatives, however, requires collaborative innovation on an unprecedented scale.

The specter of uncontrolled growth, marginalized slums, health issues, and social unrest in megacities with populations of more than 10 million also looms large. By 2013 Tokyo, New York, Mexico City, and Shanghai had populations in excess of 20 million. *The Endless City,* published in 2007, with its sequel, *Living in the Endless City* (2011), showcased writings by architects, mayors, urban planners, policy makers, and others on concerns about physical growth in cities and on how to improve the quality of life in megacities.[39] Some expressed a faith in technology to solve social and physical problems associated with growth; others put faith in visionary leadership.

Cities are places of modernity and opportunity. Nonetheless not all of tomorrow's new urbanites will relocate voluntarily. In his October 2011 speech on World Habitat Day, Dr. Joan Clos, executive director of the UN Human Settlements Programme, warned that by 2050 we can expect more than 200 million environmental refugees from the effects of floods, drought, overheating, and other climate-related disasters. Left to chance, urbanization is unlikely to proceed optimally for both the environment and the residents.

Adding 2 billion people to the planet is like adding two Chinas to the number of people alive today. Leaving aside for now the issue of whether forecasts are destiny, it is clear that large numbers of people will need food, water, and other resources on a planet that, as noted, already faces stretched resources. Leading scientists in climate-related fields have argued that human activity is already shaping climate and the web of life.

Together these megatrends call for innovation that is no less significant than a third era in the history of cities,[40] no less than a new order of things. *How can leaders today—armed with ambitious visions and complex, fallible technologies and organizations—help bring this about?* The rest of this book explores this question. See *Five Leadership Lessons for Building the Future: A Preview* for a summary of the lessons that unfold in the chapters ahead.

Overview of This Book

Chapter 2 tells the story of how a small, unlikely band of entrepreneurs from different countries and industry backgrounds teamed up to create a

Five Leadership Lessons for
Building the Future: A Preview

Lesson 1: Start with Big Vision

Building the future starts with a bold and meaningful vision—but with a twist: the vision must be open and big enough to evolve as a result of others' input and with the emerging insights derived from new experiences.

Lesson 2: Foster Big Teaming

Building the future requires teamwork that bridges industry cultures—which takes empathy and skill.

Lesson 3: Celebrate Mavericks

Future-building gets a boost from successful, credible experts who glimpse new possibilities and help shift the conversation in an industry.

Lesson 4: Embrace Small Action

Building the future is an iterative learning process—a series of small actions that help realize the evolving big vision.

Lesson 5: Balance Influence and Innovation

Building the future requires leaders to balance influencing (selling the vision) and innovating (developing the vision through small smart action).

---

new company called Living PlanIT. We get to know Steve Lewis, the CEO who envisioned the future and enrolled others to help enact it. While many were put off by Lewis's enormous claims, some were drawn to the project by his charisma and experience, others by the company's bold vision, and some by the promise of putting their talents to the highest use (not without personal sacrifice). Their stories convey the *first leadership lesson:* building the future starts with a bold and exciting vision to motivate others to join an uncertain journey with no guarantee of success. From the IT geeks to the fiercely proud mayor who gave the fledgling company a piece of land on which to build its dream of the future, we see how different these players, these strange bedfellows, really are.

Chapter 3, which positions the startup in the IT industry, is the first of five chapters portraying norms, values, and expectations in a particular industry. As we explain, innovation and information technology go hand in hand. Software and hardware engineers expect change and are even comfortable with the inevitable failures that mark the path to successful new products. Living PlanIT's early employees, for the most part, hailed from IT backgrounds. Several came from Microsoft. Some had remarkable pedigrees, with successful stints at blue-chip companies. Others were younger and less accomplished. Many, true IT enthusiasts, relished the startup environment. They believed anything was possible (and in software it's almost true). They were young, idealistic, ambitious, and sometimes naive.

It becomes clear in this chapter that Living PlanIT cannot build a city on its own. The company must team up with other organizations, with vastly different resources and skill sets, if city building is going to happen. This is the nature of the nascent smart-city industry. In this way the *second leadership lesson*—future-building requires Big Teaming across industries—begins to take shape.

Chapter 4 focuses on the role of real estate development in building the future. We show how visionary leaders with the capacity to envision a new future can shift the conversation in an industry. Often such visionary leaders are inspired by a revelation—an aha moment that allows them to imagine a new order of things. This was the experience of Adrian Wyatt, the then CEO of London's Quintain property investment and development company, who opens the chapter. In this way chapter 4 brings out the *third leadership lesson:* the importance of engaging industry mavericks who have vision as well as credibility built on past success. We examine the opportunities and the challenges of Living PlanIT's new partnership with Quintain, as well as how shared vision brought it about. But deals, especially big deals, are not built on vision alone. The challenges of Big

Teaming become especially apparent in the professional chasm that lies between IT and real estate development.

Chapter 5 introduces local government as a critical partner in the cross-industry teaming of building the urban future. These are the elected officials and civil servants who regulate the present while aspiring to build the future for their constituents. We meet Celso Ferreira, part visionary, part pragmatist, the elegant Portuguese mayor in search of a legacy. He too is a maverick—out ahead of the curve in envisioning the future city. We then meet the remarkably thoughtful policy analyst Robin Daniels, who ably bridges the worlds of technology, government, real estate, and business. Boundary spanners like Daniels, we argue, play a crucial role in building the future by facilitating Big Teaming.

In chapter 6 we dig into construction and architecture—fields with limited attention to IT historically yet central in today's plans to create new or retrofitted cities of any size. We meet two members of Quintain's construction team and recognize how their comfort with visual and tangible objects is vital to innovation. They long to see shovels hitting dirt. We also consider the role of architects—right-brain thinkers who astonish with their visual fluency, their ability to pick up a pen and an unlined piece of paper and create visions of the future. They readily glimpse new possibilities. We meet the stylish and iconoclastic Portuguese architect Pedro Balonas, who worked on a master plan for the new city Living PlanIT hoped to build. Can they team up with IT? The clash of ideology and temperament between construction and software is revealed in stark relief.

Chapter 7 explains that high-tech corporate giants embody conservatism and an appetite for innovation at the same time. Can they help bridge the gulf between the IT startup and the real estate developer? We meet two executives who joined Living PlanIT, leaving major corporate roles behind, and who seemed, at first, perfectly suited to help the young company grow up and get serious. Their pragmatism, their appetite for action, balances the visionary. Observing a flurry of meetings and memos of understanding (MOUs) that spread over months that turned into years, we see how the corporate world constitutes another distinct culture in the smart-city landscape. In the meantime Living PlanIT faces more than its share of small setbacks. We glimpse the potential hazards of successful external influencing activities that shortchange internal innovation efforts, as Lewis's penchant for the limelight, for shaping the global smart-city dialogue, grew to dominate his schedule.

Chapter 8 weaves together the insights and examples from chapters 3 through 7 to focus on teaming across industries—its challenges as well as the opportunities for overcoming them. We integrate our case study data with social psychological research to identify the culture clash that lies between industries, to examine its implications for Big Teaming, and to suggest leadership strategies for overcoming it. How can leaders bridge the psychological divides that separate industry domains? We dig more deeply into what leaders can do to build creative, psychologically safe interpersonal spaces to team up across industry "fault lines."

Chapter 9 updates the unfolding Living PlanIT story as of 2015: several promising smart-city projects were under way as we finished writing this book. This chapter highlights the *fourth leadership lesson:* the need to embrace small action as a strategy for making progress on a big vision. We reflect on the audacity and brilliance and on the naiveté and blindness (blindness in the present perhaps unwittingly caused by an intense focus on the future) that fueled and inhibited the company's progress. We conclude with the *fifth leadership lesson:* the need for future-building leaders to balance the competing goals of influencing and innovating.

CHAPTER **2**

Glimpsing the Future

Every moment in business happens only once. The next Bill Gates will not build an operating system. The next Larry Page or Sergey Brin won't make a search engine. And the next Mark Zuckerberg won't create a social network. If you are copying these guys, you aren't learning from them.

—**Peter Thiel**, *Zero to One*

ON A QUIET SUNDAY AFTERNOON IN THE SUMMER OF 2011, THE CITY OF Maia, a municipality in the northern Portugal metropolitan area of Porto, is a postindustrial stage set with empty cobblestone streets. A pair of down-and-out citizens confer on a street corner. At around five o'clock, however, Maia comes to life: elderly Portuguese women (some dressed in black) stake their places at the outdoor cafés. Skirts too short are duly noted, as are who walks arm-in-arm with whom—the matriarchy hard at work mending tears in the social fabric. On Monday morning the city reinvents itself: the outdoor cafés host a different generation: middle-aged tourists, businesspeople, shopkeepers, women shopping, and taxi drivers.

Maia, like all cities, is in a state of evolution. (Maia was, after all, the Greek goddess of growth and creativity.) Lifestyles change and cities must change, too. As futurist Stewart Brand said in his book *How Buildings Learn*, "Cities are at war with time and change . . . and they always lose."[1] The sounds of Maia are still village sounds in spite of the office towers, shopping malls, and proximity to the gleaming futuristic Porto Airport. Roosters, barking dogs, birds, the occasional midnight firecracker, and other sounds of human activity echo in the canyons created by the buildings. Behind the Hotel Central Parque, a place that figures centrally in our story, is an immaculate community garden. The hotel's bar and dining room were by all accounts the scene of audacious dreams and late-night conversations in the months stretching from late 2008 to early 2010. Walking down the empty streets of Maia, it is hard to imagine that this is where a team of future-builders, refugees from various industries, planned a bold new city, a living laboratory, a high-tech experiment called PlanIT Valley.

Years after these first meetings, the original members of the startup company that calls itself Living PlanIT—the men and women we introduce in this chapter—remember this time fondly. It was a kind of crucible in which the raw beginnings of so many of their current efforts were forged. It began with a vision. The sense of ownership they felt, and in many cases continue to feel, for that vision was powerful even as it changed and evolved, shedding some ideas and layering on others.

This, we believe, is how future-building happens. It starts when a leader glimpses a new possibility and proceeds when a diverse team commits to making it happen.

Learning in the Smart-City Trenches

When we started our research for this book in early 2009, smart cities were just starting to generate interest and excitement. We began by gathering primary and secondary data on several smart-city initiatives. We conducted interviews with architects, engineers, executives from technology companies, and government officials working on smart-city projects around the world. We gathered reports on smart cities from companies and think tanks, including McKinsey, Siemens, IBM, Cisco, Hewlett-Packard, Oracle, and Forrester. We tracked articles about smart cities, which appeared in such sources as *The Economist,* the *Financial Times,* and *Fast Company.* This background research revealed that, from 2009 onward, a growing number of stakeholders were talking about a "smart-city industry."

As our interest deepened, we wanted a firsthand look at some of the people trying to build the future. Knowing our interest, Andrew Comer, a partner and director at the global engineering firm BuroHappold, introduced us to Steve Lewis, CEO of Living PlanIT, and to his cofounder, Malcolm Hutchinson. Lewis and Hutchinson gave us full access to their startup, then in the late-night, back-of-the-envelope, vision-hatching stage. Diving into the trenches with the growing team gave us enormous insight into the interpersonal dynamics of future-building.

The more time we spent at Living PlanIT, the more we realized the scope of the challenge. We were especially struck by the difficulty of finding a common language, a common understanding of goals and opportunities, especially between Living PlanIT and its partners. In contrast to prior treatments of smart cities (high-level views of the landscape), this book focuses on the psychological and managerial factors that can make or break the realization of audacious innovation. How people work together, particularly across disciplinary boundaries, emerged in our research as critically important to the ability of future-builders to realize their dreams of innovation, to execute, and to make sure shovels hit dirt and routers meet microprocessors in real, physical ways—not just on paper and in keynote speeches.

Our background research made it clear that smart-city initiatives were complicated cross-industry collaborations. We identified a set of primary domains that had to work together to envision, design, manage, and build innovative urban spaces—notably information technology (both startups and corporate giants), real estate development, local government, and architecture and construction.

Each domain comprised its own set of ideas, values, skills, time frames, and business models. Each would be integral to building, retro-fitting, and managing the smart cities of the twenty-first century. Real estate, architecture, construction, and government have always played a role in urban development. But IT is a relative newcomer to the discussion.

To study this interplay of domains, we spent time with members of the Living PlanIT team. We shadowed them in meetings as they built a partner ecosystem. We visited them in London and Portugal. We ate plates of baked cod and Portuguese pork and drank glasses of *Vinho Verde*. We conducted dozens of interviews with company employees and with executives in other organizations working with them—including in other technology companies, real estate developers, engineers, builders, and government offices—to better understand Living PlanIT's unlikely journey forward in its quest to become a leading company in the emerging smart-city industry. It was not long before we noticed that individuals from these various domains didn't always see eye to eye.

Teaming Up in Portugal

The original players in the Living PlanIT story joined up for reasons as varied as the individuals themselves. What inspired them to leave their jobs, often their homes, and even more often their predictable paychecks to pursue an outlandish vision? Let's take a look.

In 2009 Steve Lewis was 44, a dreamer, a visionary, a driven entrepreneur in an age of entrepreneurs. He hoped to make money, certainly, yet Lewis seemed more driven by the thrill of innovation. He had already had his share of wins and losses, mostly wins. Win or lose, most of these activities were far less in the public eye than this one would be. This one would be his legacy.

People are drawn to Steve Lewis. He is one of those people whose energy and presence you remember more than the details of his appearance: medium height, medium build, graying hair, dark blue eyes. He doesn't usually look directly at the person he is speaking with, which tends to be a good thing. If he looks directly at you, it means he is going to tunnel into something you've said. Few statements can actually withstand Lewis's scrutiny. If you're lucky, he'll build on your idea. If you're not lucky, you'll be back at the starting gate in no time. In these moments Lewis's accent shifts perceptibly to the cockney intonations of his Hertfordshire childhood. As a result, perhaps a fear of his own intensity, he tends to look out and under his eyebrows, as if his head were tilted too far forward.

Perpetually casual, Silicon Valley–startup in his dress—black button-down shirts, jeans (the predominance of black, he claims, comes from being color-blind)—Lewis is almost never seen without his iPhone, which he uses frequently to describe his vision for the company. "It's a platform," he'll say, holding the phone flat in his palm, as if it could support the weight of his ideas, "a city of apps."

The Shaping of a Technology Futurist

Lewis was born on September 3, 1965, in London, the son of a carpenter. "My father was very creative," he recalls, "always making things. He worked in construction. As a kid I went to a lot of his job sites. When he moved to Saudi Arabia with the Army Corps of Engineers to do some civil construction, I went with him. He was involved with an American lady." This left young Steve with time on his hands. To amuse himself he would tinker with technology: "As far back as I can remember, I've been curious. In a masochistic way, I liked problems. I'm quite happy in the gray areas. . . . I always read a lot. I also break everything I touch. I loved to take things apart—appliances, for instance. I got my first electronics kit when I was six and a half. Then a chemistry kit. Anything that exploded. Then I got a home computer kit and locked myself away, working on juvenile software."

Lewis returned to the United Kingdom when he was 12. He remembers hanging out in the teachers' lounge: "My physics teacher had this great caustic humor. And my math teacher was one of the oddest people I've ever met." One day in school, his math teacher brought in an early-model personal computer. "It just sat there," Lewis says. "No one knew how to use it." Soon Lewis had befriended the Commodore 64 and started creating software. "Software was then, and still is, an art form," he says, like a painter talking about cadmium pigments. "It's one of the most malleable art forms—you need very little infrastructure to do an enormous number of things."

One day a representative from Hatfield Polytechnic in Hertfordshire, now a university renowned for its aerospace engineering and computer science, as well as for its focus on green technology, visited the school. Lewis, then 13, showed him what he was working on. Soon, in exchange for access to a computer, Lewis started coaching some of the staff at Hatfield on how to use it and how to create the software as well.

After high school, Lewis explains, he was on his way to playing professional soccer when he was diagnosed with leukemia. Instead of kicking a ball across a field, he spent 10 months in the hospital. Lewis is not by any stretch of the imagination an introverted guy. He thinks aloud. He thrives on debate. The mere presence of others seems to get him going and keep him going—late into the night, sometimes into the early-morning hours. Yet in those 10 months, the patient refused visits from members of his family. He recalls thinking that if they were there, he would feel their doubt and concern. Their doubt about his ability to beat the cancer would demoralize him and lessen his chances of getting better. "I didn't feel it was my time," he said in one of our first meetings.

This tells you a lot about Steve Lewis. He believes—and believes he has evidence to support it—that if your will and vision are strong enough, you can do anything. Beat leukemia. Build a city. What you must not do is let the naysayers get in your way, no matter how well meaning, no matter how much evidence they throw in your path. "My mother and stepfather were recently ill," Lewis said almost two years after our first meeting, "and they just got each other all upset about it. It's better to deal with it alone."

This way of thinking about the world—about problem solving and crisis management—became particularly interesting as we watched Lewis build the team to build the city, or perhaps just to change the way other new cities were built. Sometimes this inclination to focus on the future meant that Lewis simply refused to focus on near-term realities, such as paychecks. Keeping an eye on the ball, for Lewis, meant building on good news. The future would cantilever out on a positive meeting or a long-awaited MOU. This positive energy was and is a compelling part of Lewis's charisma, but it would also prove increasingly frustrating to several members of the team.

Just 18 and having successfully dodged death, Lewis got a job in the statistical research unit of Roussel Laboratories. To this day when he describes his most pivotal moments, his true discoveries, it is with great respect for serendipity—the chance meeting, the barroom revelation—respect for "fooling around" with machines, ideas, and possibilities to see what happens next. It was one thing to write software and another thing altogether to learn how to use the massive computing capability that was doubling itself every day. "I was just a snot-nosed kid, surrounded by doctors and surgeons." As Lewis tells it, having tinkered with machines and appliances since he was seven, his work at Roussel was fun. "I did have a strong work ethic," he says. "At night I'd work with the mainframe operators. This was tantamount to a formal education in large-scale computing."

Lewis left Roussel after a year and went to SAS software and then to Soft-Switch, a small company based in Philadelphia, where he started working on larger projects with more moving parts—system integration projects for large companies ("another dogsbody job," he says, using British slang for "drudgework"). This is where he started managing people; he recalls managing a team of 200 at age 21. "So much was happening in this time," he muses. "We knew that the way computers talked to everything else was growing like crazy." From software to hardware had been one leap. His next education would be in networking. With a growing interest in customer expectations, Lewis needed new mentors. Allen Brain, vice president of international sales at Soft-Switch ("we called him Herr Brain") taught him about the commercial side of the computing business, understanding customer needs, and developing new products. "I came to feel," Lewis says, "that as long as I created value, others would take care of me."

Five years later, in 1994, Soft-Switch was acquired by Lotus, and in 1995 Lotus was acquired by IBM. Lewis went along for the adventure, playing varied roles in product strategy, marketing, and messaging. Lewis credits Cliff Reeves, then vice president of product management at Lotus, with teaching him much about product strategy and creating markets. It was here that his entrepreneurial side began to develop. He had spent years acquiring the skills. Now he began creating his own vision of a future made better, enabled by computing. "A large part of my work has always involved trying to remain humble enough to ask questions and to realize that 50 percent of the decisions I make are going to result in failure."

By 1998 Lewis felt that he had a good sense of the marketplace for innovative products. He was ready to develop some of his own. "I'd done what I wanted. Microsoft approached me a number of times." At the end of 1998, he left IBM to work with Double Decker Studios, a small Boston-based media company with 19 people specializing in brand development, web and product user interface design, and animation. "It was fun and interesting dealing with artists," Lewis says with a grim laugh.

In 2000 Lewis was recruited by Microsoft to be general manager of market development. Eventually, he recalls, he built his baby, "dot-Net," largely by creating an extensive partner and customer ecosystem: "There I was, in one of the most dynamic, exciting industries. Technology is all about continuous, unexpected change—never static. [You never know] which invention will become important. I began to realize that it was possible to make a difference in the world, to deliver real value."

But Lewis had another revelation at this point: "Corporations think that they're invincible. This blinds them to the potential of the work. They didn't see the Internet coming; they didn't see mobile phones coming . . . they're unable to predict the future."

In his early years at Microsoft, Lewis was struck by how forthright the executives were with employees and by how much access there was to Steve Ballmer and Bill Gates and other senior executives. He remembers a leadership retreat in which some of the company's toughest problems were on the table. *Have you really got the talent?* Lewis remembers asking himself. Three business plans were discussed at that retreat. In Lewis's telling, the process of deciding to support or jettison the plans sounds something like *The Hunger Games:* "Someone would stand up to give a presentation, and Bill would interrupt with questions. Steve might argue about a fact. The guy or woman would be trembling." Lewis remembers sitting behind Ballmer and Gates: "'Was it you who hired this complete idiot?' Steve asked Bill. 'Not a single person in this room,' Steve said to the poor bloke, 'expects you to come in tomorrow morning.' . . . I've never been in a room," Lewis says, "with so much collective talent, and," he adds to his listeners' surprise, "so little ego. It was a really good education."

Glimpsing the Future of the Construction Industry

"Sometimes at Microsoft these deals would end up on your desk," Lewis recalls. "You'd be asked to look into something." In 2004 he was handed a folder containing a plan for a new development in Syracuse, New York, called DestiNY, a 1-million-square-foot technology park to house companies working on new building technologies and renewable energy, led by real estate developer Robert Congel. Congel was to become Lewis's next, and perhaps last, mentor.

Lewis's partnership with Congel on DestiNY sowed the seeds for Living PlanIT. Malcolm Hutchinson, an Australian IT entrepreneur whom Lewis had met when Hutchinson's Swiss company, WISeKey SA, became a Microsoft strategic partner in 2002, also teamed up with Congel and Lewis on DestiNY. WISeKey had two full-time staff members working solely on DestiNY, and Hutchinson made frequent trips from Geneva to Syracuse to give talks and assist with fundraising.

Born in Bacchus Marsh, Australia, the son of a schoolteacher, Hutchinson had worked as an IT specialist in the banking industry while attending college part-time. After graduation he served in several Australian government municipalities as a general manager, overseeing city employees. He then directed a national think tank studying the role of local governments. At age 40 Hutchinson changed careers, leaving the public sector to buy a partnership in an Australian IT company. Later he left Australia for Europe.

In 2006 the two men founded Living PlanIT, with a general idea of revolutionizing construction and a commitment to developing a business around it. Lewis's frustration with the construction industry, his disillusionment with large corporations, and his network from Microsoft led him, as fate would have it, to Maia, where he would encounter an unlikely cast of dreamers and visionaries.

Local Heroes

Miguel Rodrigues, a native son of Maia, is passionate about cars—*fast* cars. In the first decade of the new millennium, Rodrigues designed and built a very fast, very sleek racecar. Of medium height, fit, with dark hair and mustache, a quick smile, and charmingly broken English, Rodrigues takes us to see the beautiful expanse of 1,700 hectares of land outside town, where, he explains, PlanIT Valley will be built. Dressed in blue jeans and a crisp, white shirt, he looks like he just stepped out of an ad for a sports car. Walking with him down the street in Maia is like walking with a celebrity down Sunset Boulevard. Everyone knows him. And he knows everyone.

Rodrigues is a self-made man. He chose, he said proudly, not to go to university. "I created my own path," he told us, "my own network, my own company." That company built everything from sports stadiums to chemical plants to dams. "I never know what is going to happen when I leave my bed in the morning," he said with a shrug. But his fascination with classic cars only grew. Following a 20-year career as an entrepreneur in the global industrial construction industry, Rodrigues gave in to his passion and founded a small car company in Maia that renovated, displayed in its small "museum," and sold classic cars. The company designed and built a new racecar that debuted in July 2007 at the Historic Grand Prix of Porto.

The car caught the attention of Manuel Simas, then Microsoft's managing director for worldwide automotive. Simas, also a Portuguese native, was at the time based in Stuttgart, Germany, where he had been working for Microsoft on IT systems for Daimler's SmartCar division. He spent 30 years in the automotive industry, and SmartCar was his latest project. Simas—heavy set, outgoing, enthusiastic—seemed always on the lookout for the next big thing, the next deal. In the time we spent with him, he rarely drove the same car two days in a row. He was so often on the phone that when he was not midcall, the earphone wire hung, forlorn, over his shoulder. "I like to lead from the back," he said of his own leadership style. At Living PlanIT he was also fond of saying, "Our motto is *Work hard, play harder.*"

Aware of rumors that Porto was considering electric vehicles (EVs) as part of a transportation plan for the future, Simas contacted Rodrigues and offered to meet him in Portugal. There he discovered that Rodrigues hoped to build electric vehicles with built-in intelligent technology and that the city of Porto was in the process of developing an ambitious new public transportation plan. Collaborating with engineers and professors at the University of Porto and MIT, government officials in Porto were intent on demonstrating state-of-the-art urban transportation that would use rapid advances in sensor technology to improve scheduling and minimize energy use.

Simas introduced Rodrigues to Peter van Manen, managing director at McLaren Electronic Systems and Simas's partner on the Formula One contract. Van Manen, an Australian, had lived and worked in the United Kingdom for many years. Tall and soft-spoken, with round eyeglasses and deep technical smarts, van Manen recalled listening to Simas and thinking, quite early on, that something much bigger than an electric car factory might be possible. He agreed to help the two men develop a proposal for Porto.

Elegant, green-eyed, and with the courtly manners of another era, Celso Ferreira—born in Paredes in northern Portugal—attended university in Lisbon and worked there as a lawyer for a number of years. His father's unexpected death at a young age led Ferreira back home, leaving his Lisbon law practice to return to Paredes to run his father's furniture business. Then, in 2004, Ferreira decided to run for public office under the slogan *Doing the right things, well.* He was elected president of the Paredes municipality in 2005 and was reelected to a second four-year term in 2009, soundly beating four other opponents by garnering 58 percent of the vote. Ferreira made national headlines with his reelection by being the first candidate in Paredes to gain more than 20,000 votes, including candidates in presidential, legislative, and European Union elections.[2]

A Starter Vision

What did all these men have in common? A fascination with cars, for one. By this time sensors had been used for years in the automotive industry, most vividly for real-time feedback and control to improve the performance and efficiency of Formula One racecars but also in consumer vehicles. General Motors' OnStar subsidiary[3] uses sensor technology to provide subscription-based communications, in-vehicle security, hands-free calling, turn-by-turn navigation, and remote diagnostics systems throughout the United States, Canada, and China.[4] OnStar had more than 6 million customers by 2011. Inspired by such applications, creative minds around the world began looking at how sensors might improve efficiency and lower costs in cities.

Microsoft had partnered with McLaren Electronic Systems in 2006 to supply standard engine controls for Formula One racing teams.[5] Cliff Reeves, now general manager of Microsoft's emerging business team, suggested that Simas contact his former Microsoft colleague Steve Lewis, whom he saw as having relevant market development experience. Simas met Lewis in London in January 2008 to explain the EV strategy in which cars would communicate via an intelligent technology. As their scheduled 30-minute meeting stretched to four hours, it became clear that Lewis should travel to Portugal to meet the rest of the team.

Over the years Rodrigues had approached and been turned down by four municipal presidents in his quest to develop electric car manufacturing in Portugal. Finally, in September 2007, with the help of Simas and the backing of Microsoft, Rodrigues reached an agreement with Ferreira, then mayor of Paredes, to build a factory in Paredes.

Rodrigues and Simas made the case to Ferreira that an EV industry would provide jobs and pull the Porto region into the twenty-first century, perhaps even into a leading role. Well known for its port wine and the fine craftsmanship of its furniture makers, Porto was not a region that came to mind for high-tech jobs. And yet Porto developed top engineering talent. Graduates of the highly respected engineering programs at the University of Porto could be found in technical industries around the world, but brain drain from the region was a problem. The potential for creating value from leveraging that talent and for creating a successful business was not lost on Rodrigues.

In the spring of 2008, Rodrigues hosted two classic car rallies in Porto. In an effort to keep the forward momentum, he invited Lewis, Simas, van Manen, Ferreira, and Hutchinson to attend. Van Manen recalled, "We all got along very well. Professional respect is important, but the social side shouldn't be underestimated."

"For Living PlanIT to succeed," Simas echoed van Manen, "all the players have to get along."

"It was lovely," van Manen said. "We'd stop for meals, and every restaurant we went to decided that we should be eating the specialty of the house, which always seemed to be a pig of some type. So after three days, we had created a bond. We all enjoyed driving around to places, and it probably only took two weeks to stop having the shakes from eating so much pig. That's how it started."

After three days of driving and meetings, Lewis concluded that what Rodrigues was working on was interesting but not conceptualized at the right scale to have much of an impact. To Lewis the smaller scale made the project harder, not easier, to execute successfully. Lewis began to think about ways the project could be expanded or scaled to the necessary dimensions to have an impact. In response Rodrigues arranged a meeting with Ferreira.

Just outside the door to Ferreira's office, striking aerial photographs of 300 hectares of undeveloped land captured the visitors' attention. Ferreira explained that the land currently lacked a development plan. "I said, as a joke," recalls Simas, 'Why don't you create an automotive city like Volkswagen's?'" Simas suggested the size was right for an auto city, similar to the Autostadt in northern Germany. "My idea was to get EV investors, to create a city where automakers would meet together. Steve had been working in real estate." Ferreira offered Lewis and Simas 300 hectares.

A New Vision

After leaving the rally, Lewis returned to London and thought deeply for a few weeks about the mobility project and the opportunities in Portugal. It was then that he had the idea of building a "technology city" with the capacity to develop the elements he had previously advocated in New York and elsewhere—while still contributing to the economic development of northern Portugal. "Over the next month," Lewis recalled, "Celso and I met frequently to figure out what that might look like. It was a back-of-the-envelope proposition."

Lewis believed that Rodrigues's mobility concepts for urban environments like Porto's would not work without the new, efficient infrastructure that he and Hutchinson had contemplated. A new city, he thought, would achieve the critical mass to make the intelligent technology effective. Lewis and his growing team spent the next two or three months talking to some big companies. It was apparent that they had an interesting proposition. But, as Lewis put it, "We realized we didn't have enough land, so we went back and said that we needed more."

And they got more—much more. The municipal government, led by Ferreira, granted Living PlanIT the exclusive rights to purchase 1,670 hectares (4,125 acres) in 2008 at prerezoning values. Lewis started thinking about building PlanIT Valley according to the highest standards of efficiency and sustainability—offering an intelligent building system designed to minimize waste and increase the use of sustainable, renewable materials. He lost no time pulling together a team to form the new company.

Glimpsing the Emerald City

And the dream took shape. Soon PowerPoint decks were multiplying, capturing extensive plans—oddly detailed in some places and just as oddly vague in others—for how PlanIT Valley would generate and rely on sustainable, renewable sources of energy.

The vision encompassed a mix of centralized and distributed systems to produce, manage, and store several sources of renewable energy, including solar, wind, plasma, and biofuels. According to its energy strategy, captured in several large and growing PowerPoint decks produced in the Hotel Central Parque lounge, PlanIT Valley would produce 150 percent of the energy it needed and sell the excess energy to the surrounding region. Under the direction of Nuno Silva, Living PlanIT's chief scientist, the team also had a strategy for waste. The new city would minimize the creation of waste but convert the waste it did produce into energy in a regeneration plant. A water strategy similarly managed all aspects of the water cycle through harvesting, recycling, and integrated treatment of all water resources.

The team now described PlanIT Valley as a research city, where Living PlanIT and partner company employees would work collaboratively to develop intellectual property (IP) related to designing, testing, and selling "solutions" for cities of the future. *Solutions* meant innovations in IT, transportation (often called "mobility" by the team), construction, and energy that could improve how cities, or various components of cities, were built and managed. Living PlanIT's corporate partners would agree to set up offices in the city and to participate in the design, integration, and deployment of technology platforms in its physical operations. PlanIT Valley would thus become a "living laboratory," where high-tech companies would locate research and development (R&D) efforts focused on future cities. Ferreira was a believer, telling us in June 2011, three years after he'd first met Lewis, "PlanIT Valley will draw 250,000 people. Phase 1 is 37 hectares, 10,000 people. We don't expect 200,000 will come in 10 years. Maybe 20. We need to be practical and honest about our projections. The first phase is fundamental. This will happen within five to seven years."

While the details of the vision were not entirely clear to van Manen, he was impressed with Lewis's and Hutchinson's experiences in New York with DestiNY and especially with their ideas for using sensors to revolutionize the construction industry. "The nature of innovation," van Manen explained, is that "sometimes you have to break things or fail in order to know what to look out for next time so that you can make a whole set of new problems for yourself. As we went into 2009, the bigger picture of what could be done started to take shape."

The vision gathered momentum: Lewis and Hutchinson soon could be found explaining far and wide that PlanIT Valley would showcase technology solutions created by Living PlanIT and its partners, including intelligent buildings, "smart walls," and transport innovations such as autonomous and guided commuter and residential transportation. Connected by a software platform called the PlanIT Urban Operating System (UOS), PlanIT Valley would generate and store massive amounts of data in a large data center.

In fact, because the potential of sensors and data analytics was not yet widely understood, more and more of Lewis and Hutchinson's time seemed to be spent explaining it to potential partners or funders—*influencing*. In this way they were trying to give birth to a new industry, not just a new company, with their big and compelling vision. Listening, we conjured visions of wall-to-wall servers whirring away, of green parkways and stress-free living.

City Life

It wasn't all about technology. Besides serving as a laboratory and showcase, the new city would be welcoming and diverse, explained Bernd Herbert, vice president in charge of "PlanIT Life" who had worked with Simas at SmartCar. According to Living PlanIT's marketing materials, it would be a place to "live, work, play, and learn, a place that you would be happy to call home." The design specified a mix of homes—ranging from single family to apartment buildings—that would someday house 100,000 to 130,000 residents.[6] Corporate partners would locate research groups and operate retail establishments there. A bustling downtown area would have a mix of offices, retailers, hotels, and restaurants. Parks and entertainment centers were also planned. Simas was talking with a local international private school and Lewis with the University of Porto to locate branches of their institutions in the valley.

In 2009 Living PlanIT projected 115,000 jobs in PlanIT Valley within five years of the start of construction. Jobs included those in large partner companies, small and medium enterprises (SMEs), construction and maintenance, schools, stores, and more. Because Portugal's prestigious universities graduated thousands of software engineering students each year, there was a deep pool of local talent to fill positions and keep graduates in the region. In late 2009 Lewis said that Living PlanIT would begin construction of the data center in 2010. Subsequent phases, representing a total investment of 15 billion euros, would start soon after. Before building began, the team would develop an Experience Center in a beautiful historic building in Paredes to educate the public about the technologies, methodologies, and companies located in the new city.

To plan the design of streets and buildings, the team turned to Pedro Balonas, a prominent Portuguese architect with offices on the riverfront in Porto. When we caught up with him on a sunny day in June 2012, he explained that he believed in the future. He saw no reason why a "rich cyberlife" could not function like a neighborhood. One day, he argued over lunch in Porto, we will all be global citizens: "No more guy-next-door. . . . Airports will be the office spaces of the future. Touch tables and intelligent surfaces will keep people connected." It was clear that he enjoyed brainstorming with the Living PlanIT team, in part, he explained, because they were so different from his traditional clients. "Our clients are normally developers who want fast profits without risk," he lamented.

When building the future, timing is everything. Living PlanIT, according to Lewis and Hutchinson, was founded on an idea whose time had come. As they saw it, a small group of people came together in an unlikely way at a moment in time and hatched a dream. But as van Manen noted, making that dream a reality required a level of collaboration on a scale that none had previously experienced—a scale in which multiple professions, companies, industries, and sectors worked together to innovate—Big Teaming. That would mean developing a shared language that everyone could understand. Sharing a vision right from the start was a crucial part of this process. As we will see, vision and charisma drew many into Lewis's orbit, but city building takes more than vision.

Engineering the Future

The civil and structural engineers understood the complexity of the undertaking. Some were busy studying other companies to find products they could use to build PlanIT Valley—the latest LED lights, for example, or the best concrete in which to embed sensors. Nuno Silva, whose Portuguese heritage includes his family's celebrated port wine, was in charge of an energy and innovation team that researched solutions for smart cities in energy, waste, water, transportation, urban farming, and anything to do with new uses of technology to enhance efficiency and livability.

At 18, Silva (in his late thirties when we met him) had entered the university to study production engineering while also working in R&D for the Portuguese military. At school his unusual technical skill did not go unnoticed; in his second year, he was asked to teach courses in artificial intelligence, computer-integrated manufacturing, and more. Graduating with honors, Silva continued working in technical design for the military; then he switched to the agro-industrial sector. There he worked on product innovations that integrated sensors and advanced analytics.

During that time the Portuguese government invited a few talented engineers to join a two-year program in Italy, and Silva found himself working on the design team of Pininfarina on customized vehicles, including a special project for the sultan of Bahrain. Returning home, he was hired to work on infrastructure innovation and served on a commission reviewing new technology for the Portuguese government. The living-lab aspect of Living PlanIT's work appealed to Silva, who tends to express his rare enthusiasms in a deliberate, understated way. "The Portuguese are naturally critical," he explained, "but we always find solutions. We solve problems." Silva was interested enough to make the leap to join Living PlanIT. "I wanted," he said, "the opportunity to build the future."

Building a Corporate Culture

Many of those drawn to Living PlanIT, whether mechanical engineer or programmer, reported that traditional labels never captured their identity. "I never really thought of myself as a mechanical engineer," said one. "In that sense I have never really identified with my colleagues until now." He reported meeting Lewis for "one and a half minutes" before deciding to join him, another story one hears frequently at Living PlanIT. "This was a chance to do something that had never been done before, something really important," he explained. "It was something I couldn't have imagined until that point in my life: a wireless sensor network so big, the possibility of completely changing the way cities are made. This was not just about technology; this was about changing people's quality of life. Here was a company with an endless set of challenges—no possibility for boredom."

Shortly after the rally, Lewis decamped to Portugal with Johanna Weigelt, who was fast becoming a core member of the growing team. Weigelt, slender, blonde, and petite, with a serious-beyond-her-years expression, met Lewis before the car rally, and he invited her to come along. Born in Bratislava, the capitol of Slovakia, Weigelt had moved with her family to the United States at the age of seven. After college she contemplated law school but decided it would not give her the tools she needed to have the effect she wanted to have on the world, not to mention the downsides of the nine-to-five office lifestyle. She recalls that as an assistant for a lawyer in Massachusetts, she grew tired of working on evictions and foreclosures. *Is this,* she wondered, *what my life is going to be?*

Like so many who fell into Lewis's orbit in the early years, Weigelt followed him to London and began working for Living PlanIT. "Everyone thought I was crazy," she said, "but it was the best decision I ever made. This is a practical education, but it's also work and play combined. I've seen how a startup is built. I've been exposed to the financial, legal, and human resource aspects of that process."

Soon after Living PlanIT arrived in Portugal, Weigelt, almost 25 at the time, found herself in charge of human resources and legal affairs, a kind of glorified den mother for new employees, a solver of practical life problems for the growing team. This new role included everything from waiting for furniture to arrive to hosting meetings with executives from Cisco and other corporate partners. Weigelt was part of Lewis's trusted inner circle.

Family Dynamics

Weigelt was also the keeper of the company archives, including dozens of inside jokes still in play years after their initial delivery. The fact that Rodrigues, whose life has been spent in automobiles, had run out of gas three times in the company's brief history, for example, or that Silva's informal title is *CPO*—cut and paste officer—would not be easily forgotten if Weigelt had anything to say about it, even as the company shifted into a different gear. It wasn't hard, at this point in the company's development, to see the team as a growing family.

Living PlanIT, like all new businesses, was weaving a company culture. In those early days, it seemed as if everyone spoke the same language. Rodrigues had little patience with skeptics. "We are changing the world," he told us, talking about PlanIT Valley on a sunny spring morning in a café outside the Hotel Central Parque. "If I don't have a clear mind about what I want to do, I don't do it."

Like the 18-year-old who beat cancer, in the difficult times that followed Lewis remained uninterested in worriers and naysayers. His recurring positive predictions irritated some employees and partners. The money was always coming "in two weeks." The check was permanently in the mail. The more people clamored to be paid, the more Lewis backed into a virtual reality, with no loss of enthusiasm. But employees couldn't eat shares or pay rent with them.

In late 2009 Lewis, Weigelt, and others moved out of the Hotel Central Parque and into a *quinta*, or farmhouse, in the countryside not too far from Maia. Rosemary Lokhorst (everyone called her Rosy), one of Simas's colleagues from Microsoft's Switzerland office, joined the team, moving into a room in the *quinta*. "It took me four days, with the help of my best friend, to decide to say yes," she told us. Why? Because, she said, "It was like playing SimCity but in real life."

In 2011 several members of the team moved into condos on the Vale Pisão resort property. The new location was close to Rodrigues and not far from Ferreira's offices in Paredes. Visitors and new members of the team would often camp out with Lewis and Weigelt in the *quinta*.

Becoming Multilingual

Living PlanIT and its contemporaries (startups and corporate initiatives alike) would need to learn to speak the languages of architecture, planning, real estate, construction, and government. By 2012, one member of the team, Chrysanthos Chrysanthou, who joined from Cisco in 2011 as chief operating officer, described Living PlanIT as "a technology company enabling the development of innovative, intelligent, sustainable urban-scale environments." He explained that it brought together "people, industry, and educational institutions" to test new technologies.

Chrysanthou's description, while compelling, downplays the challenge that lay ahead. Teaming with people and companies from different professional backgrounds, who brought very different priorities, time lines, and expectations—Big Teaming, that is—would prove more difficult than anyone anticipated.

In the meantime the first wave of media stories, some skeptical, some supportive, trickled in. Lewis reported that people were stopping him in airports and restaurants to say thank you for his work and to express excitement about the potential of future buildings and cities. To a man building his legacy, this meant a great deal.

The honeymoon would not last forever. Many of the original players moved on, as we will see, with varying levels of camaraderie and disenchantment. Miguel Rodrigues called his years with Living PlanIT "the best MBA in the world." In many ways those early years were the fun part. The challenge would be to keep the essence of the original vision alive as the company, of necessity, changed.

The following five chapters explore, in turn, each of the industry domains whose expertise, commitment, and visionary leaps of faith would be essential to realizing the Living PlanIT vision.

CHAPTER **3**

Bits and Bytes

Dear, dear! How queer everything is to-day! And yesterday things went on just as usual.
I wonder if I've been changed in the night? Let me think: was I the same when I got
up this morning? I almost think I can remember feeling a little different. But if I'm not
the same, the next question is "Who in the world am I?" Ah, that's the great puzzle!

—**Lewis Carroll**, *Alice's Adventures in Wonderland*

LIKE MANY STARTUPS, LIVING PLANIT WAS MORE THAN A BUSINESS. It was a community of like-minded people who were passionate about building the future. In January 2011 Steve Lewis, Johanna Weigelt, Rosy Lokhorst, and a few others moved into sleek condominiums at the Vale Pisão resort after their *quinta* caught fire and nearly burned to the ground. Through a deal struck with the owners of the resort, Lewis and his entourage worked in the underutilized main clubhouse building—an expansive, light-filled modern space that looked out on the golf course and the fields surrounding the property. The clubhouse dining area served meals throughout the day, and a bar seemed to stay open all night, pouring local wine and other drinks that lubricated many a late-night talk among colleagues and the occasional visitors.

Many Living PlanIT employees had IT backgrounds. Some were fresh out of college, some came from another startup or two, and some brought years of experience in large companies like Microsoft or Cisco.

Lokhorst had several startups under her belt by the time she was 24, including hatchery equipment for raising chickens as well as ostrich breeding ("We IPO'd and went bust," she joked). Next came a job in a software startup. Soon she became, in her words, a "geek" through and through. She told us that she had left home at 15, lived for a time in the

United States, then in the Netherlands, and finally back in Switzerland, where she earned a master's degree in computer science and economics. "I could see that a person would never be bored in IT," she explained. "We get the opportunity to work on the future." With jobs at Siemens, Compaq, Hewlett-Packard, and Microsoft, Lokhorst shifted into consulting and business development before finding a job in Microsoft's global accounts in Switzerland. This is where Manuel Simas found her and told her about Living PlanIT.

After a few months, Lewis made Lokhorst Living PlanIT's business manager. Soon she was the team member most called upon to sit in for Lewis when he wasn't available to meet with prospective partners. Perhaps it was her utter confidence in the project that gave her this status—her underlying belief in the role technology would play in "changing the world" and lessening the "impact on Mother Earth." Perhaps it was her comfort with risk. At a point in her life when she was still free to turn on a dime, unencumbered (with the exception of her beloved dog), Lokhorst was also the team member most likely to buy up shares of Living PlanIT stock that other team members (most of whom were receiving shares in lieu of salary) might be willing to sell. "We are the new immigrants," she often said of the PlanIT Valley team. "We want to make a better life for others and for ourselves; we are designing cities we want to live in!"

Home Is Where the Work Is

People like Lokhorst who went to Living PlanIT from the IT world found a home there. Many had dreamed of a company in which they could pursue their own ideas for new applications that could change the world. They expressed an eagerness to work with like-minded people. Some had felt like outsiders in their prior workplaces; others felt they were unable to weave their visions for the future into the work they were doing. Others had ideas about the potential for smart cities but felt powerless to implement them.

If many of the early joiners felt constrained in their prior jobs, others came because they wanted to problem-solve on a larger scale. All were enthusiastic and motivated. Most valued teamwork over hierarchy. They saw innovation as a team sport, believing that few worthy innovations are accomplished alone. Most had flexibility in their lives—the ability to work late into the night and to pick up and move. All shared a passionate desire to experiment with new technologies. Many, like Lewis, began as self-taught programmers long before university. But life was catching up with some members of the team—those with families and mortgages. As Lokhorst told us in 2014, "The best employees are the ones who come in with the understanding that we are all entrepreneurs. We've all given up a lot. We do it because we want to change the world."

When we visited Vale Pisão in December 2011, we found 43 people (and 23 nationalities) working at Living PlanIT. Locals, like Nuno Silva, lived in and around Maia and commuted each day to Vale Pisão. Others had moved to Portugal from other countries, including Germany, the United States, and the Netherlands. The great room upstairs, divided by couches, a pool table, and a few small tables, served as a common office and looked every bit like the stylish, round-the-clock, loft-office startup in the popular imagination.

In fact, Vale Pisão seemed like the perfect place for a startup—no solid walls, everyone could see everyone else, information flowed, and meetings convened and unfurled in a seemingly random way. A series of stone patios flowed down onto the lawn. Eucalyptus, magnolia, pine, and palm trees lined the links. The buildings, made of stone and glass, were built into the hillsides. Here and there the developer had preserved a low stone farmhouse, which added a fleeting sense of before-ness to the landscape. People arrived in late morning and stayed until late in the evening. Lunch was served midday, and in the early evening people wandered outside to the enormous couches to sip wine and talk about the day. There was nowhere else to go: No city. No other friends. Just the team. Just the work.

This period built commitment to the vision, giving rise to a culture of openness, of psychological safety, conducive to innovation.[1] Living PlanIT may have been Lewis's baby, but it seemed to us that the people working there felt they were shaping it; they felt free to speak up, have ideas, use their imaginations. They were deeply invested, proud of the vision, and unabashed by its enormity.

Now and then visitors would arrive, often in suits. They seemed temporarily flummoxed: Who was in charge? Whom should they check in with? Where should they sit? On one occasion a team of potential investors was visiting from Japan. Their questions floated across the room: "Is it a real estate company or a tech company?" the translator asked.

"It's a platform," said Lokhorst, who was conducting the meeting in Lewis's absence.

"Who is the client?" the translator enunciated carefully.

"People," she replied without a trace of irony.

Breezes blew through the open rooms. People worked on sofas, big cushions, and patios. Coffee and plates of food were everywhere. In one corner was a meeting with people from Philips. "Tech support!" someone yelled out, joking (there was no such department, of course); the new router, a gift from Cisco, was acting up.

"I'm not a tech person," laughed Silva, Living PlanIT's chief scientist, in response. Toward the end of the day, the mood would change; the meetings were done. Someone would put on music, and the collaboration would deepen.

Okay, it's not your typical workplace. Or is it? Let's put these scenes in their proper context.

Hipsters and Geeks

When you think about a young IT company, you might picture loft offices with giant toys and newly minted programmers (mostly in their twenties) hunched in cubicles. It's a playful, slightly subversive world; a refuge for misfits, some stylish, some complete with pocket protectors; all creating the code and the gizmos that change our everyday lives.

In the 1950s when career paths in IT began to take shape, hardware engineers were the test pilots. Programming and writing code, then seen as unglamorous tasks, were often done by women. In IT skill is valued over formal education, even as over time computer science became a major department in most universities. Still it is often said that weaker programmers begin programming at university, whereas those with true talent begin long before—as did Lewis. Earning a degree, or in many cases leaving before the degree, is merely a natural continuation of a beloved hobby.

Still, programming is a kind of starting point for IT work, the crawling phase for tech professionals. It is here that they cut their teeth, prove their creativity and their commitment, identify their obsessions, develop work habits, learn a new language (not unlike musical notation), and hone their vision. Programmers like to take things apart. Examples abound: Grace Hopper, often called the first programmer, took apart and rebuilt clocks as a kid. Ken Thompson, the creator of Unix, built backyard rockets. Steve Lewis, by his own admission, went after household appliances before graduating to the Commodore 64. Toasters beware.

If You Build It, Will They Come?

Good startups depend on great programmers. In his 2006 article, "The 18 Mistakes That Kill Startups," investor Paul Graham writes, "A lot of those companies were started by business guys who thought the way startups worked was that you had some clever idea and then hired programmers to implement it. That's actually much harder than it sounds—almost impossibly hard in fact—because business guys can't tell which are the good programmers. They don't even get a shot at the best ones, because no one really good wants a job implementing the vision of a business guy."[2]

Graham's insight reflects that most people want to help shape the vision, to be heard, to matter. Many programmers go on to become software developers, and great developers understand the business they work in, not just the code. Achieving greatness as a developer is as much about business knowledge and people skills as coding smarts, wrote Dan Frost, a computer science professor at the University of California, Irvine, and technical director of 3ev, a full-service web company.[3] Developers, Frost points out, have to bridge language gaps—between, for example, programmers and users.

"My biggest challenge this year," Christian Heilmann, principal developer for Mozilla, explained to a reporter for the online *net magazine* in 2009, "is to make people who aren't techies talk to techies in a language that each party understands. The people who need and benefit most from the open web don't understand it because us techies are too much into our own lingo. What the hell's a 'password anti-pattern,' for example?!"[4] Here, Heilmann points to the very real challenges of cross-industry teaming.

IT Innovators, Then and Now

In his 1981 classic, *The Soul of a New Machine,* Tracy Kidder drew an unforgettable portrait of the computer engineering team that created the Data General Eclipse MV/8000 minicomputer.[5] Central to that portrait was a work environment in which great ideas bubbled up from the bottom of the organization. Executives were distant and often clueless. Project leaders were brilliant, mercurial, and sometimes ruthless. Team members were motivated not by the money but by the vision—building the next generation of computers. The new machine: faster, smaller, cheaper, world-changing.

Kidder's book brought the prototypical and often far from ideal—but clearly motivating—IT work environment to the attention of both the ordinary interested reader and the serious computer geek. For some readers the pace of the work—the endless hours, the odd characters, the crazy chaotic drive to be first to market, the secrecy, the technical jargon—left them grateful for their own, more sane, jobs. Still, managers everywhere longed to know the secret sauce for creating a work environment where people showed up and worked *that* hard, with that much passion and drive. (Hint: It wasn't pay.) For other readers, especially young, idealistic, and slightly unfulfilled computer scientists in starter jobs in companies around the United States, the book pulled them in as fully as if it were describing Shangri-La. Countless young men (yes, nearly all were men) inspired by Kidder's portrait, left boring jobs in search of meaning and excitement at startups or on potentially world-changing projects in larger companies.

In recent times movies like *The Social Network* present techies as young rogues who make a lot of money before they've left their college dormitories and portray tech companies as brash, fast-paced, uncivilized, sealed-off microworlds with no grownups in sight. This portrait is incomplete. Many programmers and developers work for huge corporations like Apple, Facebook, Google, and Microsoft.

Google. Facebook. A minute ago a startup; now a global behemoth. Employees work long hours and love to create new products. The atmosphere in IT is often merit based and collegial, but it can also be brutal, as readers saw in Walter Isaacson's biography of Steve Jobs, which told of employees reduced to tears by a frequently abusive boss.[6] In spite of its celebrated flexibility and openness, the IT world has no shortage of machismo. Cowboy coders and rock stars abound.

Still, in small companies the culture is usually consensus oriented, cooperative, flat. In "Discovering Microsoft's Corporate Culture," author Jia Wu writes that Microsoft Research Asia is reminiscent of "an open university that knows no boundaries."[7] Perhaps because so much of the work is solitary, performed by individuals in cubicles while staring at screens, the collegial atmosphere acts as an antidote to what might otherwise be seen as an antisocial profession.

Apple's design guru, Jonathan Ive, is eloquent on the subject of ego and teamwork. Ive, a citizen of the United Kingdom (UK) who recently received a knighthood for his role in creating such products as the iPad, has worked at Apple in California since 1992 and has been in charge of its designs since 1997. When Ive discusses his work at Apple, he talks about having room to experiment:

> What I enjoy about being here is there is a remarkable optimism, and an attitude to try out and explore ideas without the fear of failure. There is a very simple and practical sense that a couple of people have an idea and decide to form a company to do it. . . .
>
> There's not a sense of looking to generate money, it's about having an idea and doing it—I think that characterizes this area and its focus.[8]

As Ive hinted, innovation requires failure. Programmers and developers understand this, but managers often do not.

The Speed of Innovation

In some industries innovation is infrequent or slow. How we design buildings, for example, remained remarkably constant for centuries. Not so in IT. You can (and often must) turn on a dime. Software product life cycles are expressed in months rather than years or decades.[9] Learning must happen fast. The pressure to come up with the next cool thing is relentless. A March 2014 cover story in the *New York Times Magazine*, "Trouble in Start-Up Land: A Tale of Two Valleys," drew attention to the problem of what its author, Yiren Liu, called "the consumer-ification of tech." The drive to make the next cool thing creates a rift between those who want to do something useful for society (and improve "tech's infrastructure" along the way) and those who want to get rich on a new app.

Competition in IT can be intense. The global marketplace and electrons' costless travel mean that contributors around the world want to identify new possibilities before anyone else. Increasingly populated by young risk takers—some passionate about changing the world, others about fast profits—the world of software is nothing if not unpredictable.

People working in IT are used to the ever-accelerating pace of technological change. Everyone in the industry is familiar with Moore's law, named after Intel's pioneering computer scientist, Gordon E. Moore, who observed years ago that the speed of computing was doubling every 18 months while the size of computing chips was halving at the same rate. Over time it appeared that Moore's law described a pattern occurring every two years, but the rate of improvement was staggering nonetheless. Crazy short product life cycles are the inevitable result of technology's juggernaut. Fortunes are made and lost in this sector at dizzying speeds.

After the Internet bubble of the 1990s and during the so-called dot-com boom in the early 2000s, IT startups were as plentiful as stars, despite declining venture capital investments. Even a decade later, enthusiasm for starting IT companies based on new ideas remained almost absurdly high. The beauty of IT startups was how little capital one needed to get going. In 2011 Steve Lewis put it differently: "The beauty of a startup is it forces you to have ideas." He continued cheerfully, "I have a million ideas a day."

Global powerhouses take shape that didn't exist just a few years earlier. The meaning of the word *Amazon* changed from a rain forest to one of the world's largest retailers, seemingly overnight. The proverbial garages and graduate school carrels where these ideas were born made it all seem so easy. No one remembers, or in most cases even knows about, the ones that didn't make it. Countless IT entrepreneurs think about Larry Page and Sergey Brin and imagine themselves as the next major success story. Few considered how very much more likely failure was than success. The Living PlanIT team, at that time, believed that Living PlanIT could become the next Google, at least in the smart-city universe.

Only time would tell.

Fast-changing technologies and constantly shifting markets exert unexpected kinks in the trajectory of any tech company. New companies, with new-to-the-world products, sometimes must discover and create their markets at the same time. An entrepreneur who starts a hip, new, urban restaurant knows roughly what a restaurant does and whom it serves. It might take a little bit of experimenting and course-shifting to get it right, but the basic premise of the business is clear. This is not always true in IT. New markets are envisioned and created while new technological possibilities are envisioned and created. The smart-city space is one of those where the emergence of new technologies and the establishment of new markets go hand in hand. But how to reconcile the short life cycles of IT with the long life cycles of buildings was still an open question.

The Sensor Revolution

By 2010 some of the most exciting developments in IT were taking place in sensor technology. Over time, sensors had gotten smaller, less expensive, and better able to capture data generated by people's daily activities and put them to use to make things work. Sensor technology, many believed, would enable advances in construction, transportation, energy efficiency, urban planning, and more. The unprecedented scale of the resulting data sets would yield insights about how people live, enabling new efficiencies. The importance of sensors only grew in subsequent years. "The rise of objects that connect themselves to the Internet—from cars to heart monitors to stoplights—is unleashing a wave of new possibilities for data gathering, predictive analytics, and IT automation," said a November 2014 article with an exuberant headline: "Internet of Things: Software Platforms Will Become the Rage in 2015."[10]

The challenge for the Internet of things (IoT) was how to efficiently process, analyze, and use data from people's online or daily activities. There are so many data that analyzing and trading them has become a labor-intensive market of its own—the so-called big data revolution. And big data would not have been possible without dramatic advances in storage technology. In 2000 total information generated worldwide was estimated to be growing at 50 percent per year, and the cost per unit of storage was declining far faster than anticipated. This rapid acceleration of storage capacity—and shrinking of storage costs—changed everything and came seemingly out of nowhere. Where we once scrimped and saved, deleting files religiously, we now store with abandon and dream up new uses for big data, new ways to make lives, companies, and cities work efficiently. Data, it seemed, could live forever.

And yet while the technology exists to realize efficiencies in, say, construction or transportation, the business models remain underdeveloped. What markets look like, and who pays whom and how, was still taking shape in 2015. The use of IT to make cities more sustainable— through better pollution monitoring, energy-efficient municipal buildings, and intelligent transportation solutions—constitutes areas of obvious interest, but few investors were clear about how profits would be made. This was the major challenge for a company like Living PlanIT: It was sitting in a nascent industry.

A Nascent Industry

A handful of big technology companies had announced "smart-city" initiatives by 2009. Unsurprisingly, very few of these involved the creation of new futuristic cities from scratch, but the potential for innovation was clear. Wim Elfrink, the chief globalization officer at Cisco, heralded the role that smart cities would play in solving global demographic problems. We need, he said, to create new business ecosystems to realize the benefits that smart cities can offer. Elfrink described a future in which information technology would become as essential as today's three main utilities: water, gas, and electricity. New and old cities alike, he argued, were creating 10-year plans incorporating master ICT systems. Talking to a McKinsey researcher in 2010, Elfrink explained: "Worldwide spending on infrastructure and construction is about $2 trillion a year, and ICT spending is just 1.5 to 2 percent of that. But over the next decade, we will continue with advances in cloud computing, big data, and open data, and we will see 50 billion devices connected through machine-to-machine communication, which will foster the industrialization of the Internet."[11]

Elfrink predicted that "the Internet of Things will be a $1.5-trillion-a-year business—just from a technology point of view. But on top of that there will be another $2 trillion annually in new services." The business opportunities were vast. How to reap the benefits? "We just need to ensure that our investments are smarter and move technology from being an afterthought to having it embedded in our urban master plans." To do that, Big Teaming would be needed.

Elfrink went on to list five elements necessary for success in the smart-city industry: thought leadership, smart regulation, global open standards, public-private partnerships, and, most importantly, new ecosystems—four or five companies coming together, "inspired by a government initiative, to solve a big problem." Elfrink claimed optimism, in spite of the challenges: "As technology enables a host of new services over common platforms, we're going to see whole new industries arise and new waves of innovation. The future of competition will be among cities, and the ones that thrive will be those that have overall sustainability—economic, social, and environmental. From a sustainability point of view, it's a good thing for the planet. And it's probably the only way out."[12]

The potential was there. The smart-city market, valued by analysts at $526.3 billion in 2011 and at $654.7 billion by 2014, was growing. One report predicted a leap to $1.14 trillion by 2019.[13] Technology was transforming daily. Smart grids, smart metering for energy management, smart transportation dashboards for traffic management, and smart remote controls for security management were some of the growth areas. The familiar lamppost or parking meter was suddenly a potential device for capturing data. But cities are complicated and interdependent, and no single organization can build (or even easily modify) them alone.

For a while talk seemed to dominate action. The idea of embedding IT in urban systems and using the data to optimize resource allocation was taking hold a lot faster than the reality.[14] Urban transformation, as many innovators quickly learned, required more than cool new technology. Citywide or even building-wide solutions could not be designed, sold, and implemented using traditional business models. Startups thus faced a conundrum. Peter van Manen put it this way: "The biggest challenge is how to get the cash you need to support what you do. Your aspirations are generally greater than your cash. That's part of the fun of having a *big vision*. How do you crack that first customer, that first implementation, that both allows you to start delivering and fine-tuning your offering *and* allows you to say to the world, 'Someone is willing to buy this. It is real and it has value.'"

Creating a new city ready for inhabitants, van Manen explained, "would just take time." Small action, in the form of testing, demos, sales, and installations, would take delicate choreography. "If we try to do too much too early," he mused, "we fail. If we try to do too little too late, we fail because others will come in. So, it's a balancing act now of how aggressive you dare to be and how conservative you can afford to be." This tension between the visionary (wanting to change the world) and the practical (demonstrating value today) is present throughout our multiyear study of Living PlanIT.

The nascent industry around Steve Lewis and Living PlanIT was shifting fast. People talked about the future city as a machine, a high-performance vehicle, moving forward, creating energy savings and happiness at the same time. Some of the talk moved forward into experiments, in greenfield projects like Masdar City and New Songdo City, albeit far more slowly than anyone had hoped. Nonetheless the smart-city industry bandwagon seemed ready for more passengers.[15]

As our field research continued, we marveled at the enormity of the challenge. Growing a new venture in a new market is a profoundly uncertain enterprise.[16] With any new business, an entrepreneur has to develop and refine a business model that combines a compelling value proposition with an operation capable of delivering on it. But in the context of a new industry (also called a new market), knowledge about what business models might be viable, what customers might pay, and whether delivery of value is feasible is extremely limited.

Strategy scholar Tiona Zuzul describes the extreme uncertainty that entrepreneurs face in new markets and argues that people like Lewis must simultaneously build a company (looking inward) and an industry (looking outward).[17] This is not easy. Building a company requires developing an internally consistent business model, which nearly always involves false starts, new options, better and better understanding of customer needs, and lots of iteration. Building an industry means convincing a large number of people that new possibilities exist. It's about painting a consistent vision of a new market in which old and new companies sell and consume products and services that never existed before. This may mean speaking at conferences, writing papers, or demonstrating prototypes to companies or government agencies. Yet in nascent industries, an entrepreneur's externally and internally oriented activities may interfere with each other, as we explore in chapter 9. Not only do they require different skills and approaches but also pursuing one (say, selling the company story) can impair one's ability to manage the other (say, evolving the technology).

Companies are born and die all the time, but new industries are rare. They exist when it becomes clear that a set of new products, services, and markets presents viable economic opportunities that don't fit into existing industry categories. They are not cars or computers or restaurants. They're something new. History is shaped by new industries that did not exist and then sprang into being—oil, telecommunications, movies—but somehow the birth of a new industry still seems implausible at the outset. Can there be any more room for radical innovation to transform our world? (Let's hope so.) The smart-city industry, as we watched and listened, seemed to be trying to talk itself into being.

Software for Cities

John Stenlake, with his unruly hair and thick, rimless glasses, was Living PlanIT's chief technology officer. With many years of IT experience under his belt when we met him in 2011, including at Ford and Microsoft's automotive division, Stenlake had seen a lot of companies come and go with tactical but not visionary ideas for smart cities. So when Lewis and Living PlanIT came along, Stenlake was impressed. "I clearly identified with what he was trying to do," he said. "It was something we were trying to embed within Cisco. It was a direction we wanted them to grow in, but no one paid any attention because, at the end of the day, a big company cares more about the money."

Stenlake realized that the only way he could see the changes he envisioned would be by throwing in his lot with a small company. He made the leap. A lot of people asked him, "Are you crazy?" Stenlake didn't care. "We had," as he put it, "stuff that works." By the time he joined Living PlanIT, the company's Urban Operating System, which ran on Cisco software and could do real-time sensing and control, was under way. The control code was based on technology from McLaren Electronic Systems and ran inside a Cisco router—a two-unit, 19-inch device that could process data from multiple buildings to adjust their environments.

Over Chinese food in London one night, Stenlake patiently described his high-tech baby, speaking slowly and carefully, periodically checking, it seemed, to make sure we were keeping up. The first unit, called the UOSRTC (real-time controller), housed proprietary Living PlanIT code. The other unit was called an urban cloud appliance (UCA), which connected to a Cisco Unified Computing System data center platform running UOS code. A software platform tying the two units together ran Microsoft code. Stenlake explained that a mini data center would be required in actual use (for instance, in the basement of a building). He had combined the router base component (the urban network appliance, or UNA) and the UCA in one big box to facilitate demonstrations in the near term.

The problem, he said, was that they had only one box, and it was not very portable. Nonetheless they could do safety and security demos using a couple of sensors that detected stress and heat. The demo simulated a small building fire to show how the UOS could alert firefighters and security teams, map a virtual two-dimensional building display showing the location of the fire, and recommend escape routes using "intelligent" exit signs and animated arrows. This system, Stenlake continued, would work similarly to guide paramedics in a medical emergency.

In a large conference hall in Las Vegas in July 2011, Stenlake demonstrated the technology publicly, showing how sensors attached to a piece of carbon fiber could detect excessive structural stress and send an alert so that people could be evacuated before a building collapse. He explained to the crowd Living PlanIT's various planned uses for the UOS in PlanIT Valley after successful demonstrations in the Digital Enterprise Greenwich center in London. All that remained to get from demo to full-scale implementation was building an application program interface to accommodate more scenarios at a larger scale. Stenlake's corporate technologies team, comprising about 12 people in Detroit, China, Portugal, and the United Kingdom, was busy in 2011 developing proprietary code.

Stenlake had a vision for the future of his team. The UOS software platform would attract people working on apps for the real estate industry that his team had not even dreamed of—security, medical, or retail—and lure them with the promise of space to work and some support. All his team had to do was perfect the beta version of the UOS.

"It was quite a big step," van Manen explained, "moving from a beta version to something that you can deploy in real life and start adapting and controlling. At McLaren, when we talk about new systems, we know it can be quite easy to make something that works—the difficult bit is making something that can't fail." Van Manen had the patience of an experienced innovation leader: "Now we are able to demonstrate the UOS and use it for some installations, but we still need to do a lot of work."

Meanwhile, even though the world of smart-city technology was not standing still, the Living PlanIT team was sanguine on the subject of competition. The way they saw it, the size—the audacity—of the Living PlanIT vision protected them. Stenlake and Lewis believed they were ahead of the game and that it would be hard for others to catch up. "Quite honestly," Stenlake told us,

> to actually be able to scale up software development to the point where you really can have lots of people working on different pieces of it, where the whole thing actually works at the end of the cycle, is an art in itself that, actually, very few people know how to do well, which is why most large IT projects fail. They do. Beyond a certain size, the failure rate goes into something like 80 percent plus. That's the state of the industry right now.

Seeking Technology Partners

Inspired by their foray into the car world and their connections at McLaren Electronic Systems, Lewis, Simas, Miguel Rodrigues, and Malcolm Hutchinson had negotiated a strategic agreement in 2010 to apply McLaren's control and real-time data technology (so successfully used to push the limits of elite racecar performance) to a new market: next-generation buildings. Almost giddy with the potential, every team member we spoke with described this with excitement. It was a game-changing moment—cross-industry collaboration to take tried-and-tested technology from motor racing and apply it to the evolving construction and urban development market, which by some estimates was valued in the trillions. The team could so easily envision the global expanse of buildings and traffic lights that could be made smart. The problem was where to start.

In this first David-versus-Goliath deal, Living PlanIT secured a powerful collaborative relationship with a unique technology company. McLaren hoped to benefit from the collaboration in a new emerging market, and Living PlanIT would benefit from applying innovative technologies in multiple other industries. This all happened in McLaren's gleaming Norman Foster–designed headquarters in Woking, outside London, where we were later taken to see the latest racecars on display in a giant glass-enclosed exhibition space. In this magnificent futuristic building, watching a team of engineers in a control room analyze Formula One race data, in real time, from 1,000 miles away, anything seemed possible.

The first big company that Living PlanIT courted after McLaren and BuroHappold was Cisco, with its global router business. Approaching Cisco, Lewis had in mind a revenue model that was Microsoft inspired—a partner fee based on the level of partnership. Cisco and other companies would pay a PlanIT Valley participation fee, along with royalties from the use of Living PlanIT technology. "Think of Dell," Lewis explained. Imagine "we've just sold them a building. Instead of doing it on a fixed price, we charge them based on the value created."

Each new partner had an existing network of partners. In the IT industry, firms thrive in ecosystems of partners, not as stand-alone competitive entities.[18] In this way Cisco could deliver new services to its customers, in addition to its usual menu of offerings, without carrying any up-front costs. The real estate management and technology services offered by Living PlanIT would help its partners, Lewis maintained. Each new partner would add intellectual property to Living PlanIT, thereby creating more value for all. Partners, he said, would want to get in early to avoid missing out. Cisco and IBM had already started talking about building an urban software platform of some type, but—because of their size and frozen, hierarchical decision making, Lewis believed—were never able to get the project off the ground. Lewis boasted of his company's nimbleness: "We are a small company who was able to say, 'F--- it; we'll just go and build one.' That's exactly what happened with Google: a small little company that took a leap of faith and said, 'We're going to make this work.'"

Lewis and Hutchinson credited Microsoft's example for their ideas about combining IP and a partner channel to deliver value. As Lewis put it, "We started off from a shared vision of networking a whole city and applying our technology to a city from the planning stages." He continued: "PlanIT Valley is a way of dramatically accelerating adoption of that tech, by bringing together the channel in a very concentrated fashion, which drives innovation."

Hutchinson had admitted to an early lack of interest in PlanIT Valley, but he acknowledged that the Emerald City was a rallying cry: "The initial idea for PlanIT Valley was most definitely Steve's; but like so many of the ideas we have, the base idea came from Steve, and we built on it." BuroHappold, he added, had built on the idea: "This is typical of the process."

Lewis plowed on, approaching partners. As he put it, companies could not possibly do it on their own. They needed Living PlanIT, he said. At the same time, he was also suspicious of big companies simply jumping on the bandwagon.

Leaping into the Future

The company grew, hiring people and purchasing IP from tiny startups that seemed to offer necessary technology. The more Lewis's vision increased in scale, the bigger the scope Living PlanIT took on and the greater the risk for all involved. Innovation thrives amid a mix of play and discipline, chaos and focus. Ambitious goals and failure tolerance are both essential to progress.[19] But how much of Lewis's time was spent leading the team's innovation process and how much was spent giving presentations outside the company seemed to be shifting over time, in favor of influencing key players around the world.

On a breezy spring evening in 2010, we watched Lewis try to buy a startup with about 10 employees that had created an application he thought would be useful. Lewis was holding court in a London bar, moving from lunch to drinks to dinner over nine straight hours with two tables pulled together. Late in the day, Lewis reminisced about some of the risks he had taken in his life. "Leaving Microsoft was a scary moment," he admitted, "but it had become clear to me that you can have a million fantastic ideas, but if you are tied to the same old business models, they will never become real. When we launched Windows XP . . ." He switched to a happier thought: "[In one project] I was sitting around playing with my mouse, and I thought, *You can use bar codes to create algorithms that describe preferences.* I went to these two guys I'd met in a pub and said, 'What's it going to take to make this happen?' It was fast. All this collabora-tion, corporations, governments . . ." Compared with developing software apps, city building was turning out to be heavy lifting. But, on he went, seeking to close a deal.

The young man wearing a North Face sweatshirt ran the startup. While the company's business model was not entirely clear—something about fostering engagement in the design of urban environments—it was clear that Lewis liked it, and him. Lewis explained quietly to the group, "Vision is the scarcest commodity. Once in a while, you meet people who think outside the box." But it seemed to us that he was trying to convince the young man to take a leap of faith and join his merry band of city builders. His target asked nervously who all the people at the table were. "Friends," Lewis said with a smile meant to be reassuring. Lewis then offered to buy the company. The young man said okay but looked worried. After a round of drinks, clearly feeling the pressure from the audience, he nodded. "Okay," he said. "Let's do it." Lewis, by comparison the elder statesman, shook his hand and took him to the bar to buy him a drink. The mood was celebratory. On this lovely summer evening in London, for the moment, everyone believed.

And yet every step involved risk for all the players. Like many creative people in IT, those we found at Living PlanIT believed they were taking a leap—trading in the familiar for the risky, the status quo for an unknown future. Many took the leap because they saw something in Lewis or in his vision that pulled them inexorably in. Some were young and naive. Others, however, had quite of bit of experience under their belts. Stenlake, for example, fast becoming the leading technical figure at Living PlanIT, had an international reputation. He was not someone who would leap without a viable product.

That product was the UOS. But could any serious player in real estate development believe in it?

CHAPTER 4

Location, Location, Innovation

*We are not going to be able to operate our Spaceship Earth successfully
nor for much longer unless we see it as a whole spaceship and
our fate as common. It has to be everybody or nobody.*

—R. Buckminster Fuller

IT WAS A DAMASCENE CONVERSION. MILES FROM THE DAMP, NARROW London streets, whale-watching with his family on a boat off the coast of Alaska, London real estate developer Adrian Wyatt found himself in the presence of great blue whales—the largest creatures on the planet, the kings of creation. Against a backdrop of ancient mountains, primeval forests, the huge sky, and oceans teeming with life, it became suddenly and stunningly clear to Wyatt just exactly what was at stake. Words like *climate change, carbon footprint,* and *renewable energy* took on new meaning. Overwhelmed by—almost suspended in—the grandeur of the setting, he looked over at his own children watching the whales. The future wobbled on the horizon like a desert mirage.

For a moment he thought, *Nothing will ever be the same*—for himself, for his work, for his company. He thought about his legacy and future generations. Would these blinding white peaks, these awe-inspiring whales live on? Or would the future be a sci-fi nightmare, a B-movie of an industrial wasteland? This sudden connection with nature was uncharacteristic. Wyatt loved cities; he loved the density and commerce, the history, the layering. Were cities a threat to this magnificence? Were cities and whales mutually exclusive? Did human habitation necessarily trail destruction in its wake? Maybe not. Maybe there was another way to think about it.

Every industry has visionaries—mavericks, industry leaders who glimpse a new possibility and then talk about it to anyone who will listen. Wyatt, it seemed to us, was one for real estate. And to his credit, he understood that his vision could materialize only through teaming up with experts from other domains.

Wyatt founded Quintain Estates and Development in 1992 (the word *quintain,* used by medieval knights, means "target"), locating its main offices in London's swank Mayfair district. Wyatt, with his striped shirt, braces (suspenders), high pants, and face-splitting smile, looks a bit like Tweedledum from *Through the Looking-Glass.* He is not your typical real estate developer. (Steve Lewis once said, in praise of Wyatt, "I meet too many people from real estate who haven't got a bloody clue.") Perhaps he once was typical, but, now in his midsixties, Wyatt hadn't built a 2-billion-pound real estate business by magic but through hard work and acumen.

The real challenge would come post-conversion. Swimming upstream against the tide of industry norms, as we explore in this chapter, is difficult in real estate. That day in Alaska, so far from home, Wyatt had an epiphany that fueled a determination to nudge the real estate business in a new direction.

By the time we caught up with Wyatt, his epiphany had taken root. He was hardwired for change. In one of our first meetings with him, in London in September 2011, Wyatt touched on the fall of capitalism, atheism (he calls himself a "screaming atheist"), the perils of short-term thinking, and *syntopic cities* (which he explains is a "posh" term meaning "cities in which man lives in harmony with nature"). Over the past few years, he had organized meetings of government and business leaders in the Quintain offices to discuss sustainability, efficiency, and innovation in city buildings, to build the case for "responsible capitalism." He began telling everyone he met that humanity was on the brink: change or die. (We might call it a Chicken Little moment, with the exception being that the sky really was, if not falling, presiding over a slow-motion crisis.) Real estate developers and others working on the built environment, he came to believe, were on the front lines of change. He started referring to himself and others in his line of work as "custodians."

Wyatt understood what he was up against. "The trouble is," he explained, "the real estate industry is pretty conservative. What we do takes a long time." He chuckled. "The people who trade stocks think five minutes is a long time. In my view the Achilles' heel of capitalism is short-termism." The real estate business could become the "heart of the solution," he explained. The business model would have to change. Relationships among builders, designers, landlords, and tenants would have to change. The technology existed to dramatically increase the efficiency of both construction and use of buildings, but most investors lacked the imagination to grasp the long-term savings. It was hard enough to convince them on a building-by-building basis. Compelling the major players in the industry to pursue savings on a large-scale citywide basis seemed all but impossible.

Wyatt says that in that first decade of the new millennium, he felt a bit lonely, a bit out on a limb. He remained hopeful, however, buoyed by a sea change that he believed would be led by "enlightened occupiers" (Cisco, Google, and other large office-occupiers) and by a new generation that wanted to make money but that also understood the value of sustainability.[1]

And then he met Steve Lewis.

"A Kind of Love-In"

Wyatt's and Lewis's paths collided in 2009. As Wyatt recalled,

> Steve Lewis was introduced to me by a mutual friend [London public relations guru] John Milligan. He came to this building for a half-hour meeting set up by Milligan, and he stayed seven hours. I'd never met anybody so attuned to my own thought processes. It was a kind of love-in. It's one thing to know what the issues of the day are—transport, food, water. It's another thing to have a model that's basically a private town run as a business. And it's another to have the delivery mechanisms.

The two men agreed that, as soon as a master plan was ready, Quintain and Living PlanIT would begin building PlanIT Valley. Quintain also agreed to partner with Living PlanIT on two of its existing large development projects, in London's Greenwich and Wembley districts. This was a bold and important step for a startup. Having a London address would not only give Living PlanIT cachet but also attract more finance types. And finance was sorely needed.

Meeting Wyatt was a boost for Lewis in many ways. In fact, much of his career, including the leaps and risks he had taken in the past, was the result of meetings with like-minded future-builders or, in his early years, relationships with visionary mentors. The first real estate visionary who influenced Lewis was Robert Congel, the New York investor and developer who ran DestiNY: "He had a vision," said Lewis, "and he showed me how to ignore obstacles to make your vision a reality, to make it happen. He had amazing personal strength." Lewis shook his head, recalling what went wrong, and continued, "There were politics, lawsuits. . . . There were 450 to 500 people working on the project at this time, but the money disappeared."

At DestiNY, Lewis and Malcolm Hutchinson had been IT guys who wanted to build the future. Hutchinson recalled, "When Steve and I first met, we hit it off immediately. It was obvious that we clicked in terms of thought process and friendship. The two of us got along extremely well and stimulated each other's thinking." Shared vision and the camaraderie of like-minded people drive many innovation projects. But after the shared vision, after the "love-in," comes the real collaboration, often requiring working with people from diverse backgrounds who are not like-minded at all.

Soon, Lewis and Hutchinson had become discouraged with the slow pace, waste, and inefficiency of the construction business. The two men glimpsed ways to help real estate developers cut construction costs dramatically while producing buildings that were more energy efficient, productive, and livable. When they left DestiNY and founded Living PlanIT in October 2006, they were eager to identify suppliers and partners to work with them to eliminate inefficiencies in the design, production, operation, and maintenance of buildings.

Harley Blettner, a Boston real estate professional and for a time Living PlanIT's chief operating officer, is one of Steve Lewis's closest and oldest friends. They met in 1995, and later Lewis slept on Blettner's couch during a transition period in his life. Blettner, with thick silvering hair and skin tanned by the sun, is affable and generous with his time. With a pronounced Chicago accent and a firm handshake, he is one of those people you want in the room when big deals are under way. He began his career in real estate finance right out of college. Lewis contacted Blettner in 2008 for help with financial modeling in the early days of Living PlanIT. "Steve really didn't have that kind of background and wouldn't even know what kinds of questions to ask," says Blettner. He came on board full-time in October 2008.

Blettner's fondness for Lewis is obvious. "Steve's vision is pretty remarkable," Blettner told us in December 2009: "I don't think he really had a management style until recently because there wasn't a need for a management style. He's got an unbelievable vision. This vision, though, has evolved a lot over the last year and a half. . . . But a lot of the old stuff is still pretty much right on point. He's seen this vision in his mind for a long time. It certainly was born in the DestiNY project."

By all accounts, Blettner was right about DestiNY. Living PlanIT was the phoenix that rose from its ashes. By the time Lewis met Wyatt in 2009, he was determined to be an agent for change in the building business.

Mechanisms for Change

Adrian Wyatt had the philosophy part down, and Quintain had a good address, but he lacked mechanisms for change. He likened this to the Wright brothers and their pioneering forays into aviation at the turn of the twentieth century. Before them there was the desire to fly but no mechanism. He described the following alchemy, the overlapping of the real estate mentality and the IT mentality: "In my industry, I think I'm regarded as slightly avant-garde, but what Steve said blew me away. He said, 'Imagine that a town is one of these.'" Wyatt made the gesture so common to Living PlanIT employees—holding his iPhone out on his open palm, referring to Lewis's explanation of Living PlanIT's UOS: "Steve explained the concept of cities as platforms for apps—apps for energy efficiency, waste management, transportation, education, and locating available services."

Meeting a "fellow traveler" fascinated Wyatt, especially meeting one from such a different professional background. But the other thing—the penny dropping, as he called it—was a bit like his epiphany in Alaska: "There was a realization that it's one thing to talk about the principles underlying syntopic development but another thing to have the technology that enables it. His platform, if you like, of the enabling technologies fit my philosophy so fabulously. I came to the conclusion that it didn't have to be just talk anymore. There were delivery mechanisms through Living PlanIT."

Still there were questions. If, for example, apps were the main product, what would happen to property, to owning property, to buying and selling, to the heart of the real estate business—the deal? How would a city of apps change real estate development's business model?

One of the key places where change might happen, Wyatt came to see, would be at the landlord/tenant interface. If these two players, traditionally at odds, could be united by the common goal of energy and cost savings, tensions that kept the industry from progressing could dissolve. Post-epiphany, Wyatt could envision a future in which sustainability practices provided a common language, and interest in the efficient use of resources, in living in harmony with nature, was a shared goal.

"Real estate developers have five skills," Wyatt explained, "all useful in building towns. They are land acquisition, design and master planning, construction, finance, and estate management. The estate management is crucial because it's not just collecting rent and buildings. It's understanding how a development, or even a town, works holistically and how to get revenues from other activities. It might be power, it might be water, it might be transport, it might be advertising, or whatever."

Presumably, designers, planners, owners, and customers could all identify with these basic operational and business principles. Presumably, they would all jump on the bandwagon—once it pulled into town.

The rundown area with 1.8 million square feet near Wembley Stadium and the 14 million square feet on London's Greenwich Peninsula, acquired by Quintain in 1999, seemed to Wyatt the perfect places to showcase some of the ideas Lewis and other innovators had presented. "Clearly," Wyatt explained, "it's not new-build. You're taking it up as a huge place of deprivation and trying to bring economic, cultural, and social life back there with sticky jobs where people want to work, want to live, want to play."

But they ran into problems almost immediately. "One is the planning system in this country," Wyatt explained, "which is just appalling, although they're trying to do something about it at the moment. The second thing is the Treasury. For example, we've put in a device at Wembley—great big tubes underground which collect waste and sort it. You'd think that our tenants would have a rebate from local rates [taxes] because we're doing the job of the local authority, but no."

Just as Lewis had experienced frustration with the construction industry during his DestiNY experience, Wyatt was discouraged by what he saw as roadblocks to energy efficiency and waste management thrown up by local politicians: "Politicians are usually absolutely useless at urban regeneration; they don't want the private sector to be too involved because it takes away their toy set which, [at worst], sounds anarchic. Whether it's here or in the States, Europe, the Far East, or the Middle East, I think a few of us ought to get together and say, 'Call it an enterprise zone, and let's get on with it and see what we can build.'"

His palpable impatience about the industry's slow pace of change was evident. And back at Quintain headquarters, others' impatience with the Living PlanIT arrangement was equally evident. Wyatt and Lewis may have had their "love-in," but the Quintain team expected Living PlanIT to bring funding sources into the projects in Greenwich and Wembley.

Quintain's construction team, whom we meet in chapter 6, was eager to begin work on PlanIT Valley, but neither cash nor progress seemed any closer to materializing by the end of 2011. In May 2012, Wyatt stepped down as CEO of Quintain to campaign full-time, as *The Independent* noted, on "green issues and building a low-carbon economy."[2]

Teaming across Industries

As both Wyatt and Lewis were learning, building the future requires proactive and dramatic change. It also takes Big Teaming—teaming across diverse professions. Real estate developers had some experience in this. They have always had to work with designers, planners, architects, contractors, bankers and investors, businesses, communities, and government agencies (for building permits) to succeed. Clearly, it takes skill to navigate among, and sense the interests of, these different sectors. Even when the ultimate goal—serve the clients' needs and build what sells—is clear to everyone, collaboration is not easy. But Living PlanIT presented a new cultural divide, one they hadn't traversed before. Was Quintain and its ecosystem ready to journey into the culture of technology?

When we first met Wyatt, Becky Worthington was Quintain's chief financial officer, hammering out the stubborn details and commitments in the deals that happen after the lovely dinners. Many years younger than Wyatt, Worthington, lively, stylish, brisk, and every bit the Londoner, was in many ways representative of her industry. She was game for building the future with Living PlanIT, but she was skeptical:

> With Living PlanIT we're dealing with IT-based people, which is a very different world. Tech people, well, they don't have to partner with the real world. You've only got to read *The Facebook Effect* to realize how different a world it is for people like us. But at the end of the day, in the IT world, all they've got to do to make their good idea marketable, normally, is rent some service space, and that's pretty cheap. What these guys would like to do is go and build some buildings, and that ain't cheap.

A common language, in 2011, was clearly missing. While members of the real estate team at Quintain were increasingly frustrated with the IT folks, Lewis and his team were also a bit frustrated with the real estate people. As John Stenlake told us in 2011, "The partnership with Quintain helps a lot, but . . . we don't speak quite the same language."

Lewis was also impatient with the big companies in the smart-city ecosystem, behemoths like Siemens and Cisco. It took months of courtship just to sign memos of understanding. Check signing seemed perpetually frozen in the future. When we met with Lewis in the Quintain offices around this time, his phone was ringing, as they used to say, off the hook. He was dressed entirely in black, shirttails untucked, and constantly surrounded by a group of mostly men who were trying earnestly to get a word in.

Lewis's impatience waxed and waned. When Mathieu Lefevre, the young executive director of an eight-month-old think tank called the New Cities Foundation, set up a meeting with Lewis in London, he was part of a trend. Observing the meeting, we watched Lewis listen politely as Lefevre described the intentions of his organization. But soon Lewis couldn't help himself, letting Lefevre know in no uncertain terms that time was of the essence. "I need to feel what's real about your organization," Lewis told him, as if they were the only two people in a room of 12. Others looked down at the table intently. "The words *smart cities* have become meaningless—used to describe every city with a bicycle." He continued:

> Cities represent the greatest use of human technology. There are huge opportunities in building things and making sure they work. The most interesting thing about cities is how they operate in the long term. In the world of collaborative computing, everyone is scrambling to get a piece of the pie. . . . In the developing world, we have to respond to need—a destabilized India or China will not be a pretty sight. We come at these problems from the tech side. Adrian comes at them from the real estate end.

"There is a lot of noise out there," Lewis concluded, "a massive case of ADD [attention deficit disorder]." He went on, bemoaning the complexity of city building, with no discernable pause:

> Here's what we found. There are two constellations of thought on this. We're building a large ecosystem of partners. At some point we realized our plan for a city didn't fit reality. We were thinking only about the technology, about building these buildings with sensors. Then we realized that the engineers had children. And the children would need schools. And the families would need hospitals. These cities will have to be built privately because governments move too slowly.

At this point Lewis seemed impatient to build, to get off the ground. Was he getting tired of meetings and noise and of what he saw as a lack of passion? He seemed unimpressed by the other players, even as he courted them to join his ecosystem. *Can't you see there's no time to wait for these old models to work?* he seemed to be saying on that bright London afternoon. *Can't you see we have to hit the ground running—running for our lives?*

But in real estate at that point in time, *sustainability* seemed mostly a buzzword. Lewis and Wyatt harbored the shared hope that clients would start clamoring for sustainability, and real estate firms would bend, like plants to sunlight, in that direction. But for most commercial developers, the customer remained a private or public enterprise that put cost—short-term cost, that is—first. Sustainability was not rewarded and rarely dominated the thinking in the development process. Even for urban-renewal projects, developers, builders, and city governments push for low costs on building but not for low operating costs of using what gets built.[3] It was up to Living PlanIT to persuade them. But did the company have the skill set to do that? Learning to appreciate and integrate their very different skills and values would make persuasion much, much easier.

Educating the Real Estate Visionary

Compared with the offbeat paths and maverick detours taken by men and women in IT, the road to success in real estate was more defined. Success in the field, as Wyatt and Lewis noted, was largely measured financially. Most real estate developers go to four-year universities and learn the trade on the job. If sustainability did not yet play a central role in the industry culture, what did? It was financial acumen (and gain) combined with an opportunity to create something new and lasting.

The emphasis might, as Wyatt noted in 2012, be changing. Universities, he explained, were starting to offer interdisciplinary degrees in real estate–related programs, some of which were tied to the sustainability imperative. In the United States, for example, the real estate program at the Wharton School of the University of Pennsylvania offers a master's degree in urban spatial analytics, appealing directly to leaders who wish to think more holistically about problems facing the industry. Such programs may include urban ethnography, urban studies, and cartographic modeling. Students drawn to interdisciplinary programs often want to help create a better, more energy efficient or more socially just world. Whatever the motivation—building a better world or amassing wealth—in any real estate career, on-the-ground experience is highly valued.

Success in real estate depends on instinct but also on good research— that includes understanding the context in which people choose to buy homes, businesses, buildings, or land—and an ability to think ahead. Way ahead, sometimes. This is because time frames are necessarily long for large real estate developments. An ability to understand the present and future context, including demographics, macro- and microeconomic indicators, and government regulations, is critical. Stanley Gale, of Gale International, is one of those who does.

Despite a luminous family history in real estate, Gale had not planned to go into the family business. Oddly, like Lewis, Gale aspired to play professional soccer. Honored as an All-American in 1971 during his time at Florida's Rollins College, he was later placed in its sports hall of fame.[4] Immediately after college, however, Gale found himself drawn to real estate, pursued his MBA at Rollins, and then, after a stint in the family business, joined Grubb & Ellis, a growing firm in San Francisco, as senior marketing consultant. After eight years in the commercial brokerage group, Gale became the president of commercial real estate company Sammis, eventually acquiring it with his partner, Finn Wentworth.[5]

By this time, even without three generations of family real estate success, it was clear that Gale had become a force in the industry. Not content to merely pursue traditional paths, Gale sought to innovate, to realize grand visions, explaining, "My strongest tool, my strength, is strong visualization of the outcome. I set the goal, rally the troops, be sure the goal is a team goal, build consensus, and go after it with relentless pursuit."[6] His motto, *It can be done,* has driven him to undertake ambitious projects like the 100-million-square-foot New Songdo City in South Korea.

While many in real estate today prize individuality, industry leaders like Gale are intuitive, patient, and strikingly good collaborators. Asked in a recent interview for his best advice for would-be developers, Bill Hard, executive vice president of LCOR, a real estate consulting firm, said, "I think it's a very interesting business but it requires a lot of patience. If you're expecting to come in and hit one or two or three deals a year, year in and year out[,] you are probably not right for the business . . . And you've got to be able to work with a wide variety of personalities and talents[,] most of whom are probably as smart if not smarter than you are."

Not denying the economics of the enterprise, he continued:

> Having said that the rewards are terrific, you can make good money[,] but there's tremendous psychological satisfaction knowing that you've pulled off something that not a lot of people can necessarily do. And not because you're smarter but maybe you worked a little bit harder and *you were able to get a group of people together of different*

personalities to work together and find solutions. It's really a problem solving business and that to me is the satisfying part of the business.

But success took patience: "It's not for everybody because it can be very frustrating. It can be a long time between tying up a piece of property and putting a shovel in the ground."[7]

Swimming with Sharks

Designing and closing deals are skills at the heart of real estate work, formalized in detailed legal contracts and characterized by cumbersome, high-cost transactions. These activities involve great uncertainty, and mitigating risk is one of the field's essential activities.

The Deal

The deal is at the center of all aspects of real estate—development, acquisitions, sales, leasing, asset management, and certainly investment banking. The stereotypical real estate "shark," with an endless appetite for deals and sharp observations about quality, location, "comparables," tenants, and landlords, is as familiar as the IT geek in his garage. An assumption accompanying the stereotype, which we seek to challenge with our portraits of Wyatt and Gale, is that real estate people have one goal and one goal only: financial success (as opposed to community building or urban regeneration). Deals begin with networking, the foundation of the industry's culture. Plenty of formal labor organizations exist to assist people with research or professional training, but the true networking often happens at meet-and-greets. (For this reason, in stark contrast to IT, you will almost never see a real estate professional look anything less than polished.)

Transaction costs in real estate are high (including brokerage, legal, recording, and banker fees), not to mention the sheer amount of time involved in most sales. "I'm used to the world of corporate transactions," Worthington told us in London in 2011, showing considerable insight and empathy even as she lamented the challenges of teaming with Living PlanIT. "IT is fast," she said. "Real estate transactions are slow. Urban regeneration is very slow. There's no real deal closing. And Living PlanIT is so disorganized, they couldn't organize a piss-up in a brewery! Even Cisco has not been good at pairing with real estate developers. [But] I understand how difficult this must be. Real estate is so antiquated."

Arthur Segel, a professor of real estate at Harvard Business School, reminds his students that this is a sector steeped in uncertainty. "Historically," Segel has written, "perhaps more great fortunes have been made and lost in this asset class than any other."[8] If an investor puts $10,000 into the stock market, the most the investor can lose is $10,000. The same can be said for the bond market: a $10,000 investment can lead to a loss of no more than $10,000. But real estate presents much greater risk and liability.

Conflicting Interests

The implicit and explicit view in the industry that landlords and tenants have opposing interests is a long-standing barrier, say many progressive real estate developers (including Wyatt) to the upgrading of assets, to innovation—to progress. "Some mechanism for resolving this and incentivizing both parties to communicate on potential upgrade opportunities would be helpful," Wyatt has said repeatedly. The tense relationship goes way back: farmers, realizing that a well-fed army could repel desperate raiders, agreed to pay homage to a lord or king in return for security. Leading families maintained ownership by right of lineage, and royal families spread wealth to friends by signing away titles and deeds to lands, allowing holders to collect rent produced by peasants living on the land. Some say things haven't changed all that much.

There's a There There

It is important to not forget the sheer physicality of real estate. In an age where most financial assets exist only virtually (captured as electrons, ethereal projections of future valuations), real estate can be bought and sold ("I've got a bridge . . .") only if it exists physically. Physicality matters. IT, by contrast, produces products that are ephemeral. In the IT world, ideas are bought and sold regularly.

Physicality may explain the emphasis on financial success in this sector because so much is at stake so visibly. Land and money change hands. It could also account for the old-fashioned, even rigid procedures traditionally followed in real estate transactions. While the sale of ideas and intellectual property in the high-tech world happens relatively quickly (often, as we see in the case of Living PlanIT, thanks to a compelling big vision), real estate transactions can be excruciatingly slow as goods are tested and prodded like cattle until value is assessed.

To mitigate risk, those developing real estate (such as hotel chains) increasingly choose not to own the land they develop. As Bill Hard explained:

> If you look at the type of real estate we've been involved in[,] typically we do not like getting exposed on land. . . . We're not going to go out into the green fields and buy a piece of ground and take it through entitlements. . . . We'll spend the money to get through approvals[,] get entitlements [to] go through site plans, planning legal environmental and all that[,] but what we don't like to do is pay x amount of dollars for a piece of land and then have to carry it for two or three years to get it through entitlements.[9]

The real estate sector, together with construction, makes up the largest component of the global economy. In other words, Wyatt is right: if change is going to happen—in our energy usage, our carbon footprint, our overall sustainability—innovation must happen in this industry.

Breaking New Ground

Although the industry may be mired in tradition, real estate developers are entrepreneurs at heart. They take on risk and create things that didn't exist before. They spot trends. Leaders of real estate development firms are forever seeking to transform a parcel of land into something new, attractive, functional, and of course profitable. In the process they create communities, jobs, lifestyles, and businesses.

Smart-City Projects

Some, like Wyatt and Gale, are also out to develop solutions to social problems. For instance, affordable, high-quality, low-income housing as well as mixed-use, energy-efficient, and sustainably sourced projects are increasingly included in urban-renewal plans. Wyatt, it turns out, is far from being alone in seeing himself and his colleagues as custodians. In a

2012 *Forbes* article, billionaire developer Stephen Ross included the fact that he got his start in affordable housing. "Look, it's a lot of fun," said Ross. "Because it's not all about the money, really, it's about transforming something and what you leave behind. This is a legacy."[10] This idea has been fashioned into a sharp and successful marketing tool in many firms. *Forbes'* 2013 list of the world's most sustainable companies included the following five big real estate firms: Diawa House (in Japan),[11] City Developments Limited (Singapore),[12] Prologis (San Francisco),[13] Stockland (Australia),[14] and CapitaLand (Singapore).[15] In other words, sustainability looks like good business.

New Songdo City was one of the earliest attempts to build a smart city from scratch. Some 6,000 miles away from Gale International's main purlieu, ground was broken in Korea on its 100 million square feet of commercial, residential, retail, hospitality, and public space in 2001. New Songdo City, with its Songdo International Business District, is a $35 billion project 40 miles from Seoul, with plans for housing 65,000 individuals and 300,000 workers in green homes and commercial buildings. Its stated target was to emit one-third of the greenhouse gases of cities of the same size. The Songdo Aerotropolis offers easy access to one-third of the world's population in an under three-and-a-half-hour flight to the Incheon International Airport.[16] With eclectic design elements, the project draws inspiration from cities around the world: wide boulevards akin to Paris's, a 100-acre park comparable to New York's, London-style park pockets, a Venetian-style canal system, and a convention center modeled after the Sydney Opera House.

New Songdo City was intended as a demonstration of "smart, sustainable and technologically ambitious" development. In developing Songdo, Gale said he "cracked the code"[17] of urbanism, and other city mayors have expressed interest in developing similar projects. While Gale laments the slow construction of his vision, he admits, "Naturally, everyone wants to open up and have everything filled from day one. But we're adhering to the original planning and the quality and the green and the technology side."[18]

In other words, Gale recognized sustainable building, in its infancy, as a long-term play. Motivated by the climate change and urbanization megatrends, sustainable cities could be a vehicle for triggering technical innovations in the industry, ranging from more-efficient materials, better supply-chain tracking, more-sophisticated lighting systems, and more-robust modeling tools. Meanwhile social innovations have been introduced, as well, including new rating systems such as LEED (the US Green Building Council's acronym for its green building certification program, Leadership in Energy and Environmental Design), better management techniques, better-aligned incentives, and more-integrative training.

Social innovations unfortunately tend to lag behind technical ones in the built environment. By way of contrast, consider the substantial productivity gains achieved in the automotive and aerospace industries through social and organizational innovation in tandem with technical advances. In building, engineering advances outstrip social and organizational ones, leading to slow implementation.

Integrating Information Technology and Real Estate

As the desire to shape the future using the rapidly expanding technology toolbox found its way into the dreams of visionaries and mavericks in real estate development, just as it had in IT, challenges lay ahead. Bringing these two worlds together, each with its own mind-set, language, priorities, and ways of doing business, was proving difficult. Correspondingly, as our research unfolded, the difficulty of revolutionizing the built environment seemed to intensify right before our eyes. As we see in the next few chapters, Lewis's city-building plan was morphing in response. His priorities seemed to be shifting from the physical to the information world—to the Urban Operating System.

In Portugal meanwhile, the conversation about PlanIT Valley continued unabated. For most Living PlanIT employees, building a physical city was still the name of the game—requiring an actual real estate deal. Living PlanIT's team planned to acquire the land from private landowners through direct purchase or, possibly, through government-backed expropriation due to its newfound status as a Project of Potential National Interest (PIN, short for Projecto de Potencial Interesse Nacional), granted with Celso Ferreira's support. The project's PIN status would facilitate permitting and other transactions. Land acquisition would begin with the purchase of several 10-hectare plots for immediate development in phase 1. The future looked bright. The land offered to PlanIT Valley contained no residential developments and no cultural or burial sites. A new highway extension cutting through the land was already under construction. Although the tracts comprised forests and natural habitats, most contained nonnative species. Living PlanIT, moreover, intended to reintroduce native plants and designate several large areas of the site as natural reserves or parks.

Late-night conversations on the flowing patios of Vale Pisão were imaginative, even grand. "What about the churches?" someone asked the group one night, as they discussed their ideas for the perfect city. "No churches!" someone else called out. It was beginning to sound a bit like SimCity, as Rosy Lokhorst pointed out in our first interview.

But unlike SimCity—the popular game that forces players to think about the main ingredients of cities—building real cities requires skills and resources not readily available with the click of a key. In a 2014 article titled "Les Simerables" in the magazine *Jacobin,* the author analyzed the shifting relationship of the game to reality:

> Where our cities appear unpredictably chaotic and impossibly complex, *SimCity* harmoniously tames this uncertainty into a manageable landscape. It offers a micropolis . . . to serve as a model for our own. It represents our cities not as they are but as they could be: calculated, optimized, controlled.
>
> That vision is rapidly becoming our reality. The game's simulational thinking has restructured how we relate to our politics and ourselves, to our work and our play—in short, to our social space. So-called "smart" cities have already started to deploy [the game's] techniques as Silicon Valley . . . moves into the business of constructing cities.[19]

The article went on to describe the work of Living PlanIT: "Living PlanIT, a startup founded by a former Microsoft executive, has been developing what it hopes will be *the* Urban Operating System. Apps, buildings, people, traffic—all will be connected through its cloud. Living PlanIT's business model is to monetize and license its UOS for users—big players like governments and investors—to download. Their first prototype is a green smart city in the hills of Portugal."[20]

The article conceptualized the Living PlanIT model as "top-down city design" and predicted that this approach would be increasingly common.

Meanwhile, by the end of 2011, those whom we interviewed from the real estate industry were frustrated by Living PlanIT's IT types, who in turn were frustrated by the so-called laggards in the building industry, the people in construction. Construction guys, as we see in chapter 6, were frustrated by the casual (to them, flighty) nature of IT work. In turn IT was frustrated (the way an adolescent hates his parents) with big business. Real estate (and everyone for that matter) was frustrated with government, one of the biggest clients in the business of building the future.

How could anyone hope to build anything real?

CHAPTER 5

Rethinking City Hall

*When the burdens of the presidency seem unusually heavy, I always
remind myself it could be worse. I could be a mayor.*

—Lyndon Johnson

*I will say that walking down the street, getting on the subway, taking
the elevator, if there's one or two people and they say, 'Great job, Mayor,'
that is a real turn-on. I mean, anybody that wouldn't find that satisfying,
rewarding, exciting, thrilling—I think they should see the doctor.*

—Michael Bloomberg

IT WAS BECOMING INCREASINGLY CLEAR THAT MAKING BUILDINGS,
neighborhoods, and cities smarter would involve more than cool new
technology. It would require a new level of cross-sector teaming—*Big
Teaming*. In addition to IT and real estate, city government had an important role to play. Future-building technologists and real estate developers
would have to team up with visionary mayors and other government officials who aspired to innovate. As Hardik Bhatt, the director of Cisco's
Smart+Connected Communities division, put it when we interviewed
him in 2012,

> Visionary leadership is number one when it comes to transforming
> the way a city works. Generally, a powerful decision maker, such
> as the mayor, is needed to bring the key pieces together. Each facet
> of building, all of the urban planning done today, has been done
> in the same way for so many years. Every city has regulations and
> ordinances that were formed way early in the last century and haven't
> been changed to address the needs of today, for example, the way
> broadband must be considered in the way buildings are constructed.
> Our lives today revolve around technology whether we want it or not.

Visionary Mayors

Celso Ferreira, newly reelected to his second four-year term in 2009, wasn't worried. The dynamic Portuguese mayor saw investing time and resources in Living PlanIT as a strategy to put his municipality on the twenty-first-century map. His sizable region, overdue for a smart overhaul in the built environment, was poor in resources, he reasoned, but rich in *desenrascanço,* a word the Portuguese often used to describe their culture. It roughly translates as an ability to find improvised solutions to problems, to troubleshoot, to throw something together on the fly. The Portuguese, young and old, are proud of this. When Portuguese schoolchildren learn about the Dutch traders, we are told by a local engineer, they are taught that the Dutch trading ships always had a Portuguese sailor on board to take over when things went wrong.

Mayors are crucial to the revitalization of cities. Building a new city or renovating old neighborhoods and buildings demands intense participation by government agencies, officials, and regulators and by private players as well. And, once built, cities are run by municipal governments—by mayors and other elected officials. Part visionary, part pragmatist, those who work in local government control resources, enforce permitting and regulations, and depend on good relationships with businesses to get things done.

People working in government, as we explore in this chapter, see themselves as public servants. Smart-city technology seems a luxury pitted against desperately needed education, transportation, infrastructure, housing, and other improvements. And yet, as others point out, it is the job of government to keep one eye firmly fixed on the future. While elected officials must focus on election cycles, "staff are the keepers of the vision."[1] Government must consider and balance the interests of multiple entities. And the fastest-moving cog in state government, the place where decisions can be made quickly, is the mayor's office. This sometimes yields audacious innovation.

Jaime Lerner, a Brazilian architect and urban planner, takes the visionary aspect of governing seriously. Elected mayor of Curitiba, capital of the Brazilian state of Paraná, three times between 1971 and 1992, Lerner went on to become governor of the state in 1994. Leading the way in smart-city innovation, by 2001 Lerner and his master plan had put Curitiba on the technological map, as one of the smartest, most livable cities in the world. (In 2010 Lerner was nominated among the 25 most influential thinkers in the world by *Time* magazine.) Rapid transit (the famous "speedybus"), urban parks, and waste removal, along with a number of innovative social and educational programs, brought plenty of attention to Lerner as a model mayor for the twenty-first century.

With mayors and other city officials as the target audience, IBM hosted a Smarter Cities Challenge in 2012. As proclaimed in IBM's conference report, "A new generation of mayors is taking on the challenge of reinventing cities for the twenty-first century." The company's 2013 white paper, "How to Reinvent a City: Mayors' Lessons from the Smarter Cities Challenge,"[2] elaborates, presenting insights and revelations from mayors around the world. In the challenge, IBM donated $50 million in employees' time to help 100 mayors reinvent (or "Brooklynize") their cities. Insights included the exhortation to "think like a CEO," "be bold," improve citizen engagement and access to data, "exploit the long view," and collaborate across organizational and geographic boundaries to create alliances among constituents with widely varying interests (for example, tourism teaming up with petrochemicals in Siracusa, Sicily).

Ferreira, similarly, wanted to improve the lives of his constituents and leave a legacy that future generations would attach to his family name. When Steve Lewis, Manuel Simas, and Miguel Rodrigues first showed up in his office, ambitious, far-sighted development projects seemed possible: a mall, an auto city, a business park. After many meetings, building a smart city seemed the best way to create jobs, attract multinational corporations to the region, and reverse the brain drain lamented by so many.

Porto, a vibrant university town straddling the majestic Douro River, was badly in need of infrastructure and building renovation. The second-largest city in Portugal after Lisbon, Porto was home to roughly 1.3 million people (including its rapidly growing greater metropolitan area). In 1996 the city, originally an outpost of the Roman Empire, was designated a World Heritage Site by UNESCO; but engineers graduating from the University of Porto were leaving Portugal, with its precarious economy, to work for multinational corporations elsewhere. Because of the region's engineering talent, Ferreira believed that "Innovation should be our main export. If we get the right partners and the public and private support, we could start a new era." For that he needed to keep the talent from fleeing.

"I am not a politician who is afraid of failing," Ferreira told us on a brilliant spring day in Paredes. Sitting in his darkly paneled office, with the wrought iron balcony from which a mayor in another era might speak to his people, everything about Ferreira seemed to point to a slower, more elegant time. "I'm a local guy, a very creative guy," he said, opening his hands, "a sculptor and a furniture maker." Soon after coming to this office, Ferreira overhauled the schools in Paredes, beginning with the elementary schools. New buildings, complete with photovoltaics and heated with briquettes created from furniture industry waste, were just the beginning.

A New Way of Governing

As new technological solutions and products, along with advances in building materials and approaches, were being developed, it became clear that policies, permitting strategies, and even taxation would need to change to enable smart-city development. The language around smart legislation was vague at first, as in this quote from GDF Suez's Smart City Dashboard brochure: "The trend is for cities to develop policies which are global and system-based: such policies create both a synergy between the city's different key components and an expression of its different seasons and rhythms. There are economic and environmental issues at stake, as well as a need for coherence and meaning."[3]

This vagueness, uninformative on the one hand, on the other hand allowed for on-the-ground creativity and interpretation.

Ferreira, like many mayors, was game to learn a new way to get things done. He liked the term *smart legislation*—the kind of legislation that might allow a group of dreamers to build a city in his municipality. "My role is to be a facilitator," he told us. "And then get out of the way." In a 2010 interview, Ferreira explained the decision-making chain as it would relate to Living PlanIT and PlanIT Valley. "I am one step down from the minister of the economy, who is one step down from the prime minister." While Ferreira was excited about the possibilities, he also understood the obstacles. "This idea is not easy to sell," he said. "Do you explain it as a business plan, or do you explain it as a vision?"

Lewis described Ferreira as an entrepreneur, as someone willing to "just go for it" when the right opportunity came along. Ferreira saw high-technology investments as the key to Portugal's future, due to its lack of natural resources, not to mention the future of Paredes, home to almost 1,400 small furniture-manufacturing companies. He sought projects to provide opportunities for local workers and to attract foreign workers and investors. "We have to read the future," Ferreira explained. "We are close to Porto and we cannot afford to ignore the growing metropolitan area. If we have a project that can increase value and attract companies and creative people to work locally, I think it is the best way [to develop] . . . to become a hub of creative industries."

The meetings between Lewis and Ferreira had proved essential in the development of these ideas. "While talking to Celso about his munici-pality," Lewis recalled, "it became obvious that he was deeply sincere about making a difference and knew he needed to provide a richer set of industry opportunities in his municipality."

Ferreira was equally intrigued by Lewis's vision, which he believed in immediately, recalling, "What we noticed is that Steve Lewis had much more to say than what he actually said in the first night that we met. My personal duty as an official, as I understand it, is not to close any doors. We decided we should go forward with talks with Steve to understand what more he had to say."

Despite having doubts about a project so difficult to describe to inves-tors, Ferreira understood Lewis's idea: "It is not the same thing as buying a car. We are talking about a way of life. We are talking about creating the first intelligent city in the world, which has been talked about for the past 20 years, but no one has had the opportunity to make it happen." This was the kind of cross-sector teaming that we longed to see at a larger scale.

Hatching Dreams

Living PlanIT's founders wanted to demonstrate that sustainable urbaniza-tion could be achieved through high-tech, collaborative solutions. They envisioned an ecosystem of companies helping realize Ferreira's vision.

Ferreira agreed to expand the amount of land available to Living PlanIT to 1,670 hectares. That was when Living PlanIT began to refer to the vision as PlanIT Valley because the land included a large valley. And that is how a company started by a Brit who had lived for years in the United States and an Australian who'd relocated to Switzerland came to be located in Maia, Portugal.

Way back in 2008, in the aftermath of the car rally, the excitement had been palpable. Several visits to the 1,700-hectare parcel of land in northern Paredes followed soon after, always with someone's arms sweeping widely across the expansive sky, envisioning the city that would spring up in no time at all. What started as the dream of an automotive city had morphed into a smart city called PlanIT Valley, supported by a future-thinking mayor. It was a win-win. Lewis would use this vote of confidence, this credibility boost, to attract investors. Ferreira would get a bit of good publicity as the forward-thinking mayor bringing to Portugal innovative research and development in the smart-city space. The positive press continued long after the four years originally cited as the amount of time it would take to build the city, four years during which no ground was broken. Despite this, as illustrious media outlets like the *Wall Street Journal* reported, Living PlanIT was selected as one of the World Economic Forum's Technology Pioneers of 2012.[4]

For Lewis, Simas, Rodrigues, Peter van Manen, and other early members of the team, PlanIT Valley was an exciting business possibility. And it was fun. But for Ferreira, whose family went back many generations in the soil of Paredes, it was something different—a chance to put his municipality on the map, to revive its flagging economy, and to become a leader rather than a follower in world developments. When we met him in 2010, his pride in the possibilities was obvious.

Like so many others, Ferreira was drawn to Lewis but for slightly different reasons. The draw was less personal; it wasn't about charisma (Ferreira had plenty of his own). As a public servant, he saw Lewis as an invaluable link to private-sector investment:

> One thing was very important to us—his network. We saw that Steve had a high capacity in that way. The question was, *What does Steve Lewis have that we couldn't get from another project?* The answer was

that he was the leader of a team, and it's very difficult to find a leader in most projects. Steve was a visionary, and we had the possibility of talking directly to a visionary. With a very high-skilled team, we thought he could do it. We had conditions to provide him with the physical space and the municipal support to allow him to implement the project.

There was political risk: Ferreira's constituents were very conservative. "But reading the future," he told us, "means we have to create opportunities to make our area a competitive one. We have two options: either we occupy these lands correctly, or we don't do anything, and the guys that come after us will. If we have a project that can create value, that can attract global companies, it is the best way to use this land."

For many mayors, just as for Ferreira, investments in smart-city technology represented an opportunity to make a mark on history. "We live in a globalized world but with regional economies," Ferreira said. "I was interested in projects that aren't just local. We can only be part of human development if we take human resources as our raw material—by trying to achieve a new standard of innovation and efficiency from human capital. This region is focused on traditional industries, like the furniture industry, but I saw that it could have other opportunities. We are less than 70 kilometers away from four of the best five universities in Portugal."

Ferreira went on to explain that he had been looking for growth opportunities for a while: "So, in 2005, I began looking for alternative industry sectors for the region. I wasn't afraid of the decline of furniture, which is a huge industry. . . . I thought, for example, about attracting small-production car companies, making personalized cars, electric cars, etc."

Although it had been back in 2008 that Lewis had flexed his salesman muscles and triggered a new idea for Ferreira (Why not think bigger than an auto city? Why not "make it a smart urban space"?), Ferreira's excitement was still strong when we met with him two years later. He still felt that he was in the forefront of smart-city potential: "If we are the first to do it, we will be part of a new cluster of economic development—smart cities. The technology all exists—but there is no place in the world where it is all put together. We are now building a platform to do that. We are willing to work locally to facilitate a place where the technology can all come together."

Besides being attracted to the idea of PlanIT Valley, Ferreira was intrigued by the need for "smart regulations" to fast-track the project. Each municipality, he explained, has the ability to set its own regulations for architecture (e.g., fire codes), but none exists for technology. If political leaders could regulate infrastructure and technology appropriately, they could create conditions for the market to appear. City governments might have to introduce new regulations for technology, however.

Public Commitments

Ferreira was one of the first to commit publicly to smart-city building in his municipality, but soon he wasn't alone. In November 2013 the European Innovation Partnership on Smart Cities and Communities passed its "Strategic Implementation Plan" as part of the Digital Agenda for Europe. The report outlined the role of the commission (a combination of local city leaders across Europe and business leaders) in charge of the Digital Agenda to integrate ICT systems and use big data to "make our cities better places to live and work. We need to base those new systems on open standards for hardware, software, data and services which this European Innovation Partnership will develop. . . . Creating equal partnerships between cities and companies based on synergies between ICT, energy and mobility will lead to projects that make a real difference in our everyday lives."[5]

The commission had 200 million euros at its disposal to make these goals a reality.[6]

Ferreira exuded confidence in PlanIT Valley, a testament to his desire and Lewis's persuasiveness. He fully expected 250,000 new citizens to arrive by 2020. Phase 1, he said, would develop 37 hectares for 10,000 people within five to seven years. The original settlers, from places like Cisco, would soon recruit Portuguese talent.

"I saw the opportunity right away," he said proudly. "I heard Steve Lewis talking about the potential of an auto and urban sector, and I thought immediately that this could be a new global business. I believe the commercial opportunity is immense—the project is the best opportunity we could find in a lifetime. I am proud to be part of the team where this knowledge was shared and developed. To grab the idea, that's what I did."

Slow to Move

When you think of government employees, chances are terms like *risk averse, inflexible,* and *downright slow to move* come to mind. Of course, these are just stereotypes, but some of these stereotypes are grounded in actual government processes and behaviors. But governments can also make things happen when vision, opportunity, and pragmatism collide. Was this to be one of those moments? As time went on, it seemed less and less likely.

People in city and state government share a commitment to public service—along with a willingness to delay gratification. They shoulder responsibilities that include managing a justice system; maintaining highways and public transportation; implementing public welfare programs; providing education, police and fire services, water, and recreation; and regulating businesses. The diversity of tasks is staggering—and largely takes shape within thickly siloed departments.

Challenges to Progress

Cisco's director of Smart+Connected Communities, Hardik Bhatt, told us in 2014 that city governments are used to working in silos. The biggest challenge, he explained with a heavy sigh, "is when technologies are intended as a unifier across public and private applications. If visionary leadership is lacking, the collaboration does not turn out well. A city, after all, is an ecosystem: utilities are public, power might be private, and transportation might be regulated by the government."

But when silos dominate, Bhatt explained, ecosystems struggle to function: "Silos are the main challenges that anyone has to face with smart and connected cities." Even within city government, silos can get in the way. Cities, after all, are run by an uneasy combination of professional managers and elected officials. Elected councils make policy decisions and provide legislative direction. The mayor, usually the head of these councils, relies on a professional manager, who in turn manages department heads, who in turn implement policies.[7]

Local government is all about meetings—getting together face-to-face to hear concerns, offer solutions, negotiate needs, and just plain take the pulse of the constituents. Administrators work with community leaders, business leaders, and a wide variety of citizens groups.

Careers

There is no certification required to become a city official. Rather, it's a journeyman's path in which on-the-job experience earns credibility. One might go from administrative assistant in a deputy manager's office to budget analyst to city planner to assistant to the city manager, to city manager, and so on. Professional development and conferences are considered a valuable part of that experience. A background as a manager in the private sector or military experience can also translate into city administration. Leadership, particularly the ability to work with many different kinds of people with very different skills and experience, is highly valued.[8]

People in local government have generally chosen their work because of its potential to make a difference. As Jonathan Miller, secretary of finance and administration for the state of Kentucky and a 1992 graduate of Harvard Law School, put it: "I found that returning home, people really respected the fact that you could have been working on Wall Street or on Capitol Hill, but you came home to make a difference. I cannot stress the value of and the chance you have to make a difference by going back to where you came from, taking the education that less than 0.1 percent of Americans have the opportunity to get and using that to help your community and your state."[9]

Someone in the Living PlanIT orbit who understood this well was Robin Daniels.

The Boundary Spanner

Relationships with government officials would become increasingly important to Living PlanIT as time went on. Recognizing this, in 2009 Lewis teamed up with Robin Daniels. His story is important to ours because Daniels had spent most of his career collaborating across various boundaries, for instance, translating science for businesspeople or financial models for government officials. Unlike many of the early employees, Daniels was not overawed by Lewis's intelligence, vision, or charm. His career had not been spent in a silo, and he was levelheaded about the possibilities for the UOS and PlanIT Valley. Daniels embodied the kind of nimble, flexible mind and natural boundary-spanning ability that must accompany vision if progress is to be made. He could speak the language of many sectors, and was sympathetic to their priorities and entrenched processes as well.

We first spoke with Daniels in September 2011. His Clark Kent demeanor was disarming. Mild mannered, neatly dressed, efficient, and organized, Daniels looked too young to house his multifaceted career. When he spoke he betrayed a passion for his work that one might not normally associate with a policy analyst. Policy analysis, it turns out, was only a piece of Daniels's work. He had a background in engineering and manufacturing (largely in the auto industry, yes—another Living PlanIT link to cars), and he seemed at the time to be the only person on the Living PlanIT team who really understood local government channels outside Portugal. Daniels was the guy you'd want to set up your government meetings to discuss new projects. In more than one meeting that we observed, Daniels laid the groundwork and let Lewis make the pitch. He was Robin to Lewis's Batman.

In 2011 Daniels explained that he had been introduced to Living PlanIT not by Lewis but by board member Ian Taylor. In 2006 Daniels had been CEO of the Norwich Research Park, 20 miles northeast of London. At a dinner for local government officials, the guest of honor, the science minister, spoke about the fact that the conservatives had no science policy. Daniels was appalled. *Can this be true? Is there no science policy?* He fired off an e-mail after the dinner and was put in touch with former minister (and adviser to Living PlanIT) Ian Taylor. Taylor, who had been a member of the UK Parliament for 23 years until 2010, came to the Norwich Research Park to have a look around. He invited Daniels to be part of the Policy Review on Science for the Shadow Cabinet, a new policy group on science, technology, and engineering, formed prior to the general election. In 2009, when Taylor became the chairman of Living PlanIT, he invited Daniels to join the advisory board of Living PlanIT, as well.

This way of meeting with different people and talking over time is typical of the laborious chain of events—and this is just the tip of the iceberg—often required to simply have a meeting with key players in the public sector. (Contrast this with the speed of decision making in Ferreira's office or among Living PlanIT founders over coffee at the Hotel Central Parque.)

Daniels assumed that Lewis took him on out of a need for someone who could translate innovation to the private sector to inspire investment, what he called "commercializing research." With jobs in materials handling and production management in several companies, Daniels did a part-time PhD early in his career and then moved to Cambridge to run an executive master's program. While working at Cambridge, he became more and more interested in how new companies form and grow, particularly tech startups.

Throughout his career Daniels has straddled the worlds of academia, business, and government. After university at Cambridge, he became chief operating officer of a joint venture between the London Business School (LBS) and University College London (UCL) to bring together the engineering faculty of UCL with the business faculty at LBS. "From a strategic point of view," Daniels explained, in what we will come to recognize as classic Danielsese, "linkage makes sense."

He paid close attention to startups, looking for the next big thing. In 2009, he said, "The next big thing appeared to be Living PlanIT." Daniels's experience as CEO of the Norwich Research Park was also important to Lewis inasmuch as "the Park" resembled early plans for PlanIT Valley. The Park, Daniels explained, is a collection of organizations with a patchwork of different landowners. The original idea was to turn the cluster of organizations—a teaching hospital, some research institutes, and a small number of startups—into a science park. Working with real estate companies, he would create a marketing strategy and then, of course, fill the space. The United Kingdom, explained Daniels, had little experience with this sort of thing. Much of Daniels's job was managing 9,500 people employed on the site. Most were public-sector employees, either at the hospital or the university. About 40 were employed by the startups that were the real focus of the Park, and, a listener suspects, Daniels's main interest in the project.

In spite of his ability as a negotiator and bridge builder, Daniels realized that he had to get the public/private mix right for maximum job satisfaction. He enjoyed working with the academics, the companies, and the local authorities. But the job had its frustrations as well. He had an executive board, made up of all the partners in the Park, three different local authorities, and a regional development agency. "My ability to pull that community together into something cohesive, crystallize it, and sell it—this was why Steve was interested in me because he was thinking of PlanIT Valley," Daniels said.

At that point PlanIT Valley was what Living PlanIT was about. But the market Living PlanIT hoped to serve was in the developing world, where, as noted in chapter 1, the need for new cities was greatest. Daniels was asked to help Living PlanIT with business development. He was particularly interested in what the private sector could do with the public sector to help accelerate economic development. Soon his role was to help raise money and find new partners. The variety in the work was exhilarating, he said, if a little confusing: "From late summer 2009 until summer 2010, I had three or four job titles with Living PlanIT." In August 2010 Daniels threw his hat in the ring and joined Living PlanIT full-time.

Networking in the Public Sector

Because, as Daniels put it, "there was no budget for anything" and because he was familiar with development opportunities in London, that is where he chose to start looking for Living PlanIT opportunities. He began with Isabel Dedring, environment minister to the then mayor of London, Boris Johnson.

Enterprise Zones

London had launched an initiative called the Green Enterprise District, 48 square kilometers of land running from the Olympic Village down a hockey-stick shape south to the north bank of the Thames, eastward through the Royal Docks, then a bit farther east. It was earmarked as a place for investment, green-collar jobs, smart utilities, integrated transport, and other forward-thinking innovations.

Daniels explained the concept of PlanIT Valley to Dedring and suggested collaborating on a regeneration project in London. Dedring was particularly keen on having Living PlanIT corral the private sector. She had spoken with several private companies in the smart-city space and had found them more interested in selling London "a Siemens kit, an IBM kit, or a Cisco kit" than in using the space in an innovative, efficient way. Leaders in the public sector, she explained to Daniels, needed guidance. We are not equipped, she told him (and here Daniels paraphrased Dedring), "to know what's good, bad, or indifferent. We can't express a preference because there has to be due process. And actually, we're not really interested. What we want to see, long term, is new jobs, GDP growth, inward investment, and our elected bosses reelected and we keep our jobs. That's kind of the way the world works. Can you help us?"

Daniels's response was a resounding yes. He explained that the Living PlanIT business model was about bringing companies together in a place to collaborate and create new things that can be exported. Dedring, now deputy mayor for transport for London's mayor, was a good contact for Living PlanIT. She suggested convening a mayoral council—to include Celso Ferreira and New York's then mayor, Michael Bloomberg, since New York, like London, is organized by boroughs—to talk about Living PlanIT possibilities, but the idea did not come to fruition.

As it turns out, Daniels explained, "Every big city has a regeneration project, and they all want the same things. As long as your piece of regeneration land is big enough, how you do it looks like [our plans for] phase 1 of PlanIT Valley." It became clear to the Living PlanIT team that opportunity lurked in enterprise districts around the world. Lewis initiated conversations with people in Boston, Silicon Valley, Saudi Arabia, Brazil, and elsewhere. These projects, Daniels explained, are very time intensive: "You've got to coax them through, and we just didn't have the ballast."

Many conversations came close to fruition, but the effort was time-consuming for Living PlanIT's small team. Then Dedring went on sabbatical, leaving the London projects up in the air. Daniels began talking with officials in the London borough of Newham (London is organized in 52 political boroughs, each governed by a council). According to Daniels, there is tension between the mayor's office and the boroughs, and the mayor's office has more budgetary control. Newham is a poorer borough with more than 120 different first languages spoken; 54 percent of the working population is unemployed. By contrast, on the Greenwich

Peninsula, where Living PlanIT was teaming up with Quintain, there is a great deal of corporate and private wealth.

Together the Newham Council and the London Development Agency (one of the regional development agencies) own 70 percent of the land in the Green Enterprise District, so both were important players in that discussion. Daniels explained to the players that Living PlanIT could build something that looked a lot like phase 1 of PlanIT Valley, or a smaller version, if they were given the right piece of land. The Newham Council suggested a piece of land, at the edges of the Royal Docks (the world's center for shipbuilding at the end of the nineteenth century). The London City Airport sits in the middle of the Royal Docks, located next to the Greenwich Peninsula, a key site for future development.

Proposing Innovation

Living PlanIT put together a proposal. It was exciting—a real customer, with money to invest and specific questions about how it would be spent. Daniels felt that Living PlanIT, at this point, was long on vision and short on practical action. The proposal, which Living PlanIT began work on in October 2010, in his view took too long to generate. "In the public sector, they want to know, 'Well, where's the hole you're digging going to be? How big is it? When does it start? How many jobs?'" It was frustrating for Daniels, knowing that the engineering team in Portugal was chomping at the bit to begin working on a real project.

This was right around the time that Steve Lewis met Adrian Wyatt at Quintain. Quintain brought to the table its interest in developing Wembley (home of the national stadium for soccer and also a concert venue, as well as various retail and residential opportunities), along with a property the firm owned in the Brent borough in the northwest of central London. Wembley was ripe for regeneration (brown field) and retrofitting (building new technology into an existing building). Quintain asked Living PlanIT to put together a proposal for Wembley that would include modeling new technologies.

"A core part of the Living PlanIT proposition," Daniels explained, "is driving inefficiency out of construction. The money you save can be invested in technology, used to cover operating costs and add value to future buildings." Daniels brokered a deal to combine work in Greenwich, Newham, and Wembley to stimulate economic development by bringing in private companies. In the case of Wembley, Quintain was the client.

Having shown (on paper at least, in the Living PlanIT proposal) that high-tech development made commercial sense, the boroughs would, in theory, be better positioned to get financial help from the banks. In 2010 the Greenwich Peninsula had already spent 12 years mired in the development-planning process. The Living PlanIT proposal would, again in theory, help unfreeze the real estate finance challenge, lighting a fire under the permitting process. Rather than trying to simply promote Greenwich as an investment opportunity, Daniels suggested to the borough, "How about collaborating with Newham because if you look down from space at this part of London, it's much more attractive than either one of these things on the right." Despite the tendency of the boroughs to compete with one another rather than collaborate, Daniels recalled, miracle of miracles, the response was "Can you help with that?"

Cross-Council Teaming

So, Daniels brokered a collaboration deal between the Newham and Greenwich Councils. Their first goal: saving money. Daniels remembered Dedring's question a year earlier: "Can you help corral the private sector?" The public sector, he realized, felt more comfortable with Living PlanIT's relatively benign message: *We've got our own technology, but actually we're representing the global technology sector, so we can present you with something that fits with what you want, and you don't have to deal with people trying to sell you black boxes.*

Daniels's role, at this point in the game, was supporting collaboration among the boroughs and creating an economic development and investment strategy. Just before Christmas 2011, Living PlanIT provided the Newham Council with a high-level description of what technology would be required in the Royal Docks to fulfill their vision. The document helped Newham to secure economic zone status. Daniels's hope was that the mayor of London would approve the zone status with the provision that Living PlanIT do the development.

Land in cities is rarely controlled by a single owner. Moreover, ownership is moot if permits for development cannot be obtained. Quintain may have been both owner and developer of its parcel, but other developers competed for permits and usage. Daniels's hope was that banks would look at the Quintain/Living PlanIT proposal and say, "From a risk point of view, we are more comfortable providing debt for a development that is future-proofed in this way than to purely private interests at the top of the food chain." Real progress would be made when banks started saying to developers: "You need to do it the Living PlanIT way."

In the midst of these negotiations, Living PlanIT helped launch the Digital Enterprise Greenwich center in one of the buildings. The center was originally going to be a Cisco project, but Cisco decided to focus its activity on the London Olympic Village. Daniels's Cisco contact said, "Well, we'd like to do something here anyway, so why don't we say it's a Living PlanIT enterprise center with Cisco as a partner?" The space became an incubator and project office for Greenwich Peninsula development, shared by a number of companies, including Living PlanIT, Infusion, and Cisco. The project was small but, as Daniels explained, would establish a microcosm of the PlanIT Valley model. He felt this was critical because, as he put it, nothing but eucalyptus was growing in PlanIT Valley. It would be small, real action from which the team could learn.

Dueling Geographies

Almost everyone at Living PlanIT at this time lived and worked in Portugal, and yet, as Daniels pointed out, most of the action was in London. A cultural rift was growing between the people who still believed in PlanIT Valley and the people (mostly in London) who did not. The joke was that money was due to arrive in six weeks. "Don't say it," Daniels said when we spoke with him, covering his ears. "Don't say 'six weeks!'"

In late 2011, worried about the slow pace of action, Daniels began exploring possibilities in Brazil and in the United States. Living PlanIT had taken on a partner to pursue waste-to-energy anaerobic digestion technology in the United Kingdom. Daniels felt the need for a clear technology strategy to fill in gaps and drive the right partnerships with small tech companies. In each new location, Daniels explained, there is generally a mayor's office or municipal government official in the economic development role. The mayor, like Celso Ferreira, wants to be seen doing good things on his or her watch. The biggest challenge, Daniels said, was communicating with the real estate, finance, and construction communities: "They're so inefficient and they're so attached to their ways of doing things. That's why our success with Quintain is *so* critically important. It's far beyond just making a pile of money. It's about being seen and having a developer and private companies saying, 'Investing in this technology makes commercial sense for our shareholders, and so we're doing it.'"

Daniels believed that Portugal would be Living PlanIT's headquarters, at least in the short term. But Europe, North America, South America, Brazil, and Asia would be the priority areas for action. "China is seductive but difficult, so it's likely that we'll establish a presence in Singapore or something like that," he said.

"We have," Daniels reported happily one day, "a fantastic conversation developing with Hitachi. Japanese companies work in collaboration with one another. Hitachi wants to bring into a partnership discussion Fuji, Panasonic, Samsung, and all the others." While Hitachi's smart-city strategy looked similar to Living PlanIT's—the technology, how city services would be linked together—Hitachi had yet to develop an urban operating system. The idea of collaboration with Living PlanIT was on the table.

Gaining Momentum

"The technology has *really* developed significantly in a very short period of time," Daniels said of John Stenlake's tech development team. "We can demonstrate aspects of its functionality. By Christmas [2011] we'll have something real and demonstrable. There isn't one running in a building yet. Maybe by next Easter, there'll be a building somewhere with the Urban Operating System sitting in it."

We can clearly see that Living PlanIT was struggling toward a product that clients could comprehend and test. While the all-city dashboard enabled by the UOS was difficult for most—bureaucrats, builders, or banks—to imagine, the upscale, high-tech development, with its residential, commercial, and public spaces, was a familiar beast. In the absence of city leadership or smart-enough legislation, Living PlanIT might embed its technologies in this time-tested model.

Daniels believed that the shift to regeneration work in London had expanded Living PlanIT's range of offerings and products. Stenlake's team was now creating products to serve customers who might want, for example, a smart transport system *or* an energy management system, rather than buying a whole-city dashboard.

Envisioning an Alternative Future

Where was the market for these products? Daniels had great hope for the global construction marketplace, including especially emerging-market countries. He looked around the world and saw applications for Living PlanIT products and services everywhere: Africa, Brazil, the United States, and Asia. Infrastructure, healthcare—the possibilities seemed endless. His main challenge? Convincing the banks to jump in.

Daniels, like so many on the Living PlanIT team, really enjoyed the work. He felt a sense of infinite possibility. The work seemed important and useful and exciting: "I was in Norwich for five years," he told us, "and I got stuck. Before that I had been in India for more than three years. I kind of got fed up with that when it started to feel like a routine. But this is . . . I can't imagine ever feeling like that because there's always something new around the corner. In every one of these projects, . . . if you're going to be sustainable in its broadest sense, there are so many aspects to think about."

Living PlanIT needed to grow to survive. But growth required money. And most governments require substantial proof before leaping into the unknown. Daniels, like the construction guys at Quintain, was eager to get going—to meet new needs, to solve problems.

The world was not standing still, waiting for Living PlanIT to create products and services on which bureaucracies could bite down. But when we asked people like Stenlake and Daniels about the competition, the response was usually sanguine. Stenlake felt that the finest talent for building urban operating systems had been culled by Lewis. There weren't, he explained, at that point many people in the world who could build what they were building.

"It sounds very arrogant," Daniels said in response to questions about competition, "but the main competition is the noise in the marketplace— companies who have huge marketing budgets, saying, 'We're doing smart-city developments,' but when you dig into it, there are often lots of services and it's the technology that's missing." Would people try to copy the Living PlanIT model as it evolved? Yes. But Daniels felt that Living PlanIT had "first mover advantage."

Meanwhile city governments approached by Living PlanIT were increasingly worried about the news from projects like Masdar City and New Songdo City, which were being built but remained underpopulated. When potential clients mentioned these examples, Lewis would often point out that they were financed and built on "traditional real estate models: build it and they will come." But they hadn't come *yet*—and for many different reasons.

Fingers could be pointed at city and state governments for their slow decision making and cumbersome hierarchies. Mayors, like Ferreira, willing to act swiftly and decisively to support legislation that would speed smart-city developments seemed rare; yet it's not clear that blaming the public sector would be fair. Companies weren't moving all that fast, either. By the end of 2011, the smart-city buzz was deafening. City and state governments were jockeying for publicity: Who could be the greenest? Who was positioned to implement the available technology? City officials in Copenhagen, Denmark, announced their intention to make their city carbon neutral by 2025 with improvements to transportation; incorporating sensors in streetlights to provide data on parking, security information, and travel patterns; and machine-to-machine communication using a unified data platform. They sent out a request for proposals in 2012. Living PlanIT, invited by Hitachi, would be among those who responded.

Would builders and designers be ready to help?

CHAPTER **6**

Grounded Visionaries

Dream in a pragmatic way.

—Aldous Huxley

THE PLANNERS, ARCHITECTS, AND BUILDERS WHO COLLECTIVELY translate ideas into concrete reality have long played crucial roles in how any large urban project turns out. Sometimes their interdependence plays out collaboratively, other times contentiously. Innovative projects, like the exquisite Beijing Water Cube built for the 2008 Olympics, nearly always involve effective collaborations across disciplines.[1] Not all successful urban projects are innovative. Some projects rely on well-established procedures. The more routine and familiar the approach, the more easily professional responsibilities can be cleanly allocated, reducing the potential for conflict and misunderstanding.[2]

Teaming across the boundaries between even the interlinked professional domains in the built environment is fraught with conflict. Accounts of the tension between builders and architects abound.[3] Nonetheless these particular professional domains have much in common: shared experiences of undertaking large projects from start to finish, overlapping language, common time frames, and more. They also have a long history of working together across their shared boundary. Could they now team up with IT?

PlanIT Valley had gotten stalled at the vision phase. Increasingly restless, many Living PlanIT employees were anxious to break ground. So were those on the sidelines. The builders waiting to construct phase 1 of the city grew more impatient by the day with Living PlanIT's priorities and time lines.

A Dream Too Good to Waste

When we caught up with David Crump and Nigel Linscott in late 2011, they had worked together in different parts of the construction industry for 30 years. For the past decade or so, they had been managing construction projects at Quintain. It was clear, talking with them in an empty, white-walled, windowless conference room in the Quintain offices, that they knew each other well. They were polite but not afraid to interrupt or correct each other. They nodded affirmations of agreement periodically when the other spoke. Their body language was similar—slightly stooped, gracious, attentive, and something else: skeptical? Their enthusiasm for PlanIT Valley was obvious. Their enthusiasm for Living PlanIT—the company they were partnering with to build the technological wonder that would illustrate the power of innovation to improve lives and save energy—was, well, not so obvious.

"I'm caught up, swept up by the plan," said Crump.

"I've been a member of Greenpeace since 1983," said Linscott, slightly older and more stooped than Crump. "I think a lot about the environment." Both looked too large for the small space of the conference room. Linscott looked as though his body would fit perfectly around the edge of a pub bar, his hands rested on the table, positioned for a pint. "But this is a dream," he said, "that is just too good to waste."

A dream too good to waste. "Therein lies the frustration," Crump said, nodding. "There's a difference between understanding the brilliance of the dream and converting the dream into reality." Linscott looked hard at the table. Both were eager to make it clear that, while they respected Steve Lewis, it was not his charm or his charisma that brought them on board in October 2010, when they first heard about PlanIT Valley, as had been the case for so many. They were already on board. "We think it fits with our aspirations," explained Crump. "But as for Steve Lewis, well, we have our own inspirational leaders." (Here he was referring to Adrian Wyatt.) They both laughed. Imaginary clink of glasses.

"We're dealing with IT people when it comes to Living PlanIT," said Linscott. "And they're different. We actually have to build things . . ." His voice trailed off, laying bare, in that simple statement, the cultural divide between construction and IT. Linscott sighed.

Unlike others in Quintain's construction group, Crump and Linscott had interacted with the Living PlanIT team directly. "I don't think our managers understand how big that divide really is," bemoaned Linscott. "Construction is not about assembly lines. Each project is different; each project has a different concept." It seemed that he and Crump confronted a constant misunderstanding: guys in IT apparently thought construction was simple, modular. "We are not test engineers for software," Linscott said with feeling. "In the construction industry, we are always called in to fix things we didn't design." Still he was eager to get a master plan and vastly preferred working with architects and planners over IT guys.

"I've never seen him so committed," Crump said, nodding in Linscott's direction.

Aside from IT, both men agreed that it was government, local and national, that was preventing real progress in building and construction. "Look at our lack of a working Envac system," said Linscott with palpable bitterness, referring to the new sustainable urban waste management systems increasingly in use in cities around the world that stood in stark contrast to London's outdated waste collection systems. "They've been doing more-sustainable stuff in Sweden since 1948," he snorted. "In the UK there is no assistance for energy-saving technology, no rebates whatsoever, no incentives to recycle. It's a part of the jigsaw that is not in place."

When we met with them back in 2011, Crump and Linscott worried that because Living PlanIT was taking too long, another company (perhaps Cisco, Siemens, or Microsoft) would come up with something similar to the Urban Operating System. "Living PlanIT has the ability to synchronize devices, for data recovery, but we haven't seen anything we could take to market yet," said Crump, seemingly the more patient of the two.

"Cisco already has the hardware!" said Linscott. Both were anxious to see products, devices—something physical that they could install and sell. "What about Wembley and Greenwich?" asked Linscott, referring to Quintain's London redevelopment projects. "Why aren't we implementing the UOS there? If we could just start demonstrating the savings . . ."

"We're supposed to start building next week," said Crump." Both men shook their heads and stared at the table.

Linscott and Crump, like racehorses straining against the starting gate, were anxious to build a shining Emerald City. This is not how much of the world sees the construction industry, which is often blamed for holding back innovation with its adherence to established procedures, processes, and materials. But Linscott and Crump, like so many people drawn into the smart-city orbit, are not typical of their sector.

"There's something special about this project," Crump admitted. "It's like the Olympics for us," he added, looking up in search of a window in the windowless room. "But I'm not a very good hurdler. Both of us are very progressive. That's why this is such a heartbreaker for us."

They were stuck at an industry fault line.

Construction Heartbreak

As Crump and Linscott both knew, heartbreak was no stranger to professionals in the construction business, a sector known for waste, delays, insularity, failure to embrace the latest technologies, and, according to some analysts, general backwardness.[4] If sustainable building is going to happen on the kind of scale that could deflect climate change, this will have to shift. Why hadn't innovative materials and information technologies made more inroads into the built environment? The potential was clearly there.

Construction is one of the largest and most important sectors in any economy. The annual value of construction projects is a leading indicator of economic well-being in economies around the world. Why? In part because so many other industries are implicated in the activities of the construction sector—steel, lumber, asphalt, vehicles, equipment, and so on. In the United States alone, spending in construction for 2013 was about $875 billion, roughly two-thirds of it private, and one-third public.[5]

Commercial and residential buildings in the United States consume about 40 percent of total energy, including 70 percent of our electricity, 40 percent of our raw materials, and 12 percent of our freshwater. They account for 30 percent of greenhouse gas emissions around the world, and some studies show that buildings are responsible for 40 percent of all US carbon emissions.[6]

The global construction industry seemed ill prepared to tackle the challenge of sustainable urbanization. The sector is highly fragmented, inhibiting the spread of new technologies and materials, even when they may dramatically improve the lifetime performance of a building.[7] Individual construction firms have little incentive and few resources to collect, integrate, or use collective wisdom. Research on industry efficiency reveals "25 to 50 percent waste in coordinating labor and in managing, moving, and installing materials . . . ; losses of $15.6 billion per year due to the lack of interoperability . . . ; and transactional costs of $4 billion to $12 billion per year to resolve disputes and claims associated with construction projects . . ."[8] Studies suggest that up to 75 percent of construction activities add no value.[9]

Waste plagues the construction industry. In addition to inefficient building methods, the sector produces buildings that waste energy and emit substantial amounts of carbon, as reported in chapter 1. Construction material waste accounted for 60 percent of solid, nonindustrial waste. The industry wastes an estimated 30 percent of the cost of construction due to errors, unused materials, labor inefficiencies, and other problems.[10]

It's little wonder that sustainable building techniques have been slow to take hold. Construction companies are traditionally reluctant to adopt novel information technologies, yet by 2010 some were moving to cloud-based computing, and change was surely in the air, even as Living PlanIT was forming itself based on the premise that it must play a role in charting the course forward for the construction industry.[11] Green building was on the rise, with LEED certification growing rapidly for new construction projects around the world, as elaborated later in this chapter.[12]

Getting the Job Done

People in construction like to build things. It is a profession steeped in the tangible. Construction activities—endless interrelated tasks and materials—submit well to project management. Although complex, most construction tasks are knowable in advance. The industry has many segments, each with its own skill sets, apprenticeship learning curves, promotion ladders, educational backgrounds, languages, and expectations. The work is local, decentralized, and site-specific, and cultural norms can vary considerably among sites. The long-term nature of most projects reinforces these norms. Time lines and schedules can be impervious, to a large degree, to outside controls: the job gets done when the job gets done.

Those who work in construction tend to be down-to-earth, practical to the point of skeptical, risk averse, and hardworking. They often feel that a particular way of working, passed down and time-tested (as opposed to gleaned in a classroom), is the right way. A strong identification with craft and trade is carried from project to project. Change is generally not considered good—in part because the consequences of failure are so dire. Failure in construction means danger. Unlike real estate, where failure means a fallen deal or an unpredicted decrease in value, or IT, where failure means a piece of software with annoying bugs, a building failure can mean death.

For all their practicality, people in construction take on—let's face it—extremely lofty goals: build a skyscraper, a campus, a highway, or even a city. These are goals that require vision and confidence. Stand on any street in New York City and marvel at the minds and muscles that made those buildings possible—that built, on forest or farmland, a lasting metropolis to house and occupy untold numbers of people for generations—and it is easy to be reminded of the sheer crazy ambition of the whole endeavor.

There can be camaraderie, but true integration, true sharing of ideas and possibilities with co-workers over coffee does not happen on most job sites. You go to work. You do your part. You get the job done. This is why, in most annual US Department of Commerce reports on the sector, a little more than one-fourth of all the construction workers in the United States are self-employed.[13]

The Hierarchy

The construction business is riddled with hierarchies—from the labor at the bottom of the food chain to the occasional hubris at the top. Enormous disparities, in wealth especially, have created a lack of trust, if not outright hostility all the way up the ladder. "Expert" is a word often said with a sneer. "Visionary" is rarely a compliment. "The culture of construction work," writes Herbert Applebaum in his comprehensive anthropology of construction in the United States, "stresses the independence and autonomy of construction craftsmen."[14] It is what Applebaum calls "a craft culture," in which skill levels (not managerial titles) determine status. "Physical prowess and maleness are prominent."[15] The work culture, writes Applebaum, is "characterized by informality, face-to-face relationships, and loose, personalized supervision."[16] Respect is earned through demonstration of competence and skill.

This is somewhat different from hierarchies in many of today's bureaucracies, where titles and credentials, more often earned from cognitive and interpersonal abilities than physical ones, confer status. These are people who identify more with their occupation than with any particular employer.

The Green Future

Despite this conservatism, change is in the air. Industrial construction expenditures are projected to decrease. Infrastructure expenditures are expected to increase. So are expenditures for residential building. Overall construction expenditures are expected to rise 9 percent per year,[17] in part driven by the predicted need for thousands of new cities, especially in China and India.[18]

And so, in spite of the widespread perception of a sector slow to innovate, the industry has evolved substantially. By far the biggest factors forcing change have been resource scarcity and population growth. Green building has been growing over the past 30 years—especially for renovations and retrofits. According to a recent report by BBC Research, the global market for zero net energy (ZNE) commercial buildings is expected to grow to $239.7 million by 2018.[19]

According to a 2015 report from the US Green Building Council, "commercial building owners and managers will invest an estimated $960 billion globally" between the time of the report and 2023 on "greening their existing built infrastructure." The priority areas included "more energy-efficient heating, ventilation and air conditioning, windows, lighting, plumbing fixtures, and other key technologies."[20] Further, recent studies demonstrate that LEED-certified buildings use 25 percent less energy and provide a 19 percent reduction in aggregate operational costs in comparison with non-certified buildings.[21]

Sensors to the Rescue

One of the transformative innovations in the building space is the use of sensors in the construction process. Meanwhile recent advances in building controls integrate sensors and sophisticated analytics to dramatically improve energy performance.[22] Common uses of sensors are in security and in the assessment of environmental conditions, structural states, and resource flow (people, materials, traffic, water, and energy). The use of sensors was of course at the core of Living PlanIT's offering. Hoping to revolutionize the construction process and that of managing buildings and city infrastructure once built, Lewis's team coded and schemed and sought opportunities to demonstrate their work to the public.

John Stenlake explained in a 2011 interview that the UOS was a platform to take data collected by sensors and sync that data in the *cloud* (not yet a household word at the time, although used in the tech industry since the mid-1990s).[23] Whether to turn on streetlights when needed or to send a firefighting crew to the location of a kitchen fire before an occupant even knew it happened, the UOS would make urban life better. It would do this by collecting and analyzing data on building function, traffic, energy use, and more, and making the data available to applications, accessed through multiple devices, via the cloud. Just as we share photos (data) across smartphones and laptops using local applications, by sharing content via the cloud, more and more of us would be controlling everything from home thermostats to street parking spaces with the help of Living PlanIT's UOS.

Lewis and Stenlake assured us that privacy and safety were reliably protected in their system. None of this would work without embedding sensors in buildings and infrastructure during construction. Answers to practical questions—like how and when in the building process to embed the sensors, whether to build modularly, and how to design buildings to leverage the information that sensors provide—were still largely unknown in 2011. But it was clear that large shifts in the way construction was carried out and in the culture of the industry were needed. By 2014 some of the challenges of introducing sensors into the construction process had been overcome, at least for individual buildings.

Completed in 2015, the Edge in Amsterdam—touted as the world's smartest office building—boasted 28,000 sensors designed to increase human and energy efficiency. The British rating system, BREEAM (Building Research Establishment Environmental Assessment Methodology), called the Edge "the greenest building in the world."[24] Solar panels cover the southern wall; water from an aquifer beneath the building provides radiant heating and cooling, and a rainwater catchment system is used for toilets and watering the grounds. Consulting firm Deloitte was the building's main tenant in 2015 and expected a return on investment in less than 10 years. The Edge already used 70 percent less electricity than most office buildings and produced more energy than it consumed.[25]

Photos of the Edge reveal a breathtaking, enviable vision of the future workplace: clean, airy, light, and supremely hip. A smartphone app allows people who work in the Edge to check for a parking space on the way to work (the building recognizes your car), pick up coffee made to their personal specifications, and find a place to work in the building (to fit their light, temperature, meeting, and communication preferences). Twenty-five hundred people working in the Edge share 1,000 desks. A digital ceiling composed of panels full of sensors controls light, motion, humidity, and other environmental functions. Security is covered by robots, which also do much of the cleaning.

The implications for the future of construction are enormous. The next challenge was to connect smart buildings to one another. Erik Ubels, chief information officer for Deloitte in the Netherlands, was confident not only that future office buildings will look and perform much like the Edge but that they will be interconnected as well. "The multi-billion-dollar question is who is going to do it. Whoever is successful is going to be one of the most successful companies in the world."[26]

Could that company be Living PlanIT? One of the first hurdles was the completion of a master plan for PlanIT Valley.

The Elusive Master Plan

For Crump and Linscott, a master plan was the golden ticket, the go-ahead, the next best thing to a shovel hitting dirt. While they waited eagerly in London for a master plan, architects and planners involved in the early stages of PlanIT Valley were having a hard time agreeing on basic concepts.

The Mind of the Designer

On a brilliant spring day in June 2012, we met with PlanIT Valley's original architect, Pedro Balonas, and his colleague Mariana Morais at his office on the riverfront in Porto. Porto's elegant decay is everywhere apparent—buildings covered with blue and white tile stand gap-toothed and vacant on cobblestone streets that lead to stylish waterfront cafés. The Maria Pia Bridge, designed by Gustave Eiffel in 1877 and built of wrought iron, crosses the lazy River Douro, lined with picturesque barges bearing barrels of port. Porto is a living, breathing reminder that cities, like humans, have life spans and must periodically reinvent themselves to survive. Ushered into the Balonas offices, we were struck by the dramatic combination of historic and modern: spare white rooms with old wooden floors, gorgeous moldings, and broad doorways in a four-story building that once, like so many in its neighborhood, housed a single family.

Architects are a stylish and venerable breed—the Mandarins of the smart-city world. And yet, as the tools of their trade have changed in the past decade and as the construction industry lurches through its own revolution toward modularity, architects, as we will show, have had to share the stage with IT types, engineers, and contractors.

Today new information technologies are increasingly found in the toolbox of both architects and planners, allowing them to specify complex relationships among staggering numbers of elements. Gehry Technologies, an early Living PlanIT partner, developed sophisticated software to enable architects and planners to create realistic models and schedules by specifying building steps and components in extraordinary detail.

But back in 2011, these tools were still new, expensive, and often resisted by designers and planners who trusted pen and paper and often had deliberately chosen *not* to attend engineering school. Members of the Living PlanIT team had faith that these technologies would work and would help convince investors that a schedule created to build the city was realistic and affordable.

If, that is, everyone could agree on the master plan.

Over lunch with the requisite *Vinho Verde,* Balonas circled around the creation of PlanIT Valley's master plan, barely a year old and already a source of contention within the company. (Apparently, this is common with master plans, which force players to refine their philosophy, acknowledge future compromises, and bear witness to their dreams on paper.) The problem seemed to boil down to a difference in philosophy between the plan that civil engineering firm BuroHappold had created and the plan that Balonas's office in Porto replaced it with.

Hexagonal city blocks in the Balonas drawings gave the city's downtown a beehive appearance, which Balonas proudly claimed not only would allow for modular building but also recalled the successful, organic architecture of bees. "We rejected the BuroHappold plan entirely—started anew," Balonas told us. "It was a very *plan* way of planning. If you're working for a company that wants to have a revolutionary approach to planning, you need to think outside the box. This is a technology platform and not a city, so it needs to be reproducible; it must be able to translate from a smaller to a larger scale." The builders, when we discussed the plan with them, clearly sided with the engineering firm, eschewing the fanciful hexagons.

When choosing sketching over software as a way of formulating ideas, at least in the early stages of a project, architects effortlessly reveal their visual fluency—a different way of thinking. Architects, in spite of their willingness to collaborate, expect a certain freedom in the work process. They usually have strong visions of their own and do not see themselves as a "service business." If communication with a client does not go smoothly, many an architect has been known to refuse the commission.

Architects believe in the power of good design to modify the future. They can be both visionary and resistant to change at the same time. The work of the architect has changed dramatically in the past generation, perhaps more than any of the professions in our story. Today architects need and want to play a more central role in the design of new cities. "We are a profession intent on making a better world," Frank Gehry told a New York audience in 2012, "and we just need the tools to manage it. . . . Our intent is to demystify the process so that we, as architects, can control the destiny of a project from a design standpoint, guaranteeing at the end that we accomplish what we set out to do."[27] Without them programmers and engineers might create soulless cities that don't pass the livability test.

The question is, *Can they all work together?* For Big Teaming to flourish, people must periodically come together in shared physical spaces to build understanding and generate common insights. The collaboration challenge does not end with programmers and architects; urban planners and civil engineers play a vital role in building the future, as well.

Urban Planners and Civil Engineers

Urban planners are comfortable with the fact that big projects require teamwork. They are also used to not getting much credit in a major project, especially compared with big-name architects (so-called starchitects) who set out to make their mark on the world.

Civil engineers are a practical breed. They want to solve problems. They recognize that a business plan is just as important as a master plan. Many argue that business, management, and technical skills are equally critical to the work of constructing buildings. BuroHappold's Andrew Comer, trained as a civil engineer, had strong feelings about the Balonas master plan. Comer led the charge against the beehive structures: "You can't impose something like that on a landscape," he told us over coffee in London. "Very few cities have been planned in advance like this—you can't simply look at it in 2D, which doesn't allow you to see how it fits with the landscape. Balonas," he said, "is an architect, not an urban planner.

"At BuroHappold," Comer explained, "we all have a left-of-center approach to life. We tend to like the prescriptive, creative aspect of our work. We enjoy a kind of left-field thinking." But BuroHappold, he is quick to point out, has also developed quite a client pedigree, particularly when it comes to multibuilding projects and big infrastructure. The firm has moved, largely in the past decade, from single buildings to campus-style projects to "pieces of cities," like the London Olympic Park. "We understand," he says, "what makes a good urban environment and what doesn't. We are largely civil engineers, but we speak the language of designers."

BuroHappold's then chair, Rod Macdonald, had met with Lewis back in 2007 to talk about how technology could help the construction industry: how, for example, pre-construction fabrication could reduce waste. Comer then went to Portugal to meet with Miguel Rodrigues and Celso Ferreira. "It was clear," says Comer, "that we didn't just need a master plan. We needed a business plan." Comer helped the team put together an offer to the Portuguese authorities that featured a business plan, including the number of jobs created, population figures, and the need for schools, hospitals, parking, and the like. "This was not a real estate play—we were going to give it away, not sell it," he says, echoing Balonas's statement that apps, not property, would be the product.

Comer continued: "We know how to build a green building, and we have parametric modeling to help us optimize those buildings. The challenge lies in getting the money we need to make those buildings smarter on a bigger stage, to integrate city systems to realize big value." The construction industry, Comer said, is not integrated; players who make hardware make it so that builders can use only *their* hardware. It's a closed design system. In the UOS, he added, these systems will talk to one another. "You don't need an architect or an engineer to create that model," he said. "IT guys could do it without us."

Comer reflected that he had enjoyed the "whole journey," even if PlanIT Valley never got built. "You don't get many opportunities to change an industry," he said. "Society is sleepwalking toward disaster. If we carry on in this fashion, we'll be lucky to have 40 or 50 years left. I'd rather be on the vanguard of change than among the naysayers." This is a recurring theme in our research: *to build the future, it's better to be audacious—even if ostensibly unrealistically so—than to focus on why things won't work.*

In early 2012 Comer had been confident that phase 1—the master plan for PlanIT Valley—would be completed in 18 months and then phase 2, construction, would begin. A year later 1,000 people might move in. But by May 2012, in an interview in Boston, Comer seemed weary of the delays and wary of his involvement. "When we first engaged with Living PlanIT," he explained,

> we anticipated working on a city. It seemed like a clear opportunity and an area ripe for development. Steve Lewis presented some very plausible arguments about the failures of the construction industry and the potential of technology. It seemed like an obvious opportunity for BuroHappold to get ahead on new developments. Obviously, PlanIT Valley is not happening. But our partnership was based on a philosophy rather than any particular deliverables—*an investment*

in our future. Our view on Living PlanIT's value proposition hasn't shifted—really. Just the ways we can engage.

"We are not afraid of failure," he continued with a sigh, "since the basis of our business is challenging the status quo."

In 2013 Adam Greenfield, smart-city commentator and head of the organization Urbanscale, had this to say about PlanIT Valley's master plan: "Diagrams of the site released by structural engineer BuroHappold appear to allocate commercial, residential, and retail sectors around a central public space, in a radial scheme as inelastic as Disneyland's. Despite the vaguely trendy-seeming labels that orbit them ("flexi-block modular association"), nothing about the renderings suggests a capacity for adaptive reuse, organic change, or growth."

In spite of the sharp words and this critique, we were struck by the strong opinions and deep desire to do something truly radical that the architects and engineers working on both of the original master plans conveyed. Both Balonas and Comer wanted to "challenge the status quo."

Design Writ Large

Rick Robinson, an IT executive architect at IBM and a frequent blogger on smart cities, acknowledges and resents the idea that engineers are somehow less visionary by nature than architects. He pointed out that many "IT-enabled business solutions" are complex sociotechnical systems: "They are complex in an engineering sense, often extremely so; but they incorporate financial, social, operational, psychological and artistic components too; and they are designed in the context of the human, social, business, political and physical environments in which they will be used."[28]

This complexity, inherently interdisciplinary, is enormous for smart cities. As Robinson pointed out, "in any physical context—we are concerned with physical space; with transport networks; with city systems; and with human interactions." How to integrate information technology, with its complex "user interfaces, software applications, data stores, network infrastructure, data centres, laptops and workstations, wi-fi routers and mobile connectivity," was a challenge that required "IT Architects" and building architects to work together. "In Smart Cities," Robinson concluded, "we should not treat 'architecture' and 'IT architecture' as separable activities."[29]

Indeed architecture—whether computer or building—is design. And design is a critical function in building the future.

It's Not Easy Being Green

In so many ways, the dream of building PlanIT Valley had burst, Phoenix-like, from the failure of DestiNY. Living PlanIT was informed by that failure—their frustrations with the construction business, their frustration with finding investors willing to go the distance. But Lewis's faith in the IT vision left players like Crump and Linscott, valuable players with skills and the desire to jump in with both feet, feeling frustrated and disregarded.

Consider the steep learning curves, new skill sets, and cultural shifts that using new information technologies requires in the construction industry. Smart-city projects call for dramatic changes in how the construction sector works. Nonetheless, as new tools to help contractors better predict materials usage and schedule projects gain traction, embedding IT into structures may not be far behind. The IT budget on most projects (traditionally less than 1 percent) is growing rapidly with the addition of sensors and data-driven building models.[30] No one profession has all the requisite skills or perspectives. Big Teaming is thus essential.

Balonas and Morais liked working with Lewis and Living PlanIT. "We think of the house as a service, not as property," Morais said. "Steve Lewis understands this. But because we are working with a tech company, we need to think about construction in the early phases, and this can get confusing. We have to readjust the way we work. We are not moving in linear phases but are engaged in a continuous, evolving conceptual phase. We are always redefining the concept—this is the most challenging part."

Balonas and his staff had enjoyed the "brainstorming sessions with the Living PlanIT team, in part because they were so different from the architect's traditional clients," Balonas said. "Our clients are normally developers who want fast profits without risk. Working for a tech company," he explained, "means the client understands that we are working to develop IP." Balonas here resembles the Living PlanIT team in his love of ideas, yet action, for both, was still in short supply.

Balonas was frustrated by the construction industry and impatient for its inevitable evolution. Sensors would be embedded in various components. "It's all in the modularity," he explained, "and the Portuguese, with their world-famous tilework, are masters of modularity. We are combining the tile system with the tech approach."

Working with the civil engineers at BuroHappold had, in contrast, not been fun for Balonas. "This is such a unique project that we will need the best expertise and support for it. But we don't want any prima donnas—just people working toward the final result." Balonas and Morais felt that BuroHappold failed to reach the visionary level a client like Living PlanIT needed. "It's been difficult," Balonas said. "We are a small company, and that's what's hard. We are very open—and they are not. The engineers at BuroHappold fought a lot for their master plan, but they were only adding very regular concepts to PlanIT Valley. They are delivering their products," he added angrily, "rather than thinking outside the box. Steve understood our vision immediately." Here we see a glimpse of the cross-industry finger pointing that will play a central role in our analysis of the challenge of building the future.

As for Crump and Linscott, when we met in late 2011, they appeared unfazed by shifts in procedure and process, practically speaking. But they were frustrated by what they saw as unnecessary delays on the business end—the failure on Living PlanIT's part to produce a real product they could begin to embed in their process. As Crump put it, "The problem is not the conversion of this fantastic set of ideas into reality on a piece of land. That's what we do all the time. That's what our bread-and-butter is. We have the skill sets to do that." Crump and Linscott saw themselves as developers, hired as consultants by Living PlanIT "to come and help get those first spades in the ground."

Put Your Money Where Your Mouth Is

The builders' frustration seeped beyond the relationship with Living PlanIT out to a world that talked incessantly about sustainability but was unwilling to pay for it. In this way, ironically, at least in the case of these two lifelong builders, the construction industry was not the laggard, the drain on innovation toward a more efficient future; it was the consumer. The IT guys, according to Crump and Linscott, were so caught up in their vision that they failed to bring the consumer along with them. The result?

Money troubles. "I swear to you," Crump said passionately, placing the flat of his hand on the table, "even here in 2011, not one of the market research polls we had, talking to potential buyers or people who lived in the district or wherever—not one—mentioned sustainability issues. They are not interested—not interested. We, even now, cannot justify, apart from a long-term investment value, spending more money to develop a product when we know that we cannot increase the value as a result. Those are the issues that we face on a day-to-day basis."

Both men, at that time, saw Living PlanIT as their last best hope to convince the public that sustainable building could save everyone money—and the planet in the bargain. But all the talk was wearing them down. "We haven't seen anything that we can take to the marketplace from Living PlanIT," Linscott said with a scowl, "nothing we can hold up and say, 'This works. It will be sold from the shop around the corner or wherever you get your IT.' So, we can't actually say, 'This is it. Come and test it. Come and play with it. Come and feel it.'"

At the time both men agreed that the best approach would be to construct the first few buildings traditionally rather than wait for the funding that would make experimentation with new parts and processes possible. The problem, they agreed, would be the architects, already emotionally tied to their vision of PlanIT Valley. "But they're artists," Crump said. "I love working with them and letting them have their free space to go and do their bit and come up with their creative input, but then you do have to chain them up and then work within boundaries you set." As Crump put it, quite passionately:

> The big challenge for us is managing individuals who actually have such a high expectation that they're unwilling to come away from that. There's got to be a whole load of reality around this. We're both long enough in the tooth to know what has to be done. And we are both very progressive as well. We are not stuck in the mud and always looking back. We want to do it differently, and this is such a great opportunity to do it differently, as well, isn't it? That's why we want to be involved in it.

What neither one of these dedicated men realized at the time (though they probably sensed it) was that Living PlanIT would (by most accounts temporarily) jettison its plans for PlanIT Valley to earn money from the software that Stenlake and his team were busy developing.

Teaming Up to Build the Future

Crump, Linscott, Balonas, and Comer came to Living PlanIT with years of experience in their chosen fields. These fields were changing rapidly, and by teaming up with Living PlanIT they all catapulted themselves (and their families) onto the front lines of a brave new future that was waiting, clamoring, to be built. Unlocking all that virtual potential to improve daily life in cities was an appealing, worthy goal.

Meanwhile, Bernd Herbert, vice president of PlanIT Life at Living PlanIT, who had moved to Portugal with his wife and small child, spent his days researching programs to foster well-being in Living PlanIT communities. To his great dismay, he explained as we toured the Vale Pisão property in a small golf cart, there were no playgrounds, no paths, no place for a small child to walk without fear of getting hit by wayward golf balls. Herbert frequently brought his two-year-old daughter to the common living area, where the team of young engineers built on Lewis's vision, one line of code at a time, and the business team created their decks and PowerPoint presentations to educate prospective partners. In front of laptops, they sat silently, eyes darting across screens. The child careened through the room, climbing on laps and threatening keyboards. For now this would have to be her playground.

So far, there were no shovels. No dirt. Just dreams.

CHAPTER **7**

The Organization
Man Revisited

*Once upon a time it was conventional for young men to view the group life of the
big corporation as one of its principal disadvantages. Today, they see it as a positive
boon. Working with others, they believe, will reduce the frustration of work, and they
often endow the accompanying suppression of ego with strong spiritual overtones.
They will concede that there is often a good bit of wasted time in the committee way
of life and that the handling of human relations involves much suffering of fools
gladly. But this sort of thing, they say, is the heart of the organization man's job,
not merely the disadvantages of it. "Any man who feels frustrated by these things,"
one young trainee with face unlined said to me, "can never be an executive."*

—**William H. Whyte**, *The Organization Man*

HE WAS THE PERFECT MAN FOR THE JOB.

Douglas West (a pseudonym) joined the Living PlanIT team as vice
president of operations in November 2010. Clean-cut, straightforward,
reassuringly competent, West had spent 25 years in the corporate world,
working with architects, engineers, and real estate developers on large
engineering and construction projects from design through execution
and ongoing operations. Project management seemed natural to West;
tasks, time lines, and critical paths appeared on whiteboards with aston-
ishing fluency in his elegant architectural penmanship. He had all the right
qualities: vision *and* pragmatism. He was drawn to the vision of PlanIT
Valley, but he was not starry-eyed. Having spent most of his career in such
high-tech regions as Denver and Silicon Valley, West recognized the extraordinary potential of innovation to change the world. He firmly believed

that building and construction were heading into a "sea change," and he was ready and willing to oversee phase 1 in the building of PlanIT Valley.

Coming straight from a global technology giant, West was fluent in the language of the corporation, which would no doubt help corporate partners feel comfortable working with the decidedly unconventional startup. He jumped over to Living PlanIT after eight years of working in control systems and building technologies operations at his previous company. Intelligent building design, sustainability and social responsibility, customer solutions, and network technology were his specialties. He was well suited to lead the kind of external integration and internal execution that Living PlanIT badly needed. He worked hard to impose project management on the startup's casual culture, but Living PlanIT's opportunity-driven operations proved hard to tame.

Less than a year later, he was gone.

James Hovington (a pseudonym) joined Living PlanIT in early 2011 as chief investment officer. Hovington was posh, polished, and conservative, more corporate than startup in demeanor, dress, and language. He was a finance guy with extensive technology investment experience, British, well-spoken, and unabashedly cynical. The techies at Living PlanIT were at first relieved to have him aboard. After all, somebody had to understand how bankers think. But in his first few weeks, he managed to alienate several of them with his tough talk about the bottom line. For Hovington, vision was a problem, a trap, the kind of thing consultants exhort business leaders to think about, but not really serious stuff. "Money is at the root of all things," he was fond of saying. "I don't care what everybody says."

Recognizing that the company needed someone who spoke the language of money, Steve Lewis was hopeful that Hovington could bring in partners from the world of high finance. Yet some team members were concerned that Hovington didn't speak the language of technology. "He's not a technology kind of guy," one told us. "He knows nothing about that. When we had to refocus the company on the technology, James was bad at speaking that language. He couldn't really talk to potential investors from a technology point of view. He was not helping the company." Hovington passionately disputed this characterization.

A year later Hovington was gone. "He wasn't," as Lewis put it, "a guy who could sell a vision."

Corporate Culture

Every profession, every industry, has a culture, a language, a set of taken-for-granted assumptions. The world of the large corporation is no exception. Although functions within companies have their own professional cultures, the world of large corporations presents a recognizable culture of its own—one that was less easy to integrate into Living PlanIT than anticipated.

West and Hovington were both, in very different ways, cultural misfits at Living PlanIT. To us it was clear that some fluency in the languages of execution, project management, and finance was needed for the company to survive the startup phase and grow into a viable entity. Company founders may come from technology or engineering or real estate, but the diverse skills and cultures of other functional areas must be successfully integrated for longer-term survival.

Some who migrated from the corporate sector did manage to settle in comfortably. Thierry Martens had been one of the first executives to leap from corporate life at Cisco to startup life at Living PlanIT. This made him a human bridge to a company that Lewis badly wanted as a partner. Like so many at Living PlanIT, Martens gravitated toward the vision. "When I look at corporations," he told us in November 2009, then still at Cisco, stretched out on an outdoor sofa on a patio at Vale Pisão, "I understand that being profitable is a good thing, but it is not my primary driver." Martens, with his longish hair, thick glasses, and enigmatic Belgian accent, is fun to listen to. He switches easily between geek-speak and sincere personal philosophy. "I always think there needs to be a bigger goal . . . but both are important. I've certainly used that as a guiding principle in the things I've wanted to do in life."

Martens worked at Siemens right out of university. In 1993 he joined Cisco as an engineer, when there were fewer than 1,000 people working for the company in Europe. It felt like a startup, Martens says: "I always enjoyed that startup culture—rolling up your sleeves and seeing what you can do, when the rules are not that clear." At Cisco he soon became a team leader, then a manager; then he started a consulting division in Europe and later became director of technical center for Europe, Middle East, Africa. Then the tech bubble burst in 2001: "In the span of a week, we went from hiring to firing. Once Cisco caught up to reality, it reacted very fast. Maybe we should have seen this, but we all got used to hiring and hiring. In those years, if you were cautious, it was easy to regret not having moved fast enough because it was so difficult to catch up afterward."

Toward the end of the 1990s, Martens was looking for a new challenge. He jumped at the chance to work on Cisco's connected real estate initiative, located in Bangalore. "For me that was like a startup within a big organization," Martens said. "For Cisco it was a new role, and for me personally it was a new role. We were not used to having real estate people as our customers. It was a different world. We had to learn about real estate and how we could apply technology to that."

Information about Living PlanIT had crossed Martens's desk back in August 2008. Part of his job was looking at new projects with an eye to potential Cisco involvement. "I had some years of experience in dealing with real estate projects," Martens said. When he looked at new projects, there were always three criteria: One, do they own the land? Litigation due to land ownership could delay projects for years. Two, do they have the money? And three, do they have experience and have they done this before? In August 2008 Living PlanIT met none of these criteria.

Then Martens met Lewis: "I probably spent two days with Steve. On the flight back, I was summarizing this for myself, and I looked at my three criteria and said, no, no, no. It was very clear that was the end to it. And yet I felt, *Maybe this is worthwhile to follow up.* There were some positives."

Listing the positives, Martens started with "the team's background in technology." He explained, "I used to have to spend a year or two years explaining to real estate people what technology could do for them. It takes a long time to go through that. Here I spent 20 minutes. I thought, *At least that's a plus.* There wasn't anyone planning to build a city that I'd met who was so technology-savvy."

It wasn't just the tech background that was attractive. Martens continued: "What really made the difference was some of the thinking that Steve and the team had done very early on about some of the economic models. The model was still immature, but some of the ways Steve was looking at funding and monetizing the project were completely different from what anyone else was doing. I briefed my management team and decided to keep in touch."

Explaining his inconsistency, he continued, "You can either think, okay, I have these three criteria and they didn't meet them. But I thought in the reverse way: *Suppose they pull this off and get this going—they're probably going to be the leading development across the world—the model for everything else.* From Cisco's standpoint I had to ask myself, *Could we be in a position to not participate, even if we know there are some question marks?*"

Martens committed to staying in touch. Two years later, in October 2010, he left Cisco to join Living PlanIT as executive vice president of business development. He had been at Cisco for 17 years and thought, *If I want to do something else, now is the time to do it.* Plus, he was getting impatient with the large-company environment. He felt Cisco had gone from a startup with a speaking-up mentality to a more complacent mentality. Decision making had become slow and formal. "Too many people would say yes—then privately air their concerns rather than challenge people in a meeting. And that was not my style."

He liked the potential of the smart-city space. He liked the way technology trumped real estate and even construction as the lingua franca of that universe. He had spent a few privileged years working on smart-city projects for Cisco around the world. "But to me," he told us, "in terms of knowledge, in terms of potential, Living PlanIT was way ahead of anything else."

Teaming up with Cisco with its global router business clearly made sense for Living PlanIT. One thing was clear, however: It was not easy for Living PlanIT to put the talents of West and Hovington to good use. Despite shared enthusiasms, the connections remained incomplete. Was this simply culture clash, the IT startup clashing with the people of the corporation?

The People of the Corporation

The image of a typical manager working in a large company has changed dramatically since the stodgy, rule-following organization man of William

Whyte's 1956 classic eponymous book. Culturally, the public image of manager-as-rule-follower has been gradually replaced by that of the fast-moving dealmaker in movies like *Wall Street* and *The Social Network*. Yet behind the closed doors of boardrooms and conference rooms, much remains the same. Suits dominate. Hierarchy is taken seriously. While there are cracks in the monolith of conformity (once upon a time, IBM management mandated that male staff wear white shirts), today's global corporations are not exactly characterized by wild-eyed dreamers or visionaries either.

Google and Facebook aside, the corporate world rarely resembles the startup loft scene in the tech sector. The people you might see in the company headquarters of, say, Prudential, GE, or Allianz still predominantly sport suits and ties. Young people aspiring to succeed in the corporate world still flock to earn MBA degrees to accelerate their careers, dress conservatively for interviews, and dream of climbing the corporate ladder. Success is often measured in economic terms. The currency of corporations is, well, currency. *Debt, stock, salaries, options, bonuses, loans, dividends*—the vocabulary of money is vast, like Eskimo words for "snow." In this setting, players believe that it takes money to make money, growth is good, and corporate ladders exist to be climbed.

It would be wrong, of course, to assume that everyone in business is in it for the money. Nineteenth-century sociologist Max Weber cited the rational pursuit of economic gain as the overarching purpose driving businesses.[1] Since then the idea of profit as a primary goal has waxed and waned. In some eras the emphasis shifted toward social responsibility or community, in others, to stock price and shareholder returns.[2] The pursuit of a compelling vision or a noble mission fuels many successful enterprises. Companies exist to deliver products or services that solve problems for customers. They are in business to create value, not just to make a profit. Moreover, with growing appreciation of global threats like climate change and social inequality, many global companies recognize the need to embrace sustainability and social responsibility alongside profit and shareholder returns.

Overall, as widely noted, the culture of the corporate world has shifted steadily for years—from top-down command and control mind-sets to an emphasis on collaboration and teamwork, especially across disciplinary boundaries and especially for innovation.[3] While the men in Whyte's study were "joiners," embracing a social ethic that valued the group over the individual, a new emphasis on innovation in today's knowledge economy means that creativity and individuality are increasingly prized. As Whyte wrote in *The Organization Man,* however, truly creative, truly brilliant people rarely fit well in large corporations: "Management has tried to adjust the scientist to The Organization rather than The Organization to the scientist. It can do this with the mediocre and still have a harmonious group. It cannot do it with the brilliant; only freedom will make them harmonious."[4]

Indeed, the successful business magazine *Fast Company* was founded in 2001 on the principle that individuality has an important, even essential, place in corporate life.

Many in Steve Lewis's generation entered the workplace with built-in skepticism about large corporations and a pressing need to "do their own thing." A sense of individualism overwhelmed, for the most part, any large-scale corporate effort to suppress it. Starting in the 1980s, long-respected companies like IBM and GM came under attack for failing to innovate fast enough and for the staying power of their old-boy networks. Conformity, white shirts, and top-down hierarchies came under growing scrutiny. A March 2002 cover story in *Fast Company* proclaimed that radical innovation always begins as the work of a deviant.[5] Deviants celebrated! A far cry from the organization man.

What would this mean for building the future? In a 2013 interview with *The Economist,* Lewis spelled out his belief in the special ability of small companies to lead innovation:

> While large firms certainly contribute innovative ideas, small and medium enterprises (SMEs) are the catalysts for solutions, in that they provide disruptive technology, which isn't constrained by existing models. We need greater co-ordination between universities and SMEs and affordable ways for SMEs of accessing research. Government support of SMEs through regulatory means and economic incentives can support creative technologists in pursuing their ideas . . .[6]

Speed is another major theme. Traditionally, big companies had resources and credibility, while small companies would pride themselves on nimbleness. Decision making, they would claim, is faster, and flexible responses to changing markets are easier to pull off than in the corporate behemoth. Large companies struggle to determine who has the power to green-light projects and sign checks. Making fast decisions and finding ways to adapt in response to unexpected changes are of course sought-after cultural shifts. One example in IT is the change from "waterfall" software development, in which development phases are planned in advance, to "agile" development, an iterative approach that allows requirements and solutions to evolve through cross-functional collaboration as more is learned.[7] Big vision, small action conveys a similar notion: an iterative, flexible but disciplined approach to project management is needed for building the future because of its inherent novelty and uncertainty.

With the business world's newfound celebration of innovation and risk taking, it is no longer a surprise when an executive leaves a successful global company, making a leap of faith as Thierry Martens did when he left Cisco for Living PlanIT. It's been decades since newly minted MBAs or engineers would expect to stay with a single company, no matter how successful the company, for an entire career. Baratunde Thurston, who studied philosophy at Harvard, worked in management consulting, and then joined *The Onion* as director of digital, was profiled as typical of what *Fast Company* has called "Generation Flux."[8] As Thurston put it, "The uncertainty is the certainty. Change is the constant. Experimentation is rewarded. Stability is an impediment." Any company vision that does not allow for the reality of constant change is in trouble.

Vision. This was certainly a quality that Lewis had in abundance. But vision is not enough. A company's vision can clarify and inspire, but a vision is not a business model, which is sorely needed for getting traction in a new company.

Vision Is Not Enough

A business model provides the pragmatic logic that holds people and plans together—structuring action. Business models operationalize and contain a founder's vision so that it doesn't spiral out of control, gaining impossible, fanciful breadth and thwarting progress. A business model also inspires confidence in potential partners. We can think of a business model as a shared logic about a very few, very important set of agreements: namely, *what* value we hope to offer the world, *how* we produce that value (resources and processes), and *who* will pay us for it.[9] Vision inspires. Business models contain and limit. Although it might seem that limits are bad—as in, without limits anything is possible—in reality limits are essential to progress, essential to innovation.[10] By the end of 2010, we were wondering when Living PlanIT's limits would be clarified—for us, for employees, for investors and partners, and of course for potential customers.

Seeking a Business Model

Tim Gocher, Living PlanIT's general manager from April 2009 to May 2012, who joined from the investment advisory industry, told us in a March 2010 interview that, in fact, "vision" could be off-putting to people in real estate and finance:

> There are some people who are on the extreme side of vision and innovation. Without those people we would have no business model, no progress. But it's not helpful to sit in front of a banker, real estate developer, or office management company and repeat the extreme vision. You must listen with respect. For example, saying, "We won't charge any rent." Don't say that in front of anybody in real estate because to them it's clear that you can't finance it! You see that's an extreme innovation idea—a great idea, really, and someday it will work that way, but you'll never raise the money, so you'll never have a company.

Gocher saw technology as "challenging the old world of real estate," but he recognized that the challenge lay on both sides; "real estate people will pooh-pooh the technology side, and the technology side will pooh-pooh the real estate side."

In March 2015, long after Gocher had left Living PlanIT, he echoed these sentiments: "That is what I was up against as general manager—trying to drive the strategy of phase 1 and get some anchor tenants who would drive cash flow. The challenge was taking what we had in hand—the land approvals, the bodies on board, the PIN status—and using these for investor financing . . . to get someone to sign a lease."

But Gocher found that Lewis was focusing on selling licenses for the software technology, the UOS, which "wasn't ready to sell," as Gocher recalls. "I was trying to sell a lease that would give our clients the right to the technology when it was ready." Bridging cultures was proving to be as difficult as it was necessary.

Multilingual Ambassadors

Gocher believed that using the language of a traditional real estate business model was a way of building a bridge to Living PlanIT's vision of the future. Cross-industry communication was somewhat like visiting another country: one had to respect the norms. As he put it, "You have to finance property! In 2010 in Portugal, after the collapse, no one would invest without financing. No one would invest now in exchange for a stream of possible future licenses." The difficulty, as he recalled, was that every time he tried to "steer the conversation toward a lease, it would go off into software licensing." Getting Lewis to focus on generating the cash flow required to build proved difficult.

Gocher saw a lack of short-term tactics and a lack of agreement on the business plan as making it difficult for investors to get on board. In January 2010 most Living PlanIT employees were focused on the vision of building a new sustainable city in Portugal, one that was not "funded in the old-fashioned real estate development" kind of way. Living PlanIT, they argued, was a tech company, not a real estate company. The typical real estate business model was the problem, they said. Everyone believed that technology existed to do more with less, to build and manage cities in ways that were green and livable, but that it could not be implemented because of old-fashioned business thinking.

"Traditional real estate looks stupid," Lewis said. "Ultimately, if you make enough deals, you can finance real estate." Yet no financing had been secured, and people filled their calendars with meetings—with banks, private investors, anyone who would listen.

Was it the lack of a business model that delayed the partnerships? Fear of the unknown? Vast differences in organizational cultures that could not be bridged? When we spoke with Seiki Maenosono, managing director of Hitachi Consulting, in May 2012, he described the evolution of Hitachi's partnership with Living PlanIT, which began in February 2011. The "threat of colonization" (having products copied by other companies) drove Hitachi, he explained, "to allocate resources more toward social infrastructures," calling this its "Social Innovation Strategy." Smart cities were an obvious area for expansion, and in 2011 Hitachi created a Smart City Business Development Division with 70 people. This was the division that explored a partnership with Living PlanIT. Hitachi would learn from the way the Living PlanIT team developed a "marketing story" and how they communicated the value of their products (*influencing*), Maenosono explained, and Living PlanIT would benefit from Hitachi's expertise in control systems and infrastructure equipment (*innovating*).

All this was still in the future. "Most of the work hasn't started yet," Maenosono told us in 2012, "because nobody has actually come up with the business model. Who's going to monetize it; who is going to keep funding it? Et cetera, et cetera. And that's why we need to have an iconic project to prove that this model actually works."

Maenosono admitted that it had been difficult to convince people at Hitachi to go into the partnership with Living PlanIT. Why? Because Hitachi is a big corporation. Partnering with a startup like Living PlanIT seemed risky:

> Living PlanIT, they just get it. They get the idea, but for a traditional company like Hitachi with a more than 400-year history, it's a new approach to a new business opportunity. Hitachi is a manufacturing producer, so they know how to create products, but they don't know how to create a whole-city master plan, an IT master plan. So it's probably new to everyone, but it's an especially new concept and new approach for a company like Hitachi, so it took me almost six months to convince the shareholders within Hitachi group.

None of this stopped Steve Lewis, hard at work on the road, telling the story, ever the whirling dervish at the core of Living PlanIT's ambitious plans. Even back in September 2009, he had felt overwhelmed by the sheer number of phone calls, meetings, conversations, and ideas, which had only multiplied as time went on.

Financing the Dream

The future was always a little clearer than the present. In the future Living PlanIT revenues would come from partner fees and from royalties and licensing of the company's technologies (sensor-enabled software that would collect and put data to use to make the city function sustainably). At that point corporate partners would base a certain number of their employees in facilities in PlanIT Valley. Early discussions with Cisco, for example, had suggested that a sizable number of the technology giant's employees would be among those pioneers who lived and worked in PlanIT Valley. The fact that these employees would need houses, stores, schools, hospitals, and so on was not seen as a problem but rather as an exciting opportunity to design, build, and manage futuristic exemplars in each of these categories.

Back in January 2010, the team, led by Lewis, Gocher, and Malcolm Hutchinson, had signed a deal with a boutique bank to underwrite an investment of 30 million to 50 million euros. The money would be used to acquire the 1,700 hectares in Portugal, which individual owners would sell to Living PlanIT at a guaranteed appropriation price, inexpensive because the land was not yet zoned for commercial purposes. (The government had the right to purchase the land—at the same price—from any individuals who chose not to sell to Living PlanIT.) Once Living PlanIT acquired the land, the government of Paredes would rezone it for commercial purposes. The government could do this because it granted PlanIT Valley prestigious PIN status, given to projects expected to benefit the regional economy. The bank would finance all of phase 1 of the project, including construction, and would profit from the substantial growth in land value, even if PlanIT Valley became merely a mirage.

At that time a large consulting firm sent a team to Portugal to study the numbers. In a November 2009 interview, an account manager of that company told us about a meeting with Lewis the previous January: "In true Steve style, he poured out his vision as to what he thought the nature of the opportunity was. It fit well with our own initiatives around smart cities, especially smart grids. Clearly, Steve is an exceptionally visionary person. One of the problems with visionaries is how to translate vision to execution, and this is where [we are] very good."

Here he envisions the possibility of helping realize big vision through small catalyzing action. As he recalls, "We had a number of discussions with Steve and Malcolm about how to try to do this. [Our company] wouldn't get involved until the business seemed viable. We placed a team on the ground in September 2009, when Living PlanIT got the PIN status. It was a very attractive proposition, but we could see that getting financing together would be challenging for them and that if they didn't get the team right, things would fall apart."

The consulting team began working on strategic documents that would help Living PlanIT in its partner outreach efforts. But these documents required numbers and facts. Much of the emphasis had been on vision—big vision—and numbers and facts were in short supply. Members of the consulting team were both drawn in by Lewis's charisma and vision and puzzled by the lack of concrete facts and by numbers that seemed wildly exaggerated.

"Why were we there?" reflected one consultant who asked to remain anonymous. "It's really about opportunity. Everybody saw opportunity there. As consultants we were sniffing around, thinking this was going to be really big business. People can see the opportunity, but it's so difficult to quantify because the industry has yet to be created. It's not like this is a new flavor of ice cream or a new electric vehicle. This is a brand-new model."

So new, he continued, that it would be hard to sell despite its promise: "The closest thing I can think of is investing in the Internet in the 1980s. Can you imagine if someone came to your doorstep and said, 'I want you to invest $1,000 into this thing called the Internet. It's going to revolutionize the world . . . Who would have believed it? . . . [Similarly,] this is something that is so new that nobody can put a value on it—it's an unfound quantity; nobody knows what kind of animal it is."

He went on, further clarifying why it had been difficult for his company to walk away: "I can remember there was one evening when I phoned [a colleague], and I remember saying to him, 'This is crazy! I feel like I'm at the beginning of a Google. I feel like I'm observing the birth of a Google.'"

Another member of his team recalled that it took a very long time to understand what the project was about—and what was realistic and what was just a dream. One colleague worried about the project's dependence on Lewis. Would it survive without him? Meanwhile the Living PlanIT outreach team, including Rosy Lokhorst, Manuel Simas, and Miguel Rodrigues, continued to focus on building partnerships with organizations that could help push the new city forward. Lokhorst rose to take the lead on business development. Robin Daniels was asked to develop the partnership with Quintain.

By May 2010 the financing deal had fallen through. Although a number of partnerships with big players like Cisco, Hitachi, and Philips were in the works, MOUs and news releases were not translating into digging or revenues. Many members of the team expressed concern, even disillusionment. The consulting team—that steady presence of young business-suited consultants at the Hotel Central Parque headquarters—quietly left town.

A June Engagement Party

Every time morale dipped, some new tantalizing possibility would come to the fore—usually a new corporate partner who might save the day. In June 2010 it was the announcement of a Cisco–Living PlanIT partnership. "The collaboration between Living PlanIT and Cisco," explained Martens at a well-orchestrated press event, "is really the start of a new industry." PlanIT Valley, he continued, "is one of a handful of cities in the world that will serve as examples for cities of the future."

That June day well-dressed businesspeople had been spread out across the lawn outside a beautiful municipal building in Paredes to celebrate the announcement, glasses of champagne catching the summer sunlight. Excitement was palpable. Six months later, at the start of 2011, Living PlanIT signed the partnership agreement with Quintain. Quintain would take on the creation of a master plan for PlanIT Valley. You could almost hear the sound of bulldozers, of shovels hitting dirt. The possibilities seemed endless: smart-city projects, ecodistricts, and enlightened local governments with new developments planned in Chicago, Denver, Africa, Kuala Lumpur, Saudi Arabia, and China. Trips were taken. Lewis was constantly on the road, meeting with people and giving keynote speeches at conferences.

Seeking an Ecosystem

Business models in startups must shift and morph as more is learned. It is part of the entrepreneurial journey. But it was becoming clear how dependent Living PlanIT's business model was on the yet-to-be-developed ecosystem of relationships with other organizations. Far more than just needing funding, the company needed to work closely with existing corporations to develop the technology interfaces and other concrete aspects of how value would be created for partners in the ecosystem. Central among those other players were the kinds of corporate giants from which West and Hovington and Martens had sprung.

Meanwhile, as noted in chapter 3, John Stenlake's London branch of Living PlanIT was working hard to develop the UOS at the core of the company's evolving business model. Others (mostly Lewis) were out in search of the right market to demonstrate and pay for that product. To some the business model was clear—a problem-solving software product that would drive smart buildings, machine-to-machine communication, and major cost savings in new and retrofitted urban development projects around the world. Without much official talk or announcement, the dream of a smart city in Paredes slowly evaporated. Or so it seemed at the time.

By the spring of 2012, just about everyone involved with Living PlanIT was feeling anxious to move forward. Some saw a need to get rid of old thinking and move into a new phase, hopefully one that would generate significant income. Others, who had been drawn to Lewis's original vision of building a new, green city in Portugal, clung to that dream. Many people were laid off.

"In our business model," Lewis explained in 2011, "we had the same type of partner channel [as Microsoft]. We had systems integrators like IBM, technology providers like Cisco and McLaren. What we did behind it was build a unified architecture that could fit all of this together, which is the Urban Operating System." He continued: "It basically performs the functions of an operating system. At the bottom you have hardware: energy systems, water, waste, sensing, security, et cetera. [The system] might come from a bunch of different guys in the same way that a hard drive might come from a number of different sources. Multiple systems of hardware have to talk to upper-layer systems in the same way. We figured out how to unify that."

But how to pull it off (processes and capabilities) and who would pay for it were still anything but clear. Somehow, just as an iPhone gains its value from applications built by developers and added by consumers, the value of the UOS would depend on others to develop applications for managing building controls, traffic data, and waste disposal. The proposition was enormously complex. This complexity was, we noticed, downplayed.

Much of what Lewis learned about business ecosystems, he was always the first to note, he learned at Microsoft. In any ecosystem integrators are essential. These "keystone" organizations, not always the biggest entities in an ecosystem, play a critical connecting role.[11] For Living PlanIT to play this role, it would need systems integrators and specialized employees to work on security, lighting, transportation, and so on. They would also need to attract the attention of external developers. Lewis believed that Microsoft, with more than a million partners across multiple industry sectors, understood better than anybody how to "liberate and orchestrate all those guys." The point was, you couldn't do it all yourself. You had to open up the floodgates of partnership. And that was bound to be somewhat out of control.

Small Action

By the beginning of 2012, Living PlanIT's software platform was ready for experiments. In contrast to the growing number of discrete smart-city technologies (like smart trash bins that notify trash collectors when they're full), the UOS was designed to allow custom fitting for a potential client, whether a city government, mall developer, or shipping company. New projects discussed in 2012 ran the gamut from streetlights to warehouses to cities.

We've seen that Lewis was good at dreaming big. What was his appetite for small, smart projects that tackle small problems and offer incremental value?

In October 2013 Lokhorst explained that Living PlanIT was courting business on a smaller scale, for example, working with Philips to expand uses for utility poles—adding public wireless, security cameras, and environmental sensing. "We offer two categories of service," she said, "advisory and integration services." She identified several phases of business development, beginning with workshops conducted with clients to devise detailed proposals and generate white papers that tunneled into the client's needs. "The end result is a 'PlanIT Assurance Report' that defines the project," she explained. "It describes the current infrastructure, the driver, and the transformation—for example, using urban waste to create energy."

"To build the future," Lokhorst said, sighing audibly, "you need to change. Different business models' different materials, different infrastructures, different manufacturing technologies—all of these changes require helping the client understand why change is necessary." Lokhorst had experience doing this. In August 2011 she helped broker a partnership agreement with Alliander, a Dutch utility company handling roughly one-third of energy distribution in the Netherlands. The agreement included a substantial annually recurring partner fee, a licensing arrangement for the UOS, and a service package for providing training, implementation support, and project delineation. For Living PlanIT, Alliander's faith in the company and commitment to the partnership was a source of confidence.

The plan was to use the Dutch city of Almere as a test case for the UOS and its potential uses in smart homes and street lighting and as a tool for helping citizens "buy and trade homemade energy." The hope was that the city would eventually roll out the UOS citywide to ensure that both Alliander and Almere knew how to use the UOS. Lokhorst admitted that the project was a little "scary." It was the first project she would handle on her own.

The Right Scale

Living PlanIT's partnership with Quintain came to an end just before Adrian Wyatt passed the baton to his successor, Maxwell James, in May 2012. By then it was becoming clear that cities were eager to solve discrete problems with software but were not yet ready for the whole enchilada—the UOS on a citywide scale. As Daniels said in a July 2013 interview:

> Initially, we were looking just at cities. But the problem is the timing
> was wrong. We can't wait for buildings to come out of the ground to

install software. But there are interesting challenges insides cities—
retail, transport, et cetera—where you can deploy the platform. In the
Internet of things, the UOS could become the ubiquitous platform.
In an ideal world, the UOS is being deployed and you're ramping up
the relationships with partners. . . .

During the spring of 2013, it seemed that a partner ecosystem was
taking shape around Living PlanIT, with licenses and agreements, such as
the one with Alliander, defining shared R&D initiatives. One project in
London, RAPTOR, financed by a consortium that included the Technology
Strategy Board (now called Innovate UK), brought together 15 SMEs to
develop applications to work on the UOS. The project provided welcome
revenue and cemented Living PlanIT's relationship with the Greenwich
Council in London. Although there was still talk of another demo project
in Greenwich, it hadn't yet happened. We were yet to hear reassuring
sounds of shovels hitting dirt in Portugal or anywhere else.

But no one seemed to be standing still at Living PlanIT, either—least
of all Lewis, who was increasingly fascinated with data. "We had gotten
much better at managing large data sets, at gathering and coordinating
and organizing data," he said in an interview in Boston in March 2013. The
diversity of data available, thanks to ever-improving sensor technology,
was exciting, but Lewis felt that the way that data were being used in the
IoT was limited. Meanwhile a chance to experiment with the UOS was
under way in London.

A Smart Airport

Back in early 2012, the UK Technology Strategy Board announced a
government-sponsored Internet of Things Demonstrator Competition.
The winners would create a 12-month demonstration of various technologies that would interact and be deployed together. A few projects would
be chosen. Each one would receive a grant of 800,000 British pounds.
In March 2013 Living PlanIT was announced as one of eight winners of
the competition, with a proposal (led by Stenlake and Daniels) for the
London City Airport, a small urban airport used primarily by business
travelers. And Living PlanIT had an ace in the hole: a partnership with

British retail developer Milligan Retail, whose CEO, John Milligan, Lewis and Hutchinson had known from their DestiNY days. Milligan Retail had a contract to manage vendor operations at London City Airport.

There were several goals: improving the flow of passenger traffic through the airport, improving the passenger experience, and enhancing the retail experience and performance. The project would demonstrate new possibilities for the Internet of things. The team wanted to make the airport user-friendly—enhancing the customer journey by integrating airport operations, retail, food and beverage, foreign exchange, customer communications, and security together on a single platform, the UOS. Of course, airports contain extensive technology already, but much of it comprises stand-alone solutions that are difficult or expensive to integrate. The London City Airport project, in contrast, employed what Stenlake called an "integration-first" approach to design technology solutions that worked seamlessly together, coordinated by the UOS platform.

Living PlanIT pulled together a team of people from seven companies, including Hitachi, Milligan Retail, Critical Software, IBM, Juniper Networks, and Philips. They got to know the airport and discussed ways to negotiate competing goals: retailers, for example, wanted people to slow down and shop; the airport wanted people to move more quickly and efficiently.

During design, Stenlake proposed applications to allow travelers to get personalized advice about their itineraries and journey through the airport, track their luggage, estimate time needed from the train or car to the gate, and check crowds, lines, and traffic. Ultimately, the demonstration used data and automation to enable what the tech sector calls "from-your-device ordering and prepaid-to-your-location delivery" of food, beverages, and duty-free goods, helping increase retailer capacity at peak times. Behind the scenes, precise calculations were used to predict passenger arrival sequence at retail units and to sequence orders for pickup or delivery to the customer's seat or table. Meanwhile camera and active-tag-based systems monitored the movement of people and equipment in the airport, allowing operators to manage congestion and resources in real time using an interactive dashboard enabled by the UOS software platform.

Between December 2012 and July 2013, the UOS deployment went live in the London City Airport, testing all aspects of the system. Cameras and sensors counted people and tracked their movements. It was proof of concept. The impact on how airports work, near and far, would take time to fully play out.

Although Living PlanIT's work in London City Airport may not look much like building a new smart city from scratch, it was a high-profile installation in 2013. Moreover, the application of technology in the airport was easy to understand, and the improvements for customers in the contained and fast-paced environment of an urban airport would be readily apparent.

Proving Ground

The airport project was in many ways a perfect proving ground for the UOS. An airport can be seen as a kind of microcity: people, stores, restaurants, each with needs and offerings but with more-secure boundaries (which makes measuring results easier). (Okay, no schools or homes either.) "At the airport," Daniels explained, "we have the retrofit demo of the technology and the longer-term strategy. So we will be able to paint the picture that goes all the way from 'Let's just put some tech in your building' to a future-oriented master plan for an entire city."

In a news release,[12] Matthew Hall, chief commercial officer at London City Airport, proclaimed:

> LCY is the gateway to East London, which is fast establishing itself as a "tech city" within the capital. It therefore seems very fitting that we are taking a leading role in such a trailblazing project.
>
> This project will help us to manage the passenger journey through the airport and interact with our customers, track assets on-site, and utilize intelligent marketing concepts tailored to an individual's needs. We aim to set an example for airports and other businesses all over the world to follow.

Samantha Robinson, head of marketing at Milligan Retail, said in a news release, "This is a very exciting opportunity to deliver our vision for a truly enhanced and differentiated customer experience which is wholly relevant to LCY's business passenger profile."[13]

A CNN article by Daisy Carrington reported:

> Many of the more advanced features involve tracking passengers through a mix of face recognition and crowd-sourcing software that already exists in airports, plus the GPS that is already available in smart devices. For instance, a traveler who pre-orders food online or though their smartphone will be able to have it delivered to them as they arrive at the departure lounge. . . .
>
> Similar technology can insure that a passenger who booked a taxi in advance can exit the airport and step immediately into a waiting car.[14]

Daniels left Living PlanIT in the spring of 2013 after three years. "Personally," he told us later that summer, "I got to the point where I needed to move on, go back and do my own thing. Living PlanIT's like a family. That's why I still find myself using the word *we* when I talk about them. It's as dysfunctional as any family you'd like to meet. You break up and make up. But when you're up against it, you pull together."

Creating the Cake

Meanwhile fissures widened between the growing team in London and the original players back in Portugal. The London team insisted that the UOS was the heart and soul of the company. Those in Portugal talked of PlanIT Valley. Once, when we asked Manuel Simas about the business model, he had replied, "You can work to get a piece of the existing cake—where new technologies and new paradigms are involved—or you can 'create the cake.' This," he said proudly, "is the Living PlanIT business model." *Creating the cake*, we mused, was about creating a new industry.

In the dark, wood-paneled bar of a London hotel in early 2012, James Hovington was at an impasse. His influence on Living PlanIT seemed minimal, and the work was frustrating. Too proud to admit defeat much less failure, he bemoaned the failure of Living PlanIT executives to use his talents and to recognize the centrality of the bottom line.

Gocher reluctantly left Living PlanIT in May 2012: "Once I had tried everything and realized it wasn't going to happen, realized the city wasn't going to be built, even with all that goodwill from Cisco, I realized I couldn't do it. I gave it my best shot. I fully believed in the vision, but the stepping-stones required to realize the vision were not implementable in that environment."

Douglas West disappeared gracefully and soon found work elsewhere. His value as an integrator in sustainable-cities projects, an ever-growing field, was yet to be realized, leaving Living PlanIT a brief blip on his résumé.

CHAPTER 8

Confronting Culture Clash

There are two ways you encounter things in the world that are different. One is everything that comes in reinforces what you already believe and everything that you know. The other thing is that you stay flexible enough or curious enough and maybe unsure of yourself enough, or maybe you are more sure of yourself—I don't know which it is—that the new things that come in keep reforming your worldview.

—**Jane Jacobs**

Everybody is a genius. But if you judge a fish by its ability to climb a tree, it will live its whole life believing that it is stupid.

—**Anonymous**

BY THE SPRING OF 2014, IT WAS CLEAR TO ALL THAT LIVING PLANIT'S CITY building was not unfolding as initially envisioned. Why had PlanIT Valley failed to materialize, at least by that point? Big Teaming was required: With all its genius, IT could not go it alone in the smart-city space, and Living PlanIT's employees were predominantly from IT backgrounds. They saw the corporate world as stodgy and unimaginative. They saw real estate development companies as slow, antiquated, and anchored in the past. In IT anything seems possible—like creating a multibillion-dollar company out of a PhD dissertation.

This chapter examines the culture clash we discovered among the five industry domains on this future-building journey. We identify dimensions of the professional culture clash we observed, why it matters, and why it often takes a negative tone. We then offer three leadership practices that are essential to realizing the promise of the book's second leadership lesson: Foster Big Teaming.

As Living PlanIT's identity and mission shifted—from building a demonstration city to providing software to connect buildings and infrastructure to the Internet for others' smart-city initiatives, like the London City Airport or Almere's street lighting—everyone had a slightly different view of what the company did and, more importantly, where the roadblocks to progress lay. Rosy Lokhorst, describing the role of the Living PlanIT project manager, recognized this, pointing to the need to speak different "languages" to succeed: "A project manager wears many hats—internal sales and external education. We coordinate people within customer and partner companies and make sure they understand the project. These people must speak many languages—geeks have a way of talking, city planners have another way, engineers (slower), IT (anything is possible). There are many different animals around the table!"

Clients, she explained, can be "grumpy" when they don't understand the technology and there are so many different "animals around the table." She continued: "So many changes are required: different business models, different ways of building (less waste), different materials, different infra-structures, different management techniques." Bridging these knowledge gaps to build a new city was turning out to be harder than anyone had anticipated.

Recall that in 2012 the company was noticeably split between Portugal and London. As late as February 2014, Lokhorst, who had a foot in both worlds, revealed how tenaciously some clung to PlanIT Valley. "We are not giving up on it," she said, explaining that revenues from another project could help move it forward. "All the arrangements with Celso [Ferreira] and the permits are still in place," she pointed out. In June 2015, Harley Blettner reported that PlanIT Valley's plans were alive and well, with him as project manager. But still no shovels in sight.

The first casualty of Living PlanIT's growing geographical disper-sion was camaraderie. Because of the project's complexity, Steve Lewis explained, you had to be able to "grab the software guy, the hardware guy, the network guy, the construction guy, the steel guy, so their solutions come together in a visibly orchestrated fashion." Meeting face-to-face is sometimes essential. The small core of employees based at Vale Pisão offered the easy flexibility of proximity. Many a late-night conversation ended in new ideas and stronger working relationships. A deep sense of shared identity took hold. A visitor had the sense, in the balmy early hours before the first golfers arrived on the links, that building this camaraderie was an important part of what drove Lewis.

Peter van Manen touted the collaborative atmosphere for enabling integrative solutions: "It takes a little bit of a leap to go from watching a racecar go around a track to thinking, *Hang on, that could save energy in a city.* But it's exactly that type of observation, provoked through the interchange of ideas from people with different backgrounds, all keeping their eyes and ears open, that leads to their saying, 'I can see how these things can marry up and be better.' That's how you get a richer proposition."

This was an added rationale for building PlanIT Valley, van Manen explained, not just to demonstrate technology but also "to incubate this type of approach. You get clever people from a number of organizations talking to each other, and that gives you a much better chance of cross-fertilization."

Lewis, to his credit, showed bottomless stamina for reinvention. In late 2014 Lewis and Blettner were presenting Living PlanIT as a company that "solves problems for real estate developers." The company's software, they explained, can help developers reduce costs and time to market while increasing their profitability and environmental sustainability. By putting more early thought and effort into design, developers would reap later rewards. As the Internet of things gained currency in the popular imagination, Living PlanIT was positioning itself as a company that connected buildings and infrastructure to the Internet. But while the IoT typically refers to connecting consumer devices, Lewis explained, "we focus on infrastructure."

Before we judge the company's progress harshly, let's remember that we are talking about introducing a new order of things—about people with the best of intentions who underestimated the challenge of talking across industries.

Oh, for the quiet garage, the solitary work by the light of the cathode-ray tube!

Industries in the Eyes of Beholders

Living PlanIT and its partner organizations shared a common goal, but at any given point in discussing that goal these interdependent participants were likely to have wildly divergent expectations, time lines, values, priorities, and work processes. Experts live in what Rutgers professor Deborah Dougherty called their own "thought worlds," and the psychic boundaries between them can be difficult to traverse.[1] Cross-disciplinary work—even when everyone is receiving a paycheck from the same employer—is hard enough. But traversing boundaries between companies, industries, countries, and sectors is even more difficult. Not only do incentives differ but, more subtly and ultimately more powerfully, worldviews clash.

Over the course of five years, we collected and categorized issues that arose among the areas of expertise required to innovate in the built environment. Many, not surprisingly, attributed the stumbling blocks to progress to players in *other* industries. This section illustrates the characterizations and complaints leveled at fellow future-builders in IT, real estate, government, construction, planning and architecture, and the global corporation.

"The Problem with IT People"

Of all the actors in the theater of building the urban future, those in IT were the newcomers. Compared with such sectors as real estate, construction, and city government that extend back into prior centuries, IT work processes and procedures are brand-new.

In any profession one's own knowledge and assumptions seem self-evident after a while. And so, innovators seeking to bring IT into the built environment can easily fail to recognize the degree to which their skills and perspectives differ from those in other groups. Fundamental aspects of these perspectives are taken for granted. While Living PlanIT was a typical IT startup in many ways—driven young employees, odd hours, no dress code—its success would be uniquely dependent on transcending its own industry culture.

As van Manen told us in May 2012, Living PlanIT's employees had expertise but they had not collaborated on this scale before. As a result, they followed their own IT-derived rules: "They still drive me nuts. They're getting better. One of my pet hates of Living PlanIT is the culture of the organization—their time keeping is atrocious. The only thing they're quick to do is make a promise. They're very slow to deliver. And it drives me absolutely nuts because I find it terribly frustrating and terribly uncourteous."

"Uncourteous" is one way to put it. And it's apt because, in general, people interpret others' different actions as rude (and intentionally so) when they violate tacit expectations.[2] In other words, one does not have to *intend* to be rude to be seen as such. Building effective working relationships comes down first to understanding, and second to respecting, others' time frames, expectations, and work procedures.

Working with "IT types" also proved difficult for some in city government. The broad civic priorities of government officials put them at odds with the narrow technical milestones in IT. Chris Roberts, counselor for the Royal Borough of Greenwich and a leader on planning and regeneration issues for that borough, explained in a 2012 interview that he was interested not in the technology but in how it might improve the lives of his citizens. Technology, he said, gave them greater access to services, and could be

> rolled out to what you might call more excluded citizens, how this technology can enable them to be more connected and more included in society than perhaps they might feel at the moment. For me that was one of the significant things coming out of this partnership with Living PlanIT. It will enable us, I think, as public policy makers, to start stretching them [developers] as well. One of the things I think we've all got to work out is how do we connect people? Not just in digital terms . . .

Recall too how Becky Worthington, Quintain's CFO, put it in chapter 4, drawing on *The Facebook Effect* to flesh out a disparaging impression of IT's disconnect from "the real world." In Worthington's view IT companies—and Living PlanIT in particular—did not confront the same kind of responsibilities her company faced: the responsibility to actually build things. Playing with electrons isn't real work, she seemed to be saying. It's short-term; it's easy; it's reversible. Value created from nothing. Billion-dollar companies created by barely postadolescent founders. Not so in real estate.

When we analyze the many attributions we heard from other industry representatives about IT people, particularly about "startups" in IT, the portrait is one of young, creative, not always responsible, and sometimes downright disrespectful people. They are impatient, unrealistic, and casual.

But are they the only targets of aspersion? Far from it.

"The Problem with Real Estate Developers"

Many inside and outside Living PlanIT pointed to the difficulties of working with people in real estate, whose business models and operating procedures seemed to them inflexible and backward looking. John Stenlake reflected on working with Quintain in September 2011: "The partnership of Quintain helps a lot [in making progress toward the vision], but they don't necessarily tell us everything. And sometimes when they tell us things, we don't necessarily fully understand all the ramifications of it because we don't speak quite the same language in just the same way that, when we tell them stuff, they don't always quite understand the ramifications."

Stenlake expressed similar frustrations almost four years later, in March 2015: "The industries we are selling into—real estate, construction, and retail—are very conservative, with long decision cycles. I came from automotive, where long is six months! It has taken 19 to 20 months just to begin the project in Copenhagen."

In February 2015 Blettner—ironically himself a guy with a real estate finance background who was by 2015 entirely at home in Living PlanIT's IT-driven culture—expressed frustration with another ambitious project Living PlanIT was pursuing (not in Portugal), calling it a "typical real estate deal, with contractors delaying things."

Thierry Martens, who had spent most of his career at large companies, expressed a similar sentiment back in June 2010:

> The biggest competition? The traditional thinking of the real estate industry. . . . It's just that mind-set that needs to change in what is a very conservative world. So any company—whether it's IBM, Cisco, Siemens—that puts this on the agenda is a plus. You can compare this to the early days of computers. . . . It did standardize around one or

two companies, but in the early days the competition wasn't around those companies. It was around getting everyone to accept the idea of the personal computer as a platform. And that's the stage where we are with smart cities.

Even Robin Daniels, so able to span multiple worlds with respect and empathy, told us in September 2011:

> The big challenge is the real estate and construction community. They're so inefficient and they're so attached to their ways of doing things. That's why our success with Quintain is *so* critically important. It's far beyond just doing Greenwich and making a pile of money. It's about a developer and particularly a public list of companies saying, "It makes commercial sense for our shareholders to invest in this technology, and so we're doing it." That's such an important signal to send out. Quintain is small as a developer in global terms [yet] it's high-profile in terms of London. It's a very important step.

Some, like Living PlanIT's vice president of sales and marketing, Keith Hearnshaw, felt that real estate developers' traditional priorities (namely making money) precluded broader (sustainability and social) goals. In September 2011 he placed blame for his company's lack of progress squarely on the real estate developers:

> It's money. It's all about money. I think the problem is, if you look at every developer out there, they have traditional ways of doing these things. When it comes to the crunch and they're looking for cost savings, the first thing they do is say, "Well, we're not sure about this special supersystem that you're considering putting in. We'll just take that out and put in an air-conditioner." It's always the same thing. It's a very brave developer, like Quintain, that actually takes the bull by the horns and does it no matter what.

Finally, Martens, whose work with real estate traced back to his years at Cisco, echoed the theme of conservatism, saying that the challenge was changing real estate's traditional mind-set.

In sum, allowing hyperbole, in the eyes of others, real estate types were money-driven, backward looking, mired in tradition, and attached to old ways of doing things. And the cross-industry criticism doesn't stop here.

"The Problem with Politicians"

Although Living PlanIT received a critical early boost from Ferreira and the city of Paredes, it struggled to build meaningful relationships with other city governments despite their importance in urban innovation. In our research, people in government were often seen as bureaucratic, inefficient, and mired in procedures—anything but innovative. In its favor city government's priorities were seen as inclusive of social good. But people bemoaned the siloed nature of government decision making, which meant long time lines. This was difficult for IT types, used to creating solutions minute by minute.

In September 2011 Hearnshaw, six months into his job at Living PlanIT, had put his finger on what he saw as the key problem team members faced when working with city governments: "Governments make fickle customers. They're frustrating in that they have these huge mood swings. You just don't know where changes are coming from—whether there's someone in the background influencing decisions. We all know that political parties are funded by big companies trying to safeguard their profits; and maybe, sometimes, politicians make bad decisions—with somewhat good intentions."

In February 2015, after working with the London city government on the airport project, Blettner expressed similar frustrations: "Often the client doesn't understand what we do—in the case of [one project], the client did not have the technical expertise. That's why we are not moving to phase 2 as planned. Sometimes clients have a 'resistance to learning.'"

Adrian Wyatt, from the beginning, blamed city governments for the lack of progress in building more-sustainable cities. In our September 2011 interview, he said:

> In practice there are several things that slow you down. One is the planning system in this country . . . although they're trying to do something about it at the moment. The second thing is the Treasury. I think one of the other issues, which is probably unspoken, is that politicians like power. Politicians are usually *absolutely useless* at urban regeneration. They don't want the private sector to be too involved because it takes away their toy set which, [at worst], sounds anarchic.

Hardik Bhatt, director of Cisco Smart+Connected Communities, shared this perspective on working with governments in the sustainable-technology arena in April 2014: "The challenges are not new. The issue is that the city is a conglomeration of 30 to 40 independent businesses. Public safety can continue doing its business without worrying about how airports are being managed, how the streets are being managed, et cetera."

What seemed to work best, Bhatt told us, was when city officials "think of technology as a part of planning, so if you have bus stops, can you have connected bus stops? Technology is the central focus for city planning." He believed that city planners were getting better at thinking about how to incorporate technology into their process. "Right now in many places," he reported, "it is a more holistic process."

Daniels spoke frequently about the split between public and private interests, which arises when city government is the client: "The private sector says, 'We know lots of companies, and we could bring them in and work with them to produce technology and so on.' They kind of get it. But in the public sector, they want to know, 'Well, where's the hole you're digging going to be? How big is it? What services do you need? When does it start? How many jobs can be created?'"

"City governments," Daniels continued, echoing Bhatt's concerns, "are so used to working in silos. The biggest challenge," he explained with a heavy sigh, "is when technologies are intended as a unifier across public and private applications. If visionary leadership is lacking, the collaboration does not turn out well. A city, after all, is an ecosystem: utilities are public, power might be private, and transportation might be regulated by the government. It's a hybrid. Silos are the main challenges that anyone has to face with smart and connected cities."

A portrait emerges of city governments as fickle, siloed, bureaucratic, detail oriented, resistant to change, and technically unskilled. And yet a glimmer of hope could be found in these public-private partnerships. In May 2012 we spoke with Christophe Melle, senior director of channel marketing at Philips. Philips and Living PlanIT were working together on a project to refurbish streetlights in Paredes. Melle too expressed frustration with working with siloed city governments: "Each city has its own department that's managing traffic control, lighting, water. Then you have the police; then you have the firemen. Guess what? They're all competing. And, worse, they all have their own energy grid. If you talk as Philips, they will see you as a private company wanting to sell more lights. If you talk as a networker, like someone from Living PlanIT, you must explain to them how things work."

Yet, as he continued, a path forward for collaboration started to take shape: "When we started to talk to city officials, they said, 'Well, actually, you should also talk to Living PlanIT' because they're going to be the ones that will orchestrate this project. So we saw Living PlanIT as an opportunity to break through the silos and say, 'Hey guys, this is what we could achieve if we collaborate. You need to change the way you work.' So, now politicians start to get it. They are coming back to us saying, 'Okay, what should we change?'"

If technologists and politicians find common ground, are we ready to start digging? Not quite. Let's look at others' views of those who build.

"The Problem with Designers and Builders"

Although urban planners, architects, and builders come from three distinct traditions—and have their own unique history of conflicting worldviews, practical squabbles, and finger pointing—for the purposes of our study of smart-city innovation they came from a single, loosely integrated domain: those who design and build. Their work collectively culminates in enormous tangible objects—buildings, developments, campuses, and more—objects with physical permanence and occasional awe-inspiring grandeur.

Many blamed the construction sector for adhering to antiquated processes in spite of new tools and methodologies that render them obsolete. They also blame construction for the waste, inefficiency, and delays that have become synonymous with building. They often fail to appreciate the extraordinary accomplishment of reliability, of building things that last, bemoaning instead the waste and glacial pace of change.

Architects are often seen as focused on form or aesthetics rather than function or usability. The attribution is likely overstated, if not downright wrong, in today's world, but the stereotype has staying power. Today architectural firms often collaborate with engineers and software engineers to do more-interesting work, notably in iconic projects like the Beijing

Water Cube. More and more projects call for proposals that use software programs to predict materials use in specific ways so as to improve efficiency, minimize risk, and allow clients to better visualize projects in the early stages. Gehry Technologies' software includes a calendar tool to track a project's history, automate the identification and tracking of materials purchases and deliveries, provide folder and file sharing, and serve as a building information modeling data storage center.[3] These and other tools increase the power of simulations to reduce waste. This means tighter control of budgets, schedules, and quality.

Andrew Comer at BuroHappold saw architects as bridge builders: "As architects and designers have been asked more frequently to consider urban space and larger chunks of cities, they've looked for relationships with people they can talk with who understand their aspirations."

Yet, as he continued, it became clear that even the teaming between architects and civil engineers was fraught with challenges—due not so much to actual conflict about what should be done but rather to "personalities and language": "The traditional civil engineers are very different. A lot of the work they do is directly for clients. . . . A lot of the work is public-sector work and big infrastructure projects. So, they don't naturally make good bedfellows with architects because there's often this clash of not just ideas but personalities and language."

As noted, pretty much everyone complained about the slowness of the construction industry. Melle told us in May 2012, "The biggest challenge we face so far is the speed. The construction world is a very established world."

Miguel Rodrigues, with years of experience working in construction, told us in June 2011:

> The construction industry is very difficult to penetrate—but companies do adopt solutions and technology they can benefit from. For me it doesn't matter if you are talking about construction or sensors. Change always comes from suppliers. If we, the suppliers, can develop something innovative on the manufacturing side that can result in real benefits, developers will take it up. Trust from developers to suppliers is required to generate change—my network in construction is very critical. The trust and confidence a developer needs to have is critical. Right now we need to make developers understand

that technology will benefit them on the market and give them a competitive advantage.

Thus, in the eyes of beholders, the combined building efforts of architecture and construction added up to a slow, risk-averse, conflict-ridden industry stuck in traditional ways of doing things. What about the modern corporation? Surely its representatives are versatile, driven, and well positioned to facilitate innovation in this emerging business ecosystem of urban future-building.

Not so fast.

"The Problem with Corporations"

Many in our study expressed a belief that big corporations were antiquated behemoths unable to move fast enough to understand much less utilize the new technologies that might promise more-sustainable cities. Lewis put this view most succinctly when he said, "Corporations are unable to see the future much less build it."

Trying to build a partner ecosystem in the early years proved difficult when the startup team had no way of knowing whether the people they were able to get meetings with actually had decision-making power. As Lewis told us in January 2012:

> In 2008 we said we would develop this platform. At that point we hadn't named it as the UOS, but we had defined what was included there. We hadn't done our deal with McLaren but knew we had to. We knew we ultimately had to go to market with partners. We had a fair understanding of which of those partners we would be interested in—and we had a laserlike focus on Cisco at the time. That took way longer than I could have ever imagined for a bunch of reasons. The first people we were dealing with at Cisco either weren't empowered or weren't informed, so we had to hit the reset button halfway into the relationship.

In June 2011 Lokhorst explained the company's stalled progress— her causal lens aimed squarely at the corporate sector: "The market has changed; it's in crisis. Partners are much more selective; larger companies are much more regulated. We have to worry about making sure that the people who sign agreements have the right to do that. For example, our deal with Cisco was delayed by those kinds of things—people who did not know the internal processes well enough to get them circumvented as quickly as they wanted to."

In 2011 Rodrigues chalked up the difference between Living PlanIT's goals and the priorities of the big companies it was trying to attract to *values:* "Big companies are not thinking about people—they think about numbers. We think about how to bring technology to people on the street." In other words, we care about a better world; they're after profits. As always, one of the essential elements of industry culture clash is the attribution of superior motives to one's own tribe.

Recall that Isabel Dedring, the London environment minister, had complained to Daniels that it was hard for city governments to work with big companies on sustainable solutions. She argued that companies just wanted to sell their products rather than facilitate long-term growth or sustainable solutions.

By 2015 many employees were frustrated with the failure to get beyond the MOU stage to the check-cashing stage. As Blettner told us in February 2015, "We have to close the deals."

When we asked Blettner why big tech companies would want to purchase a UOS software license from Living PlanIT rather than build their own, he replied: "Because they [are] still very siloed" and would not be able to pull together the cross-disciplinary project to make it happen.

Recall too that Pedro Balonas, the architect, eschewed input from global engineering giant BuroHappold on the PlanIT Valley master plan. In his view the plan was too traditional, too rigid—a "plan way of planning."

In sum, corporations are risk averse, siloed, unimaginative, and slow. One cannot miss the echo.

Teaming in Babel

All of this finger pointing, while understandable, is counterproductive. Martens put it eloquently in June 2010: "That mix of technology, partnerships, how you bring things together—it's important. More and more with these complex issues, *it will be much more about an ecosystem, bringing people and competencies together from different industries.* It will be less about one company doing it all—it's more about partnerships; it's more about people who can bridge some of these competencies and can work across different companies."

This is possible to do, Martens mused: "In my Cisco days, some of the best-performing people were people who had passion outside the job for things like automation. You combine two things, and it becomes very powerful." But not everyone does it well. "We need people like da Vinci," he said, "who are less focused and siloed and pinpointed. The next wave of innovation will come less from going deeper into a particular space and more from ways you cross-pollinate some of these learnings."

In other words, building the future would require a new mind-set—a cross-disciplinary mind-set. Innovation researchers have long talked about the need for people with "T-shaped skills."[4] T-shaped professionals are respected experts, deep problem solvers in their own discipline capable of interacting with and understanding specialists from other disciplines.[5] In that sense the T-shaped professional is not da Vinci, wildly expert in everything, but rather is capable of reaching out across disciplinary boundaries far more readily than the typical expert. People with T-shaped skills are crucial boundary spanners in intracompany innovation projects. Can they help future-builders who span industries instead? We think the answer is yes.

Desperately Seeking da Vinci

Short of concluding that we're stuck unless we can recruit a bunch of Renaissance genius types, what can we take away from these industry stereotypes and the resulting cross-boundary frustrations? First, let's take a look at the basic dimensions along which fields of expertise differ most critically. They are both technical and interpersonal. Technical dimensions include time frame and work processes. Interpersonal dimensions include expectations, priorities, and values. Technical and interpersonal chasms are equal partners in creating confusion and inhibiting progress. Second, we will draw from our own and prior research to suggest a way to navigate industry culture clash, becoming boundary-crossing tourists, eager to learn from the other professional cultures in our midst, as a necessary first step in innovating together.

Boundaries refer to divisions between identity groups—such as gender, nationality, or, as we have seen here, occupation. Some identity groups and their corresponding boundaries are more visible than others. Gender, for example, is usually visible. Occupation is less visible—albeit easily revealed. Completely invisible, however, are the taken-for-granted assumptions and mind-sets that people hold in different identity groups. For teaming across boundaries to be successful, people must become aware that they hold different perspectives—and more importantly that they take for granted the "rightness" of their own beliefs and values. This means it's not enough to simply say, "Let's band together, and it will all work out." No matter how much goodwill is involved, boundaries limit collaboration in ways that are invisible but nonetheless powerful.

Boundaries between professions contain points of vulnerability—much like geological fault lines—that can give rise to misunderstanding and breakdown. Left to our own devices, as experts and as people, each of us has a way of communicating that enlightens or obscures, depending on the audience. And sometimes, as we have seen, it even annoys, thwarting progress.

Technical Chasms: Time Frames, Tasks, and Terminology

From the beginning, Lewis and other members of the Living PlanIT team, particularly those with IT backgrounds, were impatient with the slow pace of decision making in real estate, construction, government, and big corporations. Players in those sectors, in turn, were frustrated by what they saw as the startup's unrealistic perspectives and lack of organization. As we learned, IT moves fast due to the nature of its work, whereas real estate, construction, and government have long decision cycles. Luísa Lima, a young PhD engineer at Living PlanIT in Portugal, put it this way: "The technical people's time frames are different, and their expectations of others don't always match up to what's actually possible. If they say, 'Let's build this network two months from now,' I'll say, 'No! Are you crazy?' We may have a different understanding of the time it takes and the number of people you need to do something."

It comes as no surprise that each industry came to the party with its own ways of doing business. As we learned, closing a deal was different in an IT startup (a drink and a handshake) than at General Electric (identification of decision makers, lawyers, MOUs, and layers of signatures). Silos and hierarchies in the government and corporate worlds slowed progress.

Some took comfort only in physical signs of progress—such as those in construction we spoke with at Quintain, eagerly waiting for digging to begin. Others saw code being written as a sign of great progress. Stenlake, for instance, celebrated his company's virtual accomplishments—the (to him) tangible manifestation of exciting new ideas.

In addition to the different taken-for-granted assumptions about time frames embedded in the nature of work in each industry, the terminology—or technical jargon—experts use can also be a source of misunderstanding and confusion. Jargon obfuscates in two ways. Some terms are meaningless to nonexperts (*HyperText Markup Language* in software, for example, or *esquisse*—a first, rough sketch for an architect's design), and other terms mean different things in different fields. For example, the word *platform* means something very different to a builder (a raised level surface on which people can stand) and to a software engineer (a major piece of software, like an operating system, under which various smaller application programs can run).

Interpersonal Chasms: Values, Priorities, and Trust

Differences in priorities among players also stalled progress. In the beginning, the priority for Living PlanIT employees was creating PlanIT Valley as a high-tech showcase. Those with real estate or finance backgrounds focused on the revenue opportunities of game-changing innovation; techies wanted to create the new cool thing. Builders and planners were driven by a chance to solve practical problems with visionary solutions. Those in government were interested in creating a better future for their constituents and leaving a legacy. Meanwhile financial and political crises (like the 2010 economic downturn in Portugal) stalled carefully constructed agreements and further weakened relationships in the fragile partner ecosystem.

Some were more comfortable teaming than others. While the work in IT tended to be solitary, hammering out real estate deals involved more networking and more dependence on other players to get things done.

What did they all have in common? At 30,000 feet they all wanted to create a better world.

Stepping back it's clear that finger pointing and identification of others' limitations, along with a certain degree of blindness to one's own limitations, is deeply human. The central problem we identified in teaming across industries is how easy it is to blame people in *other* groups for problems that occur. This is neither ill-intentioned nor deliberate. It's spontaneous because it seems obvious to people that the conflicting way that those in another field are approaching the situation is wrongheaded.[6] Behavioral research has shown that we spontaneously attribute unflattering traits and motives to those who see an important issue differently—for example when a plan is being formed or a decision must be made. Because our own views feel self-evidently "right," others' expression of contrary views can seem intentionally obstructive.

Psychologist Lee Ross explored cognitive mechanisms to explain this phenomenon. Notably, what Ross calls *naive realism*—or a person's "unshakable conviction that he or she is somehow privy to an invariant, knowable, objective reality—a reality that others will also perceive faithfully, provided that they are reasonable and rational"—makes us overconfident.[7] Relatedly, people tend to see their own views as more common than they really are, leading them to assume that others share their views—the *false consensus effect*.[8] Thus when others misperceive what we view as "reality," we cannot help spontaneously seeing them as difficult. In short, people happily (and largely unconsciously) let themselves of the hook—believing that *others* need to change if progress is to be made. Human, yes, but not a strategy for effective collaboration.

Although weaknesses in formal project management also contributed to slow progress, this book emphasizes the role of cross-boundary teaming as a critical practice for audacious innovation. Other works, notably Eric Ries's book, *The Lean Startup: How Today's Entrepreneurs Use Continuous Innovation to Create Radically Successful Businesses,* provide deep insight and advice about managing the inherently uncertain journey faced by entrepreneurs, but we are unaware of other work on the role of cross-sector teaming and how to avoid being blindsided by its challenges. As a result, many would-be innovators fail to recognize its importance and its subtle dynamics and thus miss the opportunity to manage it carefully.

Leadership Practices That Enable Big Teaming

So, what can be done to enable experts to span industry boundaries successfully? Let's look first to research on teaming *within* firms, which emphasizes creating psychologically safe spaces in which people can share ideas, admit mistakes, ask questions, and offer crazy new ideas.[9] They are willing to fail in front of colleagues. This matters because no one can perform perfectly when knowledge and best practices are in constant flux—as is the case in an innovation project. As Luísa Lima put it, "If you're doing something new, you're bound to fail somewhere." Explicit recognition of this fact by project leaders helps build psychological safety. In contrast, when uncertainty is not publicly acknowledged, people tend to be risk averse and afraid to fail, which limits innovation and knowledge sharing. Emphasizing the uncertainty inherent in an innovation project helps create a climate of psychological safety because it justifies the need for candid, creative input to make progress. But psychological safety is not enough.

Drawing from several case studies of future-building, we suggest three leadership practices to help overcome both the technical and the interpersonal dimensions of culture clash.[10] First, building an adaptive shared vision provides a foundation for collaboration that helps overcome the inevitable conflicts and misunderstandings that occur in cross-disciplinary work. Second, building meaningful cross-sector relationships enables forums for intense, candid, deliberative interpersonal exchange based on trust and respect. To prevent the "fault lines" that lie between industry cultures from erupting into blame and stagnation, proactively building relationships across these cultures is vital. Understanding where these fault lines may appear will help managers and leaders avoid them. Third, building an iterative collaborative process that is designed to shift as more is learned strengthens relationships and enables timely decisions, shared understanding, rapid learning, and innovation (see the table *Leadership Strategies for Overcoming Professional Culture Clash*).

Building an Adaptive Shared Vision

The glue that held Living PlanIT together had long been the company's founding vision. The possibility of developing new technology to

Leadership Strategies for Overcoming Professional Culture Clash

Leadership Strategy	Behaviors and Tools	Behavioral Outcomes
Building an adaptive shared vision	■ Articulate a compelling vision that is bold, motivating, and open to adaptation ■ Emphasize the opportunity to contribute to shaping the vision as more is learned	■ Focuses people on exciting possible future states that motivate engagement ■ Engages people in offering ideas and running experiments to figure out what works
Building meaningful cross-sector relationships	■ Invite people to share expertise, ideas, and valued goals ■ Use boundary objects to clarify ideas, helping bridge knowledge gaps ■ Build in social time to bring people together to get to know one another	■ Mutual understanding of one another's expertise ■ Shared experiences ■ A shared vocabulary ■ Interpersonal trust
Building an iterative collaborative process	■ Identify critical interfaces (fault lines) between domains ■ Hold ad hoc meetings to make decisions at interfaces ■ Design governance structures to manage complexity ■ Use procedural transparency ■ Conduct after-action reviews to diagnose and learn from smart failures	■ Strong relationships from shared work experience ■ Timely decisions that integrate different professions' needs ■ Clear, shared understanding of process ■ Rapid learning cycles ■ Process/product innovation

demonstrate the potential of smart buildings and infrastructure in a pilot city was personally motivating, as we have seen. No one joined the company or its ecosystem of partners for long if they didn't find this vision exciting. Their enthusiasm for its unique combination of technical innovation, social good, and bold demonstration brought diverse team members together, giving them, for all their differences, a shared identity. For some the experimental city was the vision. For others it was only a tactic. But when the PlanIT Valley project waned and morphed, the company's shared identity suffered. The vision of building and distributing smart-city software to projects around the world took time to be embraced by everyone. Time would tell whether it would generate the level of enthusiasm needed to move forward together successfully, spanning boundaries along the way.

Does this mean company visions cannot change? No. It means that when they change they must be explained and celebrated to ensure buy-in. Moreover, participants must be prepared in advance for the vision to evolve further as more is learned. When leaders lay the groundwork with both a compelling vision and an explanation of the need for it to adapt as they go on, people are more committed to the near-term work they must do to make progress.

More generally, in any uncertain and risky endeavor—particularly when working with people with different expertise—it is natural for confusion, misunderstanding, and blaming to occur. A shared identity as members of a particular project or team is a counteracting force to the cultural wedges that push people apart; it makes people better able to give one another the benefit of the doubt. Shared identity makes people more likely to take into account what others are up against—rather than just seeing the (negative) impact of their behavior.[11]

The remarkable rescue of 33 Chilean miners in 2010 illustrates how a shared identity can motivate effortful, high-stakes interdisciplinary teaming. Over an excruciating 70 days, experts from multiple occupations, companies, and industries (mining, aerospace, geology, oil, military, transportation, government, and more) teamed up to innovate—that is, to develop, test, modify, and retest novel solutions to a nearly impossible technical problem.[12]

Even when a vision is singular and obvious, as in the rescue, frequently reminding people what is at stake and what they might be able to accomplish together remains essential. Moreover, in any uncertain innovation the vision must be allowed to morph. For example, the vision of rescuing the miners alive was explicitly articulated in such a way as to allow it to shift to returning their bodies to the families for formal burial, if it ultimately proved impossible to devise a solution in time to save their lives. To sustain people's energy in the inhospitable conditions of the mining site, despite lengthening odds against success, rescue leader Andre Sougarret frequently highlighted the team's core mission of saving lives. Yes, the mission was obvious, but diverse experts working together under pressure benefit from reminders of the importance of their work. In Chile the shared identity fostered by this small act of leadership helped dissolve national and professional boundaries and keep everyone's focus on the mission.

Building Meaningful Cross-Sector Relationships

As we have seen, industry differences in taken-for-granted assumptions, values, or goals give rise to conflict, misunderstanding, and stalled progress. When this happens, deliberate acts of leadership are needed to help build healthy work relationships to get things on a productive track. It starts with insisting that people share and explain their expertise, ideas, and values. The problem with expertise is that once you have it, many of its insights seem obvious. Encouraging people to be patient, thoughtful, and clear in communicating what is obvious to them to those with different expertise—to whom it's not obvious—can be enormously helpful. This often means asking those with T-shaped skills to help translate jargon and illustrate with what sociologists have called "boundary objects."

Boundary objects like drawings, prototypes, or even a shared computer screen provide tangible representations of knowledge. Tangibility makes knowledge easier to communicate than language alone. Research on new product development shows that boundary objects facilitate communication. By pointing to and discussing elements in a model or schematic drawing, experts can overcome the obfuscating nature of jargon.[13]

To those who are impatient, the process of getting together to build technical understanding can seem slow, time-consuming, and even downright wasteful. Yet a stitch in time nearly always saves nine. Investing in mutual understanding today can prevent anything from small delays to large cost overruns to major failures tomorrow. The savvy among our future-builders were acutely aware of this. As Martens told us in June 2010, the recognition that each person had a lot to learn from the others was an essential first step to effective teaming: "Technology companies have much to learn from other industries. There are a lot of companies that can learn from technology, but technology companies can also learn a lot about the challenges of running a city—what keeps a mayor awake. We can learn as much from traditional companies as the other way around. And if we can bring those learnings together, that's very powerful."

But taking the time to share expertise-derived insights in jargon-free ways is only the beginning. Going a level deeper, where the emotional content of a breakdown lives, means exploring not just expertise but also taken-for-granted values as a first step toward appreciating them. Just as in cross-cultural exploration by anthropologists (of countries, tribes, or regions), future-builders must explicitly recognize that those in other professions are not wrong to value different things. They are merely coming from a different tradition.

Deliberate relationship building was vital to the success of the Water Cube. Created by a consortium of firms teaming across continents (including global engineering firm Arup; PTW Architects, based in Sydney, Australia; and China Construction Design International in Shanghai), the project won awards for structural, aesthetic, and environmental achievements. Lead engineer Tristram Carfrae explained the importance of ensuring that the diverse team build trusting relationships across geographical, national, and professional boundaries. To bridge cultural differences (national and occupational), the firms exchanged bilingual specialists across office sites. These cultural ambassadors helped overcome the obvious language barriers between Chinese and Australian designers, but as importantly helped bridge differences in norms, practices, and expectations throughout the project. A second technique was calling ad hoc meetings for representatives of all the design partners to confront issues that arose along the way.

On a larger scale, the developers of New Songdo, South Korea's 1,500-acre greenfield city, used something called a *charrette,* a concentrated

planning event, to bring architects, engineers, planners, and environmental experts together at the project's outset to integrate expertise in
site planning, waste, transportation, materials, water, building design,
and energy.[14] This intensive week of work began with an opening-night
dinner. Informal conversation helped people get to know one another and
build shared commitment. The process led to numerous innovative solutions that saved money, time, and energy. The charrette process is increasingly used by future-builders because it addresses both the technical and
the interpersonal challenges of cross-sector teaming—building trust and
identifying novel technical solutions that live between disciplines rather
than within them.

Lake Nona is a new city in central Florida focused on healthcare
delivery and research. Building strong relationships across participating
organizations (including a real estate developer, local government, and
several research organizations and hospitals) was seen as critical from
the beginning of construction in 2003. Project leaders set up governance
structures to force conversation, brainstorming, planning, and coordination among the diverse set of organizations involved in the ambitious
project.[15] The leaders of each organization met monthly in a late-afternoon
Leadership Council, ending in a relaxed dinner that fostered strong
personal relationships. The Lake Nona Institute also organized meetings
through which other members of each organization could meet with one
another and share ideas and concerns.[16]

Building good work relationships requires trust grounded in experience, which means taking the time to get to know the other players through
shared work experiences. The early Living PlanIT participants—Steve
Lewis, Malcolm Hutchinson, Peter van Manen, Miguel Rodrigues, Manuel
Simas, Harley Blettner, Johanna Weigelt, Nuno Silva, Andrew Comer, and
Celso Ferreira—had built relationships of trust and mutual understanding
across industry and national cultures, through the shared experiences
described in chapter 2 that went well beyond conference room discussions.
With a reserve of grounded trust, diverse teams are better equipped to use
moments when conflicts break out to strengthen their relationships rather
than destroy them. Comer concurred: "I think we've evolved [to talk] very
much in the same language as urban designers, architects, and landscape

architects. We're beginning to much better understand the urban environment, what makes a good urban environment and what doesn't, and how all those elements of engineering that were starting to grow in their own right actually are very potent if you integrate them in terms of an urban context."

Building an Iterative Collaborative Process

When project interdependencies are complex, a deliberate and transparent work process is essential to overcoming culture clash. It starts with identifying fault lines and interfaces. We refer to the boundaries between any two groups at which alignment is crucial as *fault lines*.[17] Like geological fault lines, these are places where tensions may build and failures (if not outright earthquakes) may occur.[18] For example, in some companies, design and manufacturing must be in close communication to ensure the quality and cost of finished products. In others certain business units have the potential for counterproductive competition in the marketplace. Managing intergroup fault lines starts with building trusting relationships and moves on to identifying interfaces. *Interfaces* are points of overlapping work that must be coordinated to be effectively executed.

Interfaces nearly always encompass conflicting demands of different parties. In the Water Cube project, designing for the needs of athletes, officials, the media, broadcasters, workers, sponsors, and spectators was a complex task. The Arup team introduced "interface management" into the project management, dividing the work into "volumes"—each owned by a subteam responsible for identifying interfaces between volumes. Interfaces can be physical, organizational, or operational. Regular interface coordination meetings were held with relevant parties. According to an Arup project manager, "In the short term, eliminating mistakes at the interfaces . . . generated one of the largest possible savings in current industry practice."[19]

Research by Harvard doctoral student Faaiza Rashid on the use of integrated project delivery (IPD) in the design and construction of innovative new buildings found that early inclusive participant involvement, periodic co-location, and joint project management added up to *procedural transparency*.[20] Through collaborative process management, longtime industry antagonists in construction and architecture built strong trusting relationships with award-winning results. Similarly, we would argue that as Living PlanIT moved forward with multiple projects in early 2015 (summarized in chapter 9), managing the interfaces between industries would likely prove vital to its success. And this, we believe, calls for balancing hubris and humility.

Leading with Hubris and Humility

Building the future requires a unique blend of hubris (my vision is worth pursuing) and humility (no one, including me, knows how to do this yet). Often, as every pioneer knows, a focus on the future can obscure the present. For everyone involved with Living PlanIT, the future was just around the corner. Let's take a look at where the company was as our writing drew to an end and what their future-building was precariously poised to deliver.

CHAPTER 9

Balancing Influence and Innovation

Still crazy after all these years.

—Paul Simon

THIS FINAL CHAPTER CELEBRATES SMALL ACTION AS A CRITICAL component of realizing big vision. We explore the tension faced by any visionary leader trying to sell the future and build it at the same time. Like any tension, this one eludes a simple answer, but conscious management of the need for a dynamic balance—between influencing and innovating—emerges as a crucial leadership skill.

Steve Lewis and Harley Blettner remained upbeat through Living PlanIT's oscillations from infinite possibility to nagging doubt. The company's revenues were slowly growing. Although many employees had come and gone, others, like Rosy Lokhorst remained energized. "I still love it," she gushed in 2014. "I never would have had these opportunities at Microsoft selling licenses. I'm having an impact.

"In the last two years we've worked harder than ever before," she told us a year later, "and it's starting to pay off in leaps and bounds. It is very gratifying to see the growth of our company and our team. Looking back, I am also grateful for the opportunity to grow personally, and I know I'll learn a lot more in the stage we're now entering, where precision in execution is key to capturing the momentum. I believe our team and our company culture will allow us to do that, and it ignites my passion every day to be working with such a great team of people."

Lokhorst's enthusiasm aside, many on the team became increasingly skeptical as PlanIT Valley start dates moved irrevocably into the future. While Lewis's gaze remained firmly fixed on the goal, dashed expectations of shovels hitting dirt had eroded some others' confidence.

And yet there was always just enough good news to sustain hope. In 2013 Living PlanIT won a Frost & Sullivan pioneer award for the company's work on the Internet of things and new smart-city technologies.[1] This and other accolades (including another Frost & Sullivan award in 2015) seemed to indicate that Lewis's work—his never-ending efforts to educate the public—was paying off, if not in funding at least in status. But the original unifying vision of PlanIT Valley ("Let's build a cool new city!") had languished, leaving a bit of a company identity crisis in its wake.

PlanIT Valley, to be fair, had never been the end in and of itself for Lewis. As he explained in March 2010, "PlanIT Valley is a means to an end, and that end is the distribution of technology to a broad channel around the world." As noted in chapter 2, Lewis wanted to build a demonstration city to learn about what might be possible in controlled conditions. A successful pilot, he elaborated, would facilitate the adoption of his technology platform in buildings and cities around the world. And Living PlanIT would have an economic impact in Portugal. Thanks to Celso Ferreira, that possibility had seemed very real indeed. It was the perfect response to the perfect storm of urbanization, climate change, and new technologies.

While there is no question that the vision was compelling, just how coherent was it in the minds of the original team? Many had left jobs to join Living PlanIT, in no small part because of Lewis's magnetism but also because they wanted to use their skills to solve problems they found compelling and worthy. As engineer Luísa Lima put it in 2012, "If we go forward with PlanIT Valley the way we are planning, it will really help this country. I saw an article that mentioned Portugal as an example in the smart-city space. And that made me proud." Yet she too would soon leave.

In truth each member of the team had been propelled forward by his or her own version of the vision. Miguel Rodrigues, for example, had been focused on mobility—on PlanIT Valley as a testing ground for new, energy-saving transportation. He talked in 2010 about "an automotive center. We understood," he acknowledged, "that it wasn't enough to sustain the model. . . . We knew we had to expand our idea and start looking for a big picture."

Meanwhile, Malcolm Hutchinson, in 2009, had seen PlanIT Valley as a data center that needed a small citylike community around it: "Cisco said they wanted to be involved. They wanted to be able to hold executive meetings and major conferences here. So we asked what a major conference meant, and they said 30,000 people. So we would need hotel rooms for 30,000 people. That was a concept we hadn't even thought about. We realized we also would need housing for students. So, this would need to become a major city, a destination. That was a major turning point."

Hutchinson had expected Living PlanIT to be poised for building by March 2009—major deals closed with big-name corporate partners and a fully financed data center under way. But, as the DestiNY experience should have made clear, construction and real estate rarely innovate quickly. Hutchinson recalled, "We looked at other industries, such as aircraft, shipbuilding, to a lesser extent auto, to see how they revolutionized their approaches, trying to see if we could apply the same lessons in the construction industry. There were points where those industries picked up efficiencies and shot ahead. But the construction industry never found those points. Why? Because most buildings are built as one-off works of art rather than functional environments."

Hutchinson saw no reason why scale efficiencies from other industries could not be brought into construction: "If you look at an aircraft, it's a work of art, but one that's replicated. . . . We talked to people in the construction industry about why they were doing things this way, and the answer was always 'That's the way we've always done it.' This is what motivated us to do PlanIT Valley."

Manuel Simas had seen PlanIT Valley as a "merging of ideas—Miguel's car, Microsoft's intelligence and mobility, and a mayor with enough land to build a city. At that time, to be honest, we had no idea what we were talking about or how to make it happen. The glueware was Steve Lewis." But was Lewis's glue strong enough to hold all these different ideas about Living PlanIT together?

Peter van Manen understood better than anyone the distance between the idea and the reality: "In its simplest form, the evolution of PlanIT Valley is the larger equivalent of two people getting together in a diner and drawing something on the back of a napkin."

Talking the Future into Existence

Lewis traveled and networked endlessly over the years we studied Living PlanIT. He was a tireless, articulate, compelling spokesperson for his young company. Keynotes multiplied. Applause and the occasional award reinforced Lewis's confidence. As Thierry Martens explained, this was important work because of the extreme novelty of both the company and the industry. Like personal computers decades ago, the idea of smart cities had to be explained. You had to get people comfortable with the category before you could have a viable business.

Lewis and Martens intuitively understood the need for what strategy scholars call *legitimacy building*.[2] When customers and investors lack understanding of the desirability of, or use for, some product or service in a brand-new market category, innovators must educate them. They must craft and spread a message that makes the new category seem desirable—and ultimately seem inevitable.

Although most of those involved wanted to actively sell Living PlanIT's story, at least one person, Lewis's and Adrian Wyatt's mutual friend, Richard Constant, a public relations expert, warned early on against too much press too soon. When we interviewed Constant about Living PlanIT back in 2011, he reported,

> I said to the team, "I think it's just the most wonderful aspirational concept I've ever heard described in business terms because, if you get this right, you will change the way we live, work, and dwell together in the years to come, which is probably a very good thing. . . . But," I said, "from a commercial standpoint, if I were you I would be very careful about undertaking a public relations campaign before you've, first, got an anchor partner of the scale where people go, 'If they've done their technology due diligence, I don't need to disbelieve anymore.'"

Constant then added two more criteria: "Secondly, wait until you have enough financial means to get from where you are today to where it becomes more bankable. Thirdly, the media will, until it's proven, disbelieve in both your proposition and the outcome."

His reasoning? "The more you engage, the more argument there will be about whether it's a good thing. That will, in turn, color the audiences before they've even had a chance to listen to the proposition. So, I don't actually want to pitch."

Talk wasn't just for conferences. Even if he expressed disdain at times for the way big companies (those dinosaurs) operated, Lewis knew he needed them for Living PlanIT's success. They were essential partners in his model. Symbolically, he needed recognition and approval from established organizations to legitimize both Living PlanIT and the smart-city industry. Pragmatically, of course, Living PlanIT could not build a city alone—or even demonstrate new solutions in existing cities—without an ecosystem of corporate partners to help execute.

Courting big-name companies as strategic partners was, initially at least, another way to build legitimacy while navigating a novel path. Martens believed that technology companies like to move in herds, so "you have a chicken-and-egg problem: companies might not become interested if others aren't." Reaching out to Cisco was part of talking the company into existence. So was the longstanding connection with McLaren Electronic Systems, which boosted everyone's confidence. Similarly, the affiliation with BuroHappold, with its experience in large-scale construction projects including Heathrow's Terminal 5 and the London Olympics, sent a message that there were people on board who had done this before.

As Lewis pounded the pavement, it wasn't always clear who were the right people to talk to in large, complex companies. Should he meet with heads of research? With chief sustainability officers—that ambiguous new role a handful of large players, including Siemens, AT&T, and DuPont, had added to the C-suite?[3]

At a meeting in the London offices of GE in May 2011, Lewis, Robin Daniels, James Hovington, and several observers met with Keith Dawson (a pseudonym), a young, up-and-coming executive at GE. Dawson was slick and stylish, exuding confidence. He explained his place in the GE hierarchy, noting he was only "two layers from the sun" and well positioned to influence decisions about GE's relationship with Living PlanIT. "There's

a lot of noise out there on smart cities," he told the group assembled around
the enormous oval conference table. GE would pick four or five horses,
and Dawson wanted to pick the right one. He came to the room with
two concerns: "Will our widgets fit your widgets?" and, given the country's widely publicized debt issues, would doing business in Portugal be a
problem? Both concerns, thought Lewis, were easily dispelled. Each time
Dawson expressed a concern, Lewis reframed it as an opportunity.

By the end of the meeting, Lewis seemed somehow to hold all the
cards. GE was on trial here, not the startup. Lewis communicated, in an
engaging rather than offensive way, that big companies like GE needed
companies like Living PlanIT for innovation, creative new solutions,
and competitive edge. "We've got people beating down our door," he
told Dawson, "because not only are we the front runners but we are loyal
in our relationships and great to work with." Dawson seemed to agree,
suggesting one month to announce the partnership; Lewis parried, "How
about one week?"

Relationships like this are created by conversation, but they must
be nourished by action. In some form or another, everyone on the team
longed for it. Those early conversations with Ferreira had opened the
door to action in Portugal. As Martens noted, these interactions had been
unusual: "You dream of working with someone like that." Ferreira's impri-
matur would allow Living PlanIT to buy land at predevelopment prices.
The company would receive fast-track zoning approval and could use it as
collateral to secure funding. In all his work around the world, Martens had
never seen such smooth collaboration on a project of this scale. And to him
the idea of building a technology platform that could scale was bold but
sensible. Even at Cisco the dream had always been to build a technology
platform. But Cisco couldn't do it alone. As in Lewis's Microsoft-inspired
business model, you need an ecosystem of partners. And this is where
walking through the door that Ferreira opened stalls.

Why didn't talk turn into action more quickly? Culture clash between
industries, explored in chapter 8, played a major role. Another part of the
reason is that, for executives, talk is action. The leader's main job is selling
vision, purpose, direction, hope—you name it. Leaders explain, teach,
promise, and inspire. This role is especially vital in the domain of a radical

new technology or market, where communicating with external audiences—analysts, financiers, and potential customers—is a way of attracting attention and resources for a radical new enterprise.[4] Yet talk, it seems, also may inhibit action in highly uncertain enterprises.

When Influencing Inhibits Innovating

Was Living PlanIT's focus on external influence limiting its attention to internal innovation? If so, it's an easy trap to fall into. Tiona Zuzul calls this the *advocacy trap*.[5] Our research suggests that legitimacy building, although valuable, also creates risks for entrepreneurs.[6] One risk is that repeated advocacy of a clear and compelling model makes it cognitively and organizationally difficult to pivot when new experiences or feedback might otherwise point to a need to change the model.[7] The late organizational theorist Chris Argyris, studying managerial conversations inside companies, argued that advocacy suppresses genuine inquiry, in turn inhibiting organizational learning. Curiosity is inhibited by the very act of arguing one's point. The more I explain and argue, the more I believe I am right—and the more I attribute your pushback to stubbornness or ignorance. In the Living PlanIT story, we see an organizational-level analog to this interpersonal dynamic. Selling the story risks freezing the story.

A second, more obvious risk is inattention to innovation created by resource and talent scarcity. One cannot be pounding the pavement, influencing the external world, and dynamically ensuring the innovation of internal operations at the same time. While Lewis sold the gleaming Emerald City taking shape in Portugal to conference audiences and corporate executives around the world, he was not spending that time leading his senior management team in strategic decision making related to the discovery of tangible market opportunities in the smart-city space.

Did Lewis's charisma scatter and deplete his efforts, distracting him from the internal development required to push the company into a new realm? Many on the team commented on this issue as one of closure. Simas said, "We use Steve as an icon. . . . But Steve is not a closer—he doesn't close deals. But he's a fantastic opener."

Ian Taylor, chair of the advisory board, explained the tension between bold vision and fast action in late 2011: "Steve's weakness is his ability to deliver. We need to move from an entrepreneurial culture to one of execution. We'd never have gotten anywhere near this project if it wasn't for Steve—but building an effective management team will be a challenge."

Taylor continued: "Other people notice this. Celso and I had a very long talk. . . . Celso's view is that you wouldn't have gotten anything near this exciting if it wasn't for Steve, but Steve could actually be the weakness as the project goes forward." This is a common tension for entrepreneurs—their vision and their charisma are essential to the company's momentum, but they often need managers to force and structure the steady progress of small action.

Soon after, in early 2012, Tim Gocher also lamented the difficulty of execution: "Steve has a complex personality—he doesn't fit in a box. The combination of his ability to see further, his intellect, and his self-belief makes him promise things he can't deliver. It makes him too optimistic—almost pathologically." Gocher went on to illustrate: "In a recent board meeting, he said that financing is expected to come at end of year. He believes that's possible somehow—but it doesn't happen. My work has been a difficult balance of letting Steve be a leader and reining him in, going through the push-and-pull."

By May 2012 Taylor was losing patience with the overly optimistic predictions Lewis and others were making, particularly with potential clients. Taylor described his biggest challenge: "Trying to deal with the management issues of not overpromising. Trying to handle inspiring people to really get excited about what they're doing but at the same time not get carried away by unrealistic expectations of success or timing. Inculcating a culture of reality. A small company has to have a balance between cold reality and excited hyperbole. Getting that balance right is . . . the role of the chairman."

Meanwhile van Manen believed that the story was finally cohering at that time in ways that might enable action:

> The last few months have been tough—but Living PlanIT is beginning to show a new level of maturity—displaying humility, focusing on a smaller scope, looking inside the company to determine who adds value and what creates friction. The number of people has thus been greatly reduced, making it a cleaner, more sustainable organization

with a clear, focused strategy. Before, each person had a different take on Living PlanIT's vision, especially after the culture had changed. It is more aligned now.

Perhaps because Lewis had beaten leukemia as a young adult, he had little patience with naysayers. Did his willful optimism affect the company's evolution? Having heard too many predictions of future mileposts, we became inured to the excitement and certainty with which they were delivered. Construction was always about to start. But perhaps this is what future-builders must believe.

Pedro Balonas explained delays in a more expansive way. "Because we are working with a tech company," he told us in November 2011, "we need to think about construction in the early phases, and this can get confusing. We have to readjust the way we work. We are not moving in linear phases. We are engaged in a continuous, evolving conceptual phase. We are always redefining the concept and multitasking, and this is the most challenging part."

Eventually, the story did take a turn—shovels making way, in the near term at least, for software.

The Story Shifts

By the fall of 2012, when there was no denying that talk of the UOS had supplanted talk of PlanIT Valley, Lewis explained, "We found out that funding PlanIT Valley would be impossible because nobody is interested in real estate financing projects. We could have just stopped there and said we failed. Instead we used partners and technology to explore how to move forward, to develop as a tech company—which we always were. We had gotten confused, hoping that property development would drive that tech."

Andrew Comer acknowledged earlier, in May of that year:

> The focus has moved a bit from Paredes and PlanIT Valley, thankfully, to more-deliverable opportunities, which will probably be in the realm of consultancies. I think there are probably smaller physical plays Lewis can focus on. If I'm honest, I was rather anticipating—maybe naively—that within a year we would have this enormous city to design and shape. But bear in mind, when we first started it was early 2008 before everybody folded; . . . you know, it was just

another project opportunity. When we first engaged LP, we anticipated working on a city—it seemed like a clear opportunity.

Comer had seen PlanIT Valley as an opportunity because Lewis's
arguments about the construction industry made sense to him. Over time,
however, Comer recognized the need for a different approach to convert
cogent argument into tangible progress: "Lewis presented some very plau-
sible arguments about the failures of the construction industry and the
potential of technology. Obviously, PlanIT Valley is not happening. But
our partnership was based on a philosophy rather than any particular
deliverables—an investment in our future. Our view on LP's value proposition hasn't shifted—just the ways we can engage."

Before leaving Living PlanIT in 2012 to join Amazon Web Services,
Chrysanthos Chrysanthou told us that he wished he had been able to "kill
PlanIT Valley" earlier: "The culture of the company regressed tremendously
because of the ongoing financial constraints, the ongoing overpromise and
underdelivery . . . especially Steve, the ongoing market conditions that
wouldn't allow PlanIT Valley to evolve, which disillusioned the partners."

Chrysanthou felt that Lewis didn't evolve the model fast enough,
particularly related to service-delivery opportunities:

> He didn't pick up on the services aspect. So, all the things that he
> was preaching to people—excellent intellectual property that he and
> the team developed over the years—was never packaged, sold, or
> monetized. Now, in the last three months he's realized, "Holy crap,
> what an opportunity I've been missing." So, we're selling services,
> which is an additional revenue stream. The company is actually
> beginning to generate revenues and doesn't even need to go raise
> money from outside.

All of those years focusing on the real estate space, "which takes
forever to evolve and execute," he told us, "have taken a toll because big
sale cycles doesn't bring in money early enough. So, by balancing it out
with machine-to-machine or Internet of things, that is, with smaller projects—whether it's a mall or one building or a rail station . . . a transportation solution, things like that—can help. So, I think that's going to be the
evolution of the company: selling vertical solutions."

Chrysanthou had been keenly focused on hiring those who could do IT research and development. "When I came in, about 80 to 90 percent of the company was nonsales and non-R&D," he said.

Ian Taylor summed it up in 2012:

> The belief that we were a property developer as opposed to a software company was very damaging to us because of the way that capital markets have changed. So all the clever things we were going to do with the construction process—the demonstration that you can have sustainable cost/benefits from redesigning the buildings in the way that we were suggesting, the smart infrastructure, all of that that we would have done in the valley; we have built up in models and adapted software. But our first deployment will not be in PlanIT Valley.

Putting a positive spin on it, he continued, "And I think that shows a great deal of courage and entrepreneurship within the company, to adapt quickly to those circumstances."

Moving Forward

Having failed to build a pilot city in Portugal by 2015, Living PlanIT had returned to its roots as a software platform developer. Its new identity was slowly taking shape—one closer to its founders' expertise. The company's approximately 30 employees in the summer of 2015 were busy teaming up with other smart-city pioneers, pursuing a set of strikingly diverse innovation projects around the world. If a brand-new smart city was to remain elusive for a while, why not a smart microcity of some kind? A shopping mall, like an airport, can be seen as a sort of microcity. True, compared with PlanIT Valley, this was small action, but it was feasible action, not to mention a strategy for learning.

Big Vision, Small Smart Action

For the Living PlanIT team, bad news and good news flowed seamlessly into a serpentine learning curve, perhaps leaving insufficient time to learn from the bad news. As we were concluding our research for this book, members of the Living PlanIT team were flying around the globe, getting their hands dirty at last, if not with shovels at least with software. The real action, it seemed, lay in teaming up with other visionaries—just as they had always known. But this time the partnerships were taking shape in meaningful, tangible ways. The three most promising, in the wake of the London City Airport project, were the Mailbox shopping mall in Birmingham in the United Kingdom, a smart-city pilot project in Copenhagen, and the possibility of a greenfield city in Brazil. The first two projects were decidedly small, smart, and actionable.

Creating a Smart Mall

In 2012 the British developer Milligan Retail, also behind the airport project, teamed up with Living PlanIT to design an enhanced retail experience in its upscale Mailbox shopping center in Birmingham. Milligan Retail's goal was to bring new aesthetics and interconnectivity to the shopping experience. A UOS-powered smart retail platform similar to London City Airport's would improve shopper loyalty and the shopper experience. Living PlanIT got right to work, first by improving the underutilized parking garage with prebooking and better pricing for regular customers. Mailbox thus provided Living PlanIT with a second test, after the airport, of the UOS. "Although this isn't the first smart retail project we launched," John Stenlake explained, "it was the first one we planned. When this launches, it will leapfrog the competition."

Connecting Copenhagen

Recall that in 2012, the city of Copenhagen sent out a request for proposal (RFP), initially inspired by the need to replace streetlights. Søren Kvist, project manager at Copenhagen Solutions Lab and for the Copenhagen Connecting project, told us in March 2015, "We decided to explore sensor applications in streetlights. We were, and continue to be, more interested in solutions to specific problems—trash, streetlights, parking, flooding in streets, et cetera—than in big, citywide data platforms.

"Smart city" Kvist insisted, "doesn't just mean high-tech—it can also mean bike lanes. Small, smart solutions are about thinking across verticals—using sensors in streetlights, for example, for a variety of purposes, from security to energy use."

The strategy for the Copenhagen Connecting project was to engage companies, universities, and city officials to design new ways to use publicly available data. Their goals were twofold: livability for the citizens of Copenhagen and becoming a carbon-neutral city by 2025.

A left-leaning mayor focused on a climate agenda and smart solutions helped the project move through the RFP process. Copenhagen, a port city, had enjoyed a good infrastructure since the 1700s, and building and implementing new streetlights, waste bins, and parking meters (to name a few items on the wish list) did not seem daunting. The city's relatively small size would make it the perfect testing ground. And, as Kvist explained, Copenhagen had "a lot of available data"—movement patterns, CO_2 emissions, traffic flow, energy consumption. One of the first projects involved the use of smartphones for "asset tracking"; chips placed in bikes were helping with a major problem for Copenhagen citizens: bike theft.

Barriers to progress emerged early in project planning. Big organizations like telecommunications and utilities companies, Kvist explained, each had its traditional standard operating procedures—from the way meetings were conducted to the process for choosing vendors to the construction and management of utilities. Whereas data collected by city government were freely available, private companies were reluctant to share their data. Copenhagen Solutions Lab wanted to design a business model that would convince private businesses to participate.

"There is no sustainable business model for these projects," Kvist sighed. "We don't have the recipe, but we are going ahead anyway because the benefits to the city, to the public sector, are high. Political shortsightedness, silo thinking vs. platform thinking, lack of management, and organizational inertia are our biggest barriers. Our Solutions Lab acts as a bridge for all the players—Hitachi, Cisco, and the City of Copenhagen, with its seven different departments."

The city, after reviewing the submitted proposals, chose Hitachi, which had included Living PlanIT in its proposal. While Copenhagen Solutions Lab wanted to build a city dashboard using the UOS, Kvist admitted that this would require strong public-private partnerships: "Everyone would need to contribute their data to make it work—and this challenges private-sector traditional business models." Building public Wi-Fi throughout the city, for example, was something telecom companies resisted.

While Kvist was skeptical about a unified data platform in Copenhagen, Blettner, in a conversation in February 2015, expressed pure exuberance: "We will be the data platform for the entire city!"

In April 2015 Hans Lindeman, senior vice president of EMEA convergence at Hitachi Consulting, said the goal of the Copenhagen Connecting project was carbon neutrality by 2025, starting with the creation of a big-data platform that would allow citizens to innovate with data. He had worked with Critical Software, a company that had written code for Living PlanIT. In April 2015 Lindeman was consumed with building strong partnerships in the design phase: "We are in design mode, coding, software building. . . . We work together well—you need an NGO [non-governmental organization] that knows how to raise money, and you also need a large corporate company that wants to be flexible and is prepared to invest time and money. To build smart cities, you need large organizations willing to partner up."

Lindeman was also wrestling with the business model: "We don't want to pay for data, so we have to entice companies to give up data. What's our business model? With all this data, we are expecting revenue streams from app developers, SMEs, or individuals. They will pay us a subscription to get access to data. Subscriptions will be more expensive the more granular the data."

Although ambitious, the Copenhagen Connecting project was realistic. It was a fortuitous opportunity to test city software applications, to learn fast what worked and what didn't. Meanwhile dreams of building a greenfield city had not fully died down, and a new possibility seemed to be taking shape, this time in Brazil.

Teaming Up on a New Smart City in Brazil

The Brazilian company Cone SA, comprising Moura Dubeux Engineering (real estate developers) and FI-FGTS (the Brazilian government's infrastructure investment fund), is one of the largest engineering and development firms in Latin America.[8] Cone provides industrial infrastructure and logistics platforms for port regions. In 2013 Living PlanIT entered a Strategic Alliance Agreement with Cone and its newer subsidiary, Convida, to team up on a project to design an innovative city in the Brazilian state of Pernambuco and provide a high living standard for its residents by leveraging the Internet of things to transform mobility, sustainability, education, and leisure. The carefully planned city would prioritize walkability and security.

In partnership with other companies, the Living PlanIT team anticipated building an integrated technology platform for the new city to reduce construction time and building, operating, and maintenance costs, as well as to increase revenues from leases—all while reducing environmental impact. The UOS would capture data from sensors and use them to manage security, safety, and traffic in and around the warehouses, residential areas, and port functions.

Steve Lewis and Marcos Roberto Dubeux, the handsome 31-year-old CEO and co-founder of Cone and the son of Cone's other founder, Marcos Dubeux Sr., hit it off immediately. Over many months that followed, they hammered out an initial agreement. The idea of turning an ordinary real estate development deal into a smart city that would revitalize a region and put that region on the high-tech map appealed to the younger Dubeux. Lewis and Dubeux envisioned the new city of Convida, 10 minutes from the oil refineries and shipyards of the Suape Port, as home for 100,000 people. Workers who previously had to commute from Recife (a city of 4 million) 90 minutes each way, would have a place to live.

Dubeux had spent three years on permits and funding. "In 2004 we had 60 million euros to finance the project," he explained when we met up with him in February 2015. "In 2009 we received a 200-million-euro bond from the Brazilian government to build residential units. By 2010 we had 6.5 billion euros in finance." Most people recognized the critical economic importance of this long-neglected region, internally and externally, as a foreign trade zone. (Suape is the closest Latin American port to Africa.) Dubeux created teams to build the industrial park, the dry port, a gas station, a rail yard, an expressway, a shopping center, a convention center, hotels, offices, restaurants, and more. The business plan was full of numbers that grew exponentially into the billions. "We are still in the dream phase," he said. "In 2011 this land was sugar cane. I was almost afraid to start."

Living PlanIT intended to start small, contracting to build security systems for the warehouses—something that seemed both feasible and consistent with the company's vision. But Lewis, as usual, reveled in the scale of the project. The Living PlanIT team began with a report to outline the possible residential and commercial structures. The team would use the UOS, Lewis explained, to help Convida store, share, and manage renewable energy: "The traditional revenue stream for a developer like this is rent, leases. The UOS allows them to layer on additional services, like solar power, data analytics run on Amazon Cloud, for their tenants."

Lewis explained further that the UOS would control the 176,000 solar panels planned for the first phase of construction. It would handle conversion into energy and distribution to customers, including the government. In February 2015 Lewis, Blettner, and Nuno Silva convened executives from Convida and Gehry Technologies to plan. Lewis, we noticed, tended to speak in the present, making it difficult for a listener to discern what is planned and what has already been built. "Our focus is on solving these problems for developers," he said, "reducing their capex [capital expenditures] and their time to market, and increasing their ROI and the project's environmental sustainability. This requires they put more effort into the design, and their costs are lower later."

A few weeks later, however, Blettner was glum. The project seemed to have stalled.

From our perspective the Mailbox, Convida, and Copenhagen projects were great experiments—profoundly useful learning opportunities. Would one of them demonstrate to investors Living PlanIT's value and viability for the longer term? Only time would tell. No matter what happens, however, we were impressed by the team's doggedness in the face of hurdles. Living PlanIT's story vividly illustrates the principles listed in *Five Leadership Lessons for Building the Future: A Review*.

As we contemplate these innovative projects, each with its enormous challenges, it is impossible not to wonder how tomorrow's green, livable, energizing cities will be built. Who will take the lead?

Five Leadership Lessons for
Building the Future: A Review

Lesson 1: Start with Big Vision

Big vision compels and motivates people—at different ages and from different backgrounds—to take personal and professional risks to pursue a dream.

People must feel able to contribute to the vision, to help adapt it, and to move it along as more is learned. This adaptation should be an explicit part of the initial design.

Making sure everyone knows that vision adaptation is expected, especially in nascent industries, is crucial. This means being explicit about both the exciting possibilities *and* how little is known at the outset.

Lesson 2: Foster Big Teaming

Audacious innovation, such as building a new city, requires bridging industry cultures—with more empathy and skill than comes naturally.

People have a tendency to emphasize the negative attributes of other professions and to place blame on other groups when progress stalls.

Overcoming these negative dynamics requires task- and leisure-focused cross-sector exchanges through which people gain understanding of what each group brings and faces in its area of expertise.

Increased mutual understanding across groups enables innovation.

Lesson 3: Celebrate Mavericks

Future-building flourishes when successful, credible experts glimpse new possibilities and help shift the conversation.

Industry mavericks are often frustrated by the slow pace of change, but their vision and reputations provide vital encouragement that helps others believe and push onward.

continued

Five Leadership Lessons for Building
the Future: A Review *(continued)*

Lesson 4: Embrace Small Action

When pursuing a big vision, small action is essential, but it can seem inadequate and unappealing when considered alongside the vision.

Leaders must therefore reframe small action as valued data—learning events that are mission critical to progress and to building a bold new future.

A series of small but highly innovative projects allows a company to learn in action, as a way of technically and financially realizing the evolving big vision.

Lesson 5: Balance Influence and Innovation

Building the future requires leaders to balance influencing (selling the vision) and innovating (developing the vision through small smart action).

Influencing is essential when it represents a new and unfamiliar possibility; a growing number of people must grasp the need for the innovation, to build a foundation for realizing it.

Innovating (experimenting to develop new technologies and business models) is essential to making progress.

Balancing influencing and innovating is more challenging than it might first appear:

- Influencing takes founders' limited time and resources away from innovating.

- Influencing brings more-certain and more-immediate rewards than innovating—in the form of applause, awards, and prestigious contacts, making it natural to prefer and emphasize influencing.

Balance must be struck with deliberation and care.

Building Tomorrow's Cities

Who should take the lead in creating tomorrow's cities? At a 2012 conference, UN Human Settlements Programme executive director Joan Clos laid responsibility for new-city building squarely at the feet of urban planners: "The place to start is with the street network. Without this you can't lay pipes or run trams. It's the foundations of urbanism, and without foundations you're building on sand. Yes, we can have subways that cut across and beneath the street network, and data packets that travel through the airwaves over the tops of buildings, but if these aren't serving human interactions in effectively laid-out street networks, then they are to little avail."

Adam Greenfield's book-length critique of smart-city building by corporations similarly bemoans the tendency to leave out architects and urban planners.[9] According to Greenfield corporations have "taken on the mantle of urbanists without taste for history or texture or any familiarity with history of urbanist discourse." Generic-looking master plans, he writes, created by IT architects who used algorithms to predict human behavior served little more than to pave the way for privatization of municipal services and corporate profit making: "The deep involvement of large-scale commercial actors in the germination of ideas about the design and equipment of cities does make it somewhat unusual in the history of urbanism. It's as if the foundational works of twentieth-century urbanist thought had been collectively authored by United States Steel, General Motors, the Otis Elevator Company and Bell Telephone, rather than Le Corbusier or Jane Jacobs."

As we have seen, IT certainly cannot forge the future-building path alone. The idea that any city could be built without the benefit of multiple areas of expertise seems patently ridiculous. In the time we have been working on this book, criticism of the fact that corporations like IBM, Cisco, Philips, and Siemens are the main drivers of smart-city research and development has grown louder. Where are the urban planners? critics say. Where are the statespeople, the historians, the architects, the visionaries?

Where are the leaders?

The Future-Building Leader

In a recent interview, New Songdo City's Stan Gale described himself as a visionary *and* a manager: "My strongest tool, my strength, is strong visualization of the outcome. I set the goal, rally the troops, be sure the goal is a team goal, build consensus, and go after it with relentless pursuit."[10] In our research we discovered visionaries (mavericks) in every industry domain. Such individuals span the boundary between the past and the future. They understand their industry and how it works but also glimpse a better way. There was Steve Lewis, of course, from IT; Adrian Wyatt in real estate; Celso Ferreira in government; Nigel Linscott and David Crump in construction; Andrew Comer from civil engineering and planning; Pedro Balonas from architecture; Peter van Manen and Thierry Martens from the corporate sphere; and also Robin Daniels, who had a foot (think of the game of Twister) in several of these worlds.

As we have seen, vision is not enough. Future-building leaders also must create conditions for Big Teaming across industries. The deeply held biases that pervade any professional sphere must be unearthed and overcome to allow people to see and celebrate the strengths each domain brings, rather than to simply bemoan the limitations. Finally, future-building leaders must insist on a disciplined process of small, fast, iterative action. Whatever new solutions will work best, one thing is for sure: We will not know them fully in advance. Only through smart experiments, fast failure, and even faster learning will they materialize.

What the
Future Holds

SLOWLY BUT SURELY, THE WORLD WAS CATCHING UP WITH STEVE LEWIS'S vision. In the July/August 2015 issue of *Harvard Magazine,* author Stephanie Garlock wrote: "The Internet of Things promises to change the way consumers live. But the industrial shift—forcing companies far beyond Silicon Valley to join the tech world—might be even more significant."[1]

As Garlock's article went to press, our small band of future-builders came together from around the world to assess their own future. Living PlanIT's executive team met in June 2015 in a rented house in Gloucester, Massachusetts, the setting for the book and movie *The Perfect Storm,* a story that has become a metaphor for the collision of unlikely events. Joining them were the company's two latest hires, both familiar names— Richard Constant and Peter van Manen—having suddenly taken a leap of faith into future-building.

Imagine the scene: Lewis, Constant, van Manen, Thierry Martens, Johanna Weigelt, and Harley Blettner are huddled around a laptop, working on a PowerPoint deck with nearly 200 slides, a presentation for a private equity firm. (To be fair, at least 120 or so comprise backup data.) All are a little sunburned from time outdoors the day before.

This could be the proverbial garage scene—innovators hard at work—but the house is too nice, the views too resplendent, the participants showing off the company's new website too experienced. And perhaps, in their forties and fifties, a decade too old for the garage. This meeting is to strategize about how best to attract investors. Outside the windows the gray Atlantic, frosted with whitecaps, stretches into the future.

Out come the fish chowder and the steamers, still a bit sandy, and some new language: the phrase *edgeless computing,* apparently a frontier bigger than the IoT, looms ahead. The Living PlanIT team assures us that this new market makes the IoT look tiny. Half the GDP of the planet, someone says, will be spent on edgeless computing.

The future is never finished. As for the present, the shopping mall in Birmingham will go live before this book hits the shelves. Then will come Copenhagen, with a planned launch of the initial phase in early 2016, followed by a smart-nation platform in Singapore, a few smart malls throughout Asia, and some security work with the UK's National Health Service.[2] The biggest risks they see now? Poor timing. Missing the opportunity.

Everyone agrees that now is the time to move into execution mode. Execution, Constant points out, means leveraging partners. Living PlanIT may have been founded almost a decade earlier, but its presentation to the world, its debutante ball, would happen in 2016. We listen intently, and hear that the world was not ready in 2008. Cloud hosting was not a reality until 2014; 2016 will be the year of edgeless computing; 2017 will see advanced analytics and modeling; and 2018 will be the year of edgeless intelligence. The UOS, a tool built for the non-centralized use of data, will be a central piece of this velvet revolution. Links between the real and virtual worlds, operating in much the way that building information modeling allowed builders to envision their plans in 3D, will allow cities to interpret and predict the effects of polluted air and water and the spread of disease.

But how to fund it? Most IoT companies, says Lewis, don't have business models, and they're hobbled by short-term views of the market, by greed. Their executives are not visionaries. "There is," he says, "no channel strategy in their models."

Still his team needs to capture some of the money flowing into new ventures. "You can't build a product like this in three to four years," he says in hindsight. "It took time for the product to mature. As for the market, it is still immature. The real estate guys are really just beginning to get it—the need for core infrastructure and for integrating the data sources that they need for operations. They may not be sophisticated, but they are sick of proprietary systems."

The dream of PlanIT Valley, it turns out, is still alive. This will be where edgeless computing will become a reality, where the mutual learning that will give rise to new models for future projects will occur. The good old-fashioned shovel, that symbol of human industry and human hopes, will, we are once again assured, hit dirt.

Until then the rain beats down on the Massachusetts shore, perhaps with more ferocity than in centuries past, perhaps not. Inside, a team of very creative, very optimistic thinkers continues to do what future-builders do: eat, drink, share ideas, and learn, one small step at a time, how to work together.

Notes

Preface

1. "Hold Please: George Coy Launched the First Commercial Telephone Exchange," New England Historical Society website, accessed October 28, 2015, http://www.newenglandhistoricalsociety.com/hold-please-george-coy -launched-first-commercial-telephone-exchange.

2. This extensive case study builds on our prior case studies of audacious innovation, including research on the Beijing Water Cube, Florida's brand-new Lake Nona Medical City, and the rescue of 33 Chilean miners: Robert G. Eccles, Amy C. Edmondson, and Dilyana Karadzhova, "Arup: Building the Water Cube," Harvard Business School Case 410-054, February 2010 (revised June 2010); Amy C. Edmondson, Sydney Ribot, and Tiona Zuzul, "Designing a Culture of Collaboration at Lake Nona Medical City," Harvard Business School Case 613-022, October 2012; and Amy C. Edmondson, Faaiza Rashid, and Herman B. "Dutch" Leonard, "The 2010 Chilean Mining Rescue (A) and (B)," Harvard Business School Cases 612-046 and 612-047, November 2011 (revised October 2014). We believed that focusing the book on a single unusual case study would be the best way to develop and convey our ideas about audacious innovation.

3. Erin Griffith, "Why Startups Fail, According to Their Founders," Fortune, September 25, 2014, http://fortune.com/2014/09/25/why-startups-fail -according-to-their-founders.

Chapter 1: Building the Future

1. Faaiza Rashid, Amy C. Edmondson, and Herman B. Leonard, "Leadership Lessons from the Chilean Mine Rescue," Harvard Business Review, July–August 2013, 91, 113–19; and Amy C. Edmondson, Teaming: How Organizations Learn, Innovate, and Compete in the Knowledge Economy (San Francisco: Jossey-Bass, 2012).

2. "Online Extra: Fred Smith on the Birth of FedEx," Bloomberg.com, September 19, 2004, http://www.bloomberg.com/bw/stories/2004-09-19/online-extra -fred-smith-on-the-birth-of-fedex.

3. Edmondson, *Teaming*.

4. Amy C. Edmondson and Tiona Zuzul, "The Advocacy Trap: When Leaders' Legitimacy Building Inhibits Organizational Learning," Harvard Business School Working Paper 11-099, September 17, 2015.

5. Note that this research was done in collaboration with London Business School professor Tiona Zuzul, formerly at Harvard Business School.

6. Built environment. Accessed November 3, 2015, http://en.wikipedia.org/wiki /Built_environment.

7. Federico Casalegno and William J. Mitchell, *Connected Sustainable Cities* (Cambridge, MA: Mobile Experience Publishing, 2008).

8. Anthony M. Townsend, *Smart Cities: Big Data, Civic Hackers, and the Quest for a New Utopia* (New York: W. W. Norton, 2014), 15.

9. *Ecocities, sustainable cities, smart cities, resilient cities,* and *living cities* are all terms in this literature, each with a subtly different emphasis. Today the term *smart cities* has become the most common, especially in the corporate world, although many companies, such as Siemens, have begun replacing that term with *resilient cities,* as two megatrends—urbanization and climate concerns— merge into a single problem. Resilient cities are prepared for climate change. Governments, businesses, and communities around the world are seeing an ever-increasing frequency of extreme weather–related events. These events are playing out against a backdrop of global population growth and urbanization. Resilient cities have adapted for the effective and reliable operation of infrastructure systems to deliver energy, mobility, water, sanitation, shelter, information, emergency response, and other critical services.

10. This is both because of higher-than-average consumption by residents of most cities and because cities house considerable manufacturing.

11. United Nations Department of Economic and Social Affairs, *World Economic and Social Survey 2013: Sustainable Development Challenges,* accessed November 6, 2015, https://sustainabledevelopment.un.org/content /documents/2843WESS2013.pdf.

12. Daniel Hoornweg, Lorraine Sugar, and Claudia Lorena Trejos Gómez, "Cities and Greenhouse Gas Emissions: Moving Forward," *Environment and Urbanization* 23, no. 1 (2011): 207–27.

13. "Big Cities Are Not Always Biggest Polluters," Phys.org, January 26, 2011, http://phys.org/news/2011-01-big-cities-biggest-polluters.html.

14. David Owen, *Green Metropolis: Why Living Smaller, Living Closer, and Driving Less Are the Keys to Sustainability* (New York: Riverhead Books, 2009).

15. Edward Glaeser, *Triumph of the City: How Our Greatest Invention Makes Us Richer, Smarter, Greener, Healthier, and Happier* (New York: Penguin Press, 2011).

16. Owen, *Green Metropolis.*

17. Peter Calthorpe, *Urbanism in the Age of Climate Change* (Washington, DC: Island Press, 2010).

18. "Interview with Peter Calthorpe," American Society of Landscape Architects website, accessed November 3, 2015, http://www.asla.org/ContentDetail .aspx?id=30566.

19. Casalegno and Mitchell, *Connected Sustainable Cities.*

20. Richard Dobbs, Jeremy Oppenheim, and Fraser Thompson, "Mobilizing for a Resource Revolution," *McKinsey Quarterly,* January 2012, http://www .mckinsey.com/insights/energy_resources_materials/mobilizing_for_a _resource_revolution.

21. "Buildings and Emissions: Making the Connection," Center for Climate and Energy Solutions website, accessed November 6, 2015, http://www.c2es.org /technology/overview/buildings.

22. Jock Herron, Amy C. Edmondson, and Robert G. Eccles, "Beyond Platinum: Making the Case for Titanium Buildings," in *Constructing Green: Sustainability and the Places We Inhabit,* ed. Rebecca Henn and Andrew Hoffman (Boston: MIT Press, 2013).

23. Rajendra K. Pachauri and Andy Reisinger, eds., *Climate Change 2007: Synthesis Report.* Intergovernmental Panel on Climate Change, accessed October 28, 2015, https://www.ipcc.ch/publications_and_data/publications _ipcc_fourth_assessment_report_synthesis_report.htm.

24. Herron, Edmondson, and Eccles, "Beyond Platinum," 77–100.

25. Thomas L. Friedman, *Hot, Flat, and Crowded: Why We Need a Green Revolution—and How It Can Renew America* (New York: Farrar, Straus and Giroux, 2008).

26. Shane Greenstein, *How the Internet Became Commercial: Innovation, Privatization, and the Birth of a New Network* (Princeton, NJ: Princeton University Press, 2015).

27. "Cisco to Bring 21st Century Remote Learning Programs to Colorado Higher Education Institutions" (news release), Cisco website, January 18, 2011, http://newsroom.cisco.com/press-release-content?type=webcontent& articleId=5875476.

28. Mark Fischetti, "The Smartest Cities Will Use People as Their Sensors" (video), *Scientific American* website, August 16, 2011, http://www.scientificamerican .com/article/ratti-smartest-cities-use-people-as-sensors.

29. James Kanter, "As Sea Levels Rise, Dutch See Floating Cities," *Green* (blog), *New York Times,* October 27, 2009, http://green.blogs.nytimes.com/2009/10/27 /as-sea-levels-rise-dutch-see-floating-cities.

30. Michael Moyer and Carina Storrs, "How Much Is Left? The Limits of Earth's Resources," *Scientific American* 3, no. 3 (2010), 74–81.

31. Joachim von Braun, "The World Food Situation: New Driving Forces and Required Actions," International Food Policy Research Institute website, accessed October 28, 2015, http://www.ifpri.org/sites/default/files/publi cations/pr18.pdf.

32. Cynthia Rosenzweig and Martin L. Parry, "Potential Impact of Climate Change on World Food Supply," *Nature* 367, no. 6495 (1994): 133–38.

33. Mathis Wackernagel (doctoral dissertation, University of British Columbia, 1992). See Erling Holden, "Ecological Footprints and Sustainable Urban Form, *Journal of Housing and the Built Environment* 19, no. 1 (2004): 91–109.

34. Duncan Pollard, ed., *Living Planet Report 2010: Biodiversity, Biocapacity and Development* (Gland, Switzerland: WWF International, 2010).

35. Geoffrey McNicoll, "The United Nations' Long-Range Population Projections," *Population and Development Review* 18, no. 2 (1992): 333–40.

36. Mark R. Montgomery, "The Urban Transformation of the Developing World," *Science* 319, no. 5864 (2008): 761–64.

37. McNicoll, "The United Nations' Long-Range Population Projections."

38. Ian Johnson, "China's Great Uprooting: Moving 250 Million into Cities," *The New York Times,* June 15, 2013, http://www.nytimes.com/2013/06/16/world /asia/chinas-great-uprooting-moving-250-million-into-cities.html.

39. See Richard Burdett and Deyan Sudjic, eds., *The Endless City: The Urban Age Project by the London School of Economics and Deutsche Bank's Alfred Herrhausen Society* (London: Phaidon, 2007); and Ricky Burdett, Deyan Sudjic, and Omer Cavusoglu, eds., *Living in the Endless City* (London: Phaidon, 2011).

40. Casalegno and Mitchell, *Connected Sustainable Cities.*

Chapter 2: Glimpsing the Future

1. Stewart Brand, *How Buildings Learn: What Happens after They're Built* (New York: Penguin, 1994).

2. Robert G. Eccles, Amy C. Edmondson, Susan Thyne, and Tiona Zuzul, "Living PlanIT," Harvard Business School Case 410-081, February 2010 (revised November 2013).

3. General Motors. Accessed January 4, 2015, http://en.wikipedia.org/wiki /General_Motors.

4. Remote diagnostics. Accessed January 4, 2015, http://en.wikipedia.org/wiki /Remote_diagnostics.

5. "Microsoft and McLaren Electronic Systems Win Race to Provide Electronic Technology to the FIA Formula One World Championship for 2008 to 2010," Microsoft website, December 11, 2006, http://news.microsoft .com/2006/12/11/microsoft-and-mclaren-electronic-systems-win-race-to -provide-electronic-technology-to-the-fia-formula-one-world-champion ship-for-2008-to-2010.

6. Eccles, Edmondson, Thyne, and Zuzul, "Living PlanIT."

Chapter 3: Bits and Bytes

1. Amy C. Edmondson, *Teaming to Innovate* (San Francisco: Jossey-Bass, 2013).

2. Paul Graham, *The 18 Mistakes That Kill Startups* (blog), October 1 2006, http:// www.paulgraham.com/startupmistakes.html.

3. Dan Frost, "How to Be a Great Developer," Creative Bloq website, June 11, 2012, http://www.creativebloq.com/design/how-be-great-developer-6126259.

4. "Christian Heilmann" (interview), Creative Bloq website, November 4, 2009, http://www.creativebloq.com/netmag/christian-heilmann-11097140.

5. Tracy Kidder, *The Soul of a New Machine* (Boston: Little, Brown, 1981).

6. Walter Isaacson, *Steve Jobs* (New York: Simon & Schuster, 2011).

7. Jia Wu, " January 5, 2009, http://research.microsoft.com/en-us/news/asia /features/ciw_mscorpculture.aspx.

8. Mark Prigg, "Sir Jonathan Ive: The iMan Cometh," *Evening Standard,* March 12, 2012, http://www.standard.co.uk/lifestyle/london-life/sir-jonathan-ive -the-iman-cometh-7562170.html.

9. Frost, "How to Be a Great Developer."

10. Frank Gillett, "Internet of Things: Software Platforms Will Become the Rage in 2015," ZDNet, November 13, 2014, http://www.zdnet.com/internet-of -things-software-platforms-will-become-the-rage-in-2015-7000035783.

11. Wim Elfrink, "The Smart-City Solution," McKinsey website, October 2012, http://www.mckinsey.com/insights/public_sector/the_smart-city_solution.

12. Ibid.

13. Smart Cities Market by Smart Home, Intelligent Building Automation, Energy Management, Smart Healthcare, Smart Education, Smart Water, Smart Transportation, Smart Security, & by Services—Worldwide Market Forecasts and Analysis (2014–2019). Marketsandmarkets.com, January 2015, http:// www.marketsandmarkets.com/Market-Reports/smart-cities-market-542 .html.

14. John Vidal, "Masdar City—a Glimpse of the Future in the Desert," *The Guardian*, April 26, 2011, http://www.theguardian.com/environment/2011 /apr/26/masdar-city-desert-future. See also http://travel.cnn.com/korea -8city-tourism-hub-incheon-789461 and http://www.urenio.org/2012/09/13 /indias-ambitious-plans-for-7-new-smart-cities-across-the-delhi-mumbai -industrial-corridor.

15. Jacquelyn Smith, "The World's Most Sustainable Companies," Forbes.com, January 23, 2013, http://www.forbes.com/sites/jacquelynsmith/2013/01/23 /the-worlds-most-sustainable-companies/3.

16. Amy C. Edmondson and Tiona Zuzul, "The Advocacy Trap: When Leaders' Legitimacy Building Inhibits Organizational Learning," Harvard Business School Working Paper 11-099, September 17, 2015.

17. Ibid.

18. Smith, "The World's Most Sustainable Companies."

19. Amy C. Edmondson, *Teaming to Innovate* (San Francisco: Jossey-Bass, 2013).

Chapter 4: Location, Location, Innovation

1. Adrian Wyatt, "Adrian Wyatt, OBE on Climate Change at Ecobuild 2012" (video), August 1, 2012, https://www.youtube.com/watch?v=aiW0mFgJoI0.

2. Russell Lynch, "Spotlight On . . . Adrian Wyatt, Quintain Founder and Chief Executive," *Independent*, May 25, 2012, http://www.independent.co.uk /news/people/news/spotlight-on-adrian-wyatt-quintain-founder-and-chief -executive-7786219.html.

3. Jock Herron, Amy C. Edmondson, and Robert G. Eccles, "Beyond Platinum: Making the Case for Titanium Buildings," in *Constructing Green: Sustainability and the Places We Inhabit,* ed. Rebecca Henn and Andrew Hoffman (Boston: MIT Press, 2013).

4. Rollins Sports Hall of Fame Roster (1989), Rollins College website, accessed November 6, 2015, http://www.rollinssports.com/ViewArticle .dbml?ATCLID=1549231.

5. "Nothing but Net," Lehigh University website, accessed November 6, 2015, http://www1.lehigh.edu/news/nothing-net.

6. Regina Raiford, "Stanley Gale—Chairman and Chief Operating Officer, Gale & Wentworth, Florham Park, NJ," Buildings.com, December 3, 2001, from http://www.buildings.com/article-details/articleid/486/title/stanley-gale -chairman-and-chief-operating-officer-gale-wentworth-florham-park-nj .aspx.

7. Henry Odeniran and Jeff Leighton, "Real Estate: Exclusive Developer Interview with LCOR Executive Vice President Bill Hard," Metro Business Media, January 6, 2012, http://www.metrobusinessmedia.com/article/real -estate-exclusive-developer-interview-lcor-executive-vice-president-bill -hard-010612 (emphasis added).

8. Sarah Jane Johnston, "Real Estate: The Most Imperfect Asset," Harvard Business School website, August 30, 2004, http://hbswk.hbs.edu/item/4342 .html.

9. Odeniran and Leighton, "Real Estate: Exclusive Developer Interview with Bill Hard."

10. Morgan Brennan, "The Last Master Builder," Forbes.com, March 7, 2012, http://www.forbes.com/forbes/2012/0326/billionaires-12-united-states -stephen-ross-new-york-related-companies-developer-master-builder.html.

11. Daiwa House Group website, accessed October 29, 2015, http://www.daiwa house.co.jp/English/greetings/index.html.

12. City Developments Limited website, accessed October 29, 2015, http://www .cdl.com.sg/app/cdl/index.xml.

13. "Environmental Stewardship," Prologis website, accessed October 29, 2015, http://www.prologis.com/en/corporate-responsibility/environmental -stewardship.html.

14. "About Stockland," Stockland website, accessed October 29, 2015, http://www .stockland.com.au/about-stockland.htm.

15. "CapitaDNA," CapitaLand website, accessed October 29, 2015, http://www .capitaland.com/about-capitaland/capitadna.

16. John D. Kasarda and Greg Lindsay, *Aerotropolis: The Way We'll Live Next* (New York: Farrar, Straus and Giroux, 2011).

17. Don Southerton, "Songdo IBD—An Aerotropolis," February 27, 2011, http:// www.songdoibdcitytalk.com/blog/?tag=stan-gale.

18. Dan Frommer, "Sim City: Inside South Korea's $35 Billion Plan to Build a City from Scratch," ReadWrite, July 31, 2012, http://readwrite.com/2012/07/31 /sim-city-inside-south-koreas-35-billion-plan-to-build-a-city-from -scratch#awesm=~oeqMHdTBgdQJ9D.

19. Ava Kofman, "Les Simerables," *Jacobin*, accessed October 29, 2015, https:// www.jacobinmag.com/2014/10/les-simerables/.

20. Ibid.

Chapter 5: Rethinking City Hall

1. We are grateful to reviewer Josh O'Connor, an urban planner and infrastructure specialist, for this insight.

2. IBM Smarter Cities, "How to Reinvent a City: Mayors' Lessons from the Smarter Cities Challenge" (white paper), January 2013, http://smartercities challenge.org/scc/executive_reports/IBM-SCC-How-to-Reinvent-a-City -Jan-2013-v2.pdf.

3. GDF Suez, "Smart City Dashboard: Visibility and Simplicity in a Complex World" (brochure), September 2012, http://www.engie.com/wp-content /uploads/2012/10/smartcity_EN.pdf.

4. Ben Rooney, "Portuguese Smart City Wins WEF Global Award," *Wall Street Journal,* September 5, 2011, http://blogs.wsj.com/tech-europe/2011/09/05 /portuguese-smart-city-wins-wef-global-award.

5. "Making Europe's Cities Smarter" (news release), November 26, 2013, http:// europa.eu/rapid/press-release_IP-13-1159_en.htm?locale=FR.

6. European Innovation Partnership on Smart Cities and Communities, *Operational Implementation Plan: First Public Draft,* accessed October 29, 2015, http://ec.europa.eu/eip/smartcities/files/operational-implementation -plan-oip-v2_en.pdf.

7. International City/County Management Association, "Local Government Management: It's the Career for You!," 2003, accessed October 29, 2015, http:// www.momanagers.org/pdf_files/Careers.pdf.

8. Ibid.

9. Katie Nihill and Lisa D. Williams, "Careers in State and Local Government," 2009, http://hls.harvard.edu/content/uploads/2008/06/statelocal_09.pdf.

Chapter 6: Grounded Visionaries

1. Robert G. Eccles, Amy C. Edmondson, and Dilyana Karadzhova, "Arup: Building the Water Cube," Harvard Business School Case 410-054, February 2010 (revised June 2010).

2. For a fuller discussion of the implications of well-understood work, see chapter 1 of Amy C. Edmondson, *Teaming: How Organizations Learn, Innovate, and Compete in the Knowledge Economy* (San Francisco: Jossey-Bass, 2012).

3. For example, see Tracy Kidder, *House* (New York: Houghton Mifflin, 1999).

4. James Woudhuysen, Ian Abley, Stefan Muthesius, and Miles Glendinning, *Why Is Construction So Backward?* (Chichester: Wiley-Academy, 2004).

5. US Census Bureau, "December 2103 Construction at $930.5 Billion Annual Rate" (news release), February 3, 2014, https://www.census.gov/const/C30/release.pdf.

6. John F. Kennedy, "Technological and Investment Reasons to Require Net-Zero Energy Today" (white paper), 2010, http://images.autodesk.com/adsk/files/whitepaper_investing_in_net-zero_energy_final.pdf.

7. Jock Herron, Amy C. Edmondson, and Robert G. Eccles, "Beyond Platinum: Making the Case for Titanium Buildings," in *Constructing Green: Sustainability and the Places We Inhabit,* ed. Rebecca Henn and Andrew Hoffman (Boston: MIT Press, 2013).

8. Modular Building Institute, *Improving Construction Efficiency & Productivity with Modular Construction* (white paper), accessed November 6, 2015, http://www.modular.org/marketing/documents/Whitepaper_Improving ConstructionEfficiency.pdf.

9. Robert E. Chapman and David T. Butry, "Measuring and Improving the Productivity of the US Construction Industry: Issues, Challenges, and Opportunities," National Institute of Standards and Technology, July 17, 2008, http://www.researchgate.net/publication/237214517_Measuring_and _Improving_the_Productivity_of_the_U.S._Construction_Industry_Issues _Challenges_and_Opportunities.

10. Ibid.

11. Tomio Geron, "Webcor Moves Construction Industry to the Cloud," Forbes .com, August 21, 2013, http://www.forbes.com/sites/tomiogeron/2013/08/21 /webcor-moves-construction-industry-to the-cloud.

12. "A Second Look at Green Buildings: The Rise of Certifications around the World," Institute for Building Efficiency website, August 2011, http://www .institutebe.com/Green-Net-Zero-Buildings/green-buildings-second-look .aspx.

13. Herbert Applebaum, *Construction Workers, U.S.A.* (Westport, CT: Greenwood Press, 1999).

14. Ibid., 1.

15. Ibid., 2.

16. Ibid., 2.

17. "World Construction Aggregates," Freedonia website, January 2012, http:// www.freedoniagroup.com/industry-study/2838/world-construction-aggre gates.htm.

18. Geoffrey McNicoll, "The United Nations' Long-Range Population Projections," *Population and Development Review* 18, no. 2 (1992): 333–40.

19. Mike Hower, "Global Market for Zero Net Energy Buildings to Reach $240 Million by 2018," Sustainable Brands website, November 19, 2014, http://www.sustainablebrands.com/news_and_views/cleantech/mike_hower/global_market_zero_net_energy_buildings_reach_2397_million_2018.

20. "The Business Case for Green Building," US Green Building Council website, February 10, 2015, http://www.usgbc.org/articles/business-case-green-building.

21. US General Services Administration Public Buildings Service, "Green Building Performance: A Post Occupancy Evaluation of 22 GSA Buildings," August 2011, http://www.gsa.gov/graphics/pbs/Green_Building_Performance.pdf.

22. For a recent review of advances in building control technology, see the report by real estate services firm Jones Lang LaSalle, "The Changing Face of Smart Buildings: The Op-Ex Advantage," accessed December 2, 2015, http://www.joneslanglasalle.com/MediaResources/AM/Email/Chicago/Corporate%20Solutions%20Marketing/EIUJLLSmartBldgsFINALhires.pdf.

23. Antonio Regalado, "Who Coined 'Cloud Computing'?" *MIT Technology Review,* October 31, 2011, http://www.technologyreview.com/news/425970/who-coined-cloud-computing.

24. Tom Randall, "The Smartest Building in the World: Inside the Connected Future of Architecture," Bloomberg Business website, September 23, 2015, http://www.bloomberg.com/features/2015-the-edge-the-worlds-greenest-building.

25. Ibid.

26. Ibid.

27. Frank Gehry at an October 2012 press event at the Center for Architecture in New York City.

28. Rick Robinson, "The New Architecture of Smart Cities," The Urban Technologist website, September 26, 2012, http://theurbantechnologist.com/2012/09/26/the-new-architecture-of-smart-cities.

29. Ibid.

30. "Residential Construction Contractors Industry Profile," First Research website, accessed October 29, 2015, http://www.firstresearch.com/Industry-Research/Residential-Construction-Contractors.html.

Chapter 7: The Organization Man Revisited

1. Max Weber, *The Protestant Ethic and the Spirit of Capitalism,* 2nd Roxbury ed. (Los Angeles: Roxbury, 1998).

2. Eduardo Porter, "Motivating Corporations to Do Good," *New York Times,* July 15, 2014, http://www.nytimes.com/2014/07/16/business/the-do-good -corporation.html?_r=1.

3. See, for example, Amy C. Edmondson, *Teaming: How Organizations Learn, Innovate, and Compete in the Knowledge Economy* (San Francisco: Jossey-Bass, 2012).

4. William H. Whyte, *The Organization Man* (New York: Simon and Schuster, 1956), 213.

5. Ryan Matthews and Watts Wacker, "Deviants, Inc.," *Fast Company,* February 28, 2002, http://www.fastcompany.com/44620/deviants-inc.

6. "The Innovation Imperative: Interview with Steve Lewis, CEO and Founder, Living PlanIT," *The Economist,* December 12, 2013, http://europesenergy future.economist.com/innovation-imperative-2.

7. "What Is Agile Software Development?" Agile Alliance website, accessed October 29, 2015, http://www.agilealliance.org/the-alliance/what-is-agile.

8. Robert Safian, "Generation Flux: Baratunde Thurston," *Fast Company,* January 9, 2012, http://www.fastcompany.com/1806751/generation-flux -baratunde-thurston, 2014/04/03.

9. Andrea Ovans, "What Is a Business Model?" *Harvard Business Review,* January 23, 2015, https://hbr.org/2015/01/what-is-a-business-model.

10. Amy C. Edmondson, *Teaming to Innovate* (San Francisco: Jossey-Bass, 2013).

11. Marco Iansiti and Roy Levien, *The Keystone Advantage: What the New Dynamics of Business Ecosystems Mean for Strategy, Innovation, and Sustainability* (Boston: Harvard Business School Press, 2004).

12. Nick Vivion, "The Internet of Things and Travel: London City Airport Takes Off," Tnooz.com, http://www.tnooz.com/article/the-internet-of-things-and -travel-london-city-airport-takes-off.

13. "Milligan and Living PlanIT to Lead the World's First 'Smart Airport Experience' with London City Airport" (news release), Milligan Retail website, April 2014, http://www.milliganretail.com/media/9845/press-release_worlds -first-smart-airport-experience-at-london-city-airport_25march13_sr -_2_.pdf.

14. Daisy Carrington, "London to Create Airport of the Future with 'Internet of Things,' CNN.com, May 2, 2013, http://www.cnn.com/2013/05/02/travel /london-city-airport-internet-of-things.

Chapter 8: Confronting Culture Clash

1. Deborah Dougherty, "Interpretive Barriers to Successful Product Innovation in Large Firms," *Organization Science* 3, no. 2 (1992): 179–207.

2. Seminal research by Stanford professor Lee Ross identifies a psychological phenomenon called the actor-observer bias, along with the fundamental attribution error, both of which describe the spontaneous human tendency to interpret others' actions in a less favorable light compared with one's own actions.

3. For more information about Gehry Technologies, see http://www.gehry technologies.com/en/services/.

4. The earliest known reference to the term *T-shaped skills* can be found in a 1991 article in the London *Independent:* David Guest, "The Hunt Is On for the Renaissance Man of Computing," *The Independent,* September 17, 1991. It has been elaborated and discussed at length by Dorothy Leonard-Barton and Marco Iansiti and others at Harvard Business School.

5. Dorothy Leonard-Barton, *Wellsprings of Knowledge: Building and Sustaining the Sources of Innovation* (Boston: Harvard Business School Press, 1995); and Marco Iansiti, *Technology Integration: Making Critical Choices in a Dynamic World* (Boston: Harvard Business School Press, 1997).

6. See Amy C. Edmondson and Diana McLain Smith, "Too Hot to Handle? How to Manage Relationship Conflict," *California Management Review* 49, no. 1 (2006): 6–31.

7. Robert J. Robinson, Dacher Keltner, Andrew Ward, and Lee Ross, "Actual versus Assumed Differences in Construal: 'Naive Realism' in Intergroup Perception and Conflict," *Journal of Personality and Social Psychology* 68, no. 3 (1995): 405.

8. Lee Ross, "The False Consensus Effect": An Egocentric Bias in Social Perception and Attribution Processes," *Journal of Experimental Social Psychology* 13, no. 3 (1977): 279–301.

9. Amy C. Edmondson, "Making It Safe to Team," in *Teaming: How Organizations Learn, Innovate, and Compete in the Knowledge Economy* (San Francisco: Jossey-Bass, 2012).

10. For earlier research that helped lay the foundation for this study, see Faaiza Rashid and Amy C. Edmondson, "Risky Trust: How Multi-entity Teams Develop Trust in a High Risk Endeavor," in *Restoring Trust,* eds. Roderick Kramer and Todd Pittinsky (New York: Oxford University Press), 129–50; and Robert G. Eccles, Amy C. Edmondson, and Dilyana Karadzhova, "Arup: Building the Water Cube," Harvard Business School Case 410-054, February 2010 (revised June 2010).

11. Edmondson and Smith, "Too Hot to Handle?"

12. Faaiza Rashid, Amy C. Edmondson, and Herman B. Leonard, "Leadership Lessons from the Chilean Mine Rescue," *Harvard Business Review,* July–August 2013, 91, 113–19.

13. Paul R. Carlile, "A Pragmatic View of Knowledge and Boundaries: Boundary Objects in New Product Development," *Organization Science* 13, no. 4 (2002): 442–45; and Beth A. Bechky, "Sharing Meaning across Occupational Communities: The Transformation of Understanding on a Production Floor," *Organization Science* 14, no. 3 (2003): 312–30.

14. Amy C. Edmondson, Sydney Ribot, and Mary Saunders, "Building Innovation at Terrapin Bright Green," Harvard Business School Case 613-053, March 2013 (revised May 2013); and Glen David Kuecker, "Building the Bridge to the Future: New Songdo City from a Critical Urbanism Perspective," University of London Working Paper 85159, June 5, 2013, https://www.soas.ac.uk /koreanstudies/overseas-leading-university-programmes/soas-aks-working -papers-in-korean-studies-ii/file85159.pdf.

15. Amy C. Edmondson, Sydney Ribot, and Tiona Zuzul, "Designing a Culture of Collaboration at Lake Nona Medical City," Harvard Business School Case 613-022, October 2012.

16. Ibid.

17. In geology, *faults* are cracks in the earth's crust that result from differential motion within the crust, and *fault lines* are areas of intense pressure and heat, with the potential to erupt into earthquakes, volcanic activity, or tidal waves. We refer instead to boundaries in organizations that, if not communicating well, have the potential to give rise to serious divisions in the firm and lost potential. See Dora C. Lau and J. Keith Murnighan, "Interactions within Groups and Subgroups: The Effects of Demographic Faultlines." *Academy of Management Journal* 48, no. 4 (2005): 645–59.

18. Edmondson and Smith, "Too Hot to Handle?"

19. Robert G. Eccles, Amy C. Edmondson, and Dilyana Karadzhova, "Arup: Building the Water Cube," Harvard Business School Case 410-054, February 2010 (revised June 2010).

20. Rashid and Edmondson, "Risky Trust."

Chapter 9: Balancing Influence and Innovation

1. Mireya Espinoza, "Frost & Sullivan Congratulates Living PlanIT for Growth and Leadership in IoT and Smart City Markets," Frost & Sullivan website, September 2, 2014, http://www.best-practices.frost-multimedia-wire.com /livingplanit-14.

2. Howard E. Aldrich and C. Marlene Fiol, "Fools Rush In? The Institutional Context of Industry Creation," *The Academy of Management Review* 19, no. 4 (1994): 645–70.

3. Robert Strand, "Strategic Leadership of Corporate Sustainability," *Journal of Business Ethics* 123, no. 4 (2014): 687–706.

4. Aldrich and Ruef note that many entrepreneurs spend much of their time giving speeches or connecting with prestigious individuals or companies. See Howard E. Aldrich and Martin Ruef, *Organizations Evolving*, 2nd ed. (London: Sage, 2006).

5. Amy C. Edmondson and Tiona Zuzul, "The Advocacy Trap: When Leaders' Legitimacy Building Inhibits Organizational Learning," Harvard Business School Working Paper 11-099, September 17, 2015.

6. Ibid.

7. This idea is consistent with research on the advocacy effect by Cialdini in Robert Cialdini, *Influence: Science and Practice,* 4th ed. (Boston: Allyn and Bacon, 2001), which shows that spokespersons for an argument become closed to disconfirming evidence by virtue of being asked to defend even a randomly assigned viewpoint.

8. See "Moura Dubeux Creates Company to Perform Project of 15 Million Square Meters," Grandes Construções website, https://translate.google.com /translate?hl=en&sl=pt&u=http://www.grandesconstrucoes.com.br/br/index .php%3Foption%3Dcom_conteudo%26task%3DviewNoticia%26id%3 D4423&prev=search.

9. Adam Greenfield, *Against the Smart City* (Part 1 of *The City Is Here for You to Use*), Do Projects, 1.3 ed. (New York: Amazon Digital Services, 2013).

10. Regina Raiford, "Stanley Gale—Chairman and Chief Operating Officer, Gale & Wentworth, Florham Park, NJ," Buildings.com, December 3, 2001, from http://www.buildings.com/article-details/articleid/486/title/stanley-gale -chairman-and-chief-operating-officer-gale-wentworth-florham-park -nj.aspx.

Epilogue: What the Future Holds

1. Stephanie Garlock, "Why the Internet of Things Is Big Business," *Harvard Magazine,* July-August 2015, http://harvardmagazine.com/2015/07/why-the -internet-of-things-is-big-business.

2. For the latest updates, see http://living-planit.com/news.html.

Index

Acknowledgments

First we want to thank the people at Living PlanIT, who allowed us to study their young company, opening the door for all of us to learn from their adventures. We are grateful for their enthusiasm and time. We also wish to thank the Division of Research at Harvard Business School for the generous financial support that funded the several years of research reported in this book.

Tiona Zuzul—a doctoral student at Harvard when we started the project and now a professor at London Business School—was a full collaborator in the field research reported in this book. Tiona conducted many of the interviews at Living PlanIT and did much of the analytical work to help identify themes and examples to illustrate them. In particular, the ideas fleshed out in chapter 9 on the challenges of simultaneously influencing and innovating comprise joint work with Amy Edmondson, as cited in that chapter. The book's thinking about the significance of nascent industries, discussed in chapters 1 and 3, draws heavily from Tiona's dissertation research.

Steve Piersanti at Berrett-Koehler (BK) played an indispensable role in shaping our work. We are grateful for his coherent, appreciative, and experienced thinking about what this book could become. In a series of thoughtful conversations over several months, much like a graduate school seminar conducted by telephone—and every bit as demanding—Steve pushed us to sharpen our ideas and focus our narrative and message. Our title, *Building the Future*, emerged in one of those early sessions to clarify the book's core purpose; our subtitle took shape later, in a spontaneous brainstorming session in a sunny BK conference room with Steve, Charlotte Ashlock, Michael Crowley, and Neal Maillet. Thanks also to

Ed Schein who first suggested that we talk to BK, with its inspiring mission of helping "create a world that works for all."

Charlotte Chang and Sydney Ribot provided superb research assistance in the early years of this study, particularly in conducting much background research on smart cities and on the different industry domains explored in the book. Natalie Bartlett managed references, permissions, and many of the other endless details that go into a project like this with skill, precision, and remarkable good cheer. Thanks also to Josh O'Connor, Molly Thomas, and Nic Albert—reviewers wisely chosen by Berrett-Koehler. Their insightful and thorough comments on the manuscript greatly strengthened the book.

Our husbands, George Daley and Douglas Harp, were endlessly patient as we grappled with ambiguous data from our multiyear study and put more and more time into writing. Words cannot fully express our love and gratitude.

Finally, we thank our children—Jack and Nick Daley and Sam, Ellie, and Amelia Reynolds—for giving us space and encouragement to shed light on the promise and perils of audacious innovation. We are profoundly aware that their lives, even more than ours, will be shaped by the courage, creativity, and determination of today's future-builders.

About the Authors

Evgenia Eliseeva

Amy C. Edmondson

Nearing graduation from Harvard College three decades ago, Amy Edmondson took a leap of faith and wrote a letter to a personal hero, seeking advice about employment. To her surprise Buckminster Fuller wrote back. His letter arrived barely a week later with far more than advice. The legendary inventor, architect, and futurist offered her a job. Spending the next three years as Fuller's "chief engineer," trying to keep up with the peripatetic octogenarian while running calculations for new geodesic projects and producing old-fashioned engineering drawings with pencil and paper (just before personal computers and well before affordable CAD/CAM software), Amy developed an intense and enduring interest in innovation in the built environment. Fuller was a passionate future-builder, whose ideas about the built environment outpaced reality by decades. His remarkable legacy did not answer the question of how visionaries can make practical progress in the world.

Today, as the Novartis professor of leadership and management at the Harvard Business School, Amy studies leaders seeking to make a positive difference in the world through the work they do in organizations of all kinds. The research described in this book was an opportunity to blend her early interests in the built environment and her later studies in organizational behavior. She has been on the Harvard faculty since 1996 and teaches courses in leadership, teaming, and organizational learning.

Amy's writings have been published in *Harvard Business Review* and *California Management Review,* as well as in academic journals such as *Administrative Science Quarterly* and the *Academy of Management Journal.* Before her academic career, she was director of research at Pecos

River Learning Centers, where she worked with CEO Larry Wilson to design and implement change programs in large companies. In this role she discovered a passion for understanding how leaders can build organizations as places where people can learn, grow, and contribute to making a better world.

Amy's prior books—*Teaming: How Organizations Learn, Innovate, and Compete in the Knowledge Economy* (San Francisco: Jossey-Bass, 2012) and *Teaming to Innovate* (San Francisco: Jossey-Bass, 2013)—explore the challenges and opportunities of teamwork in dynamic, unpredictable work environments. Her first book, *A Fuller Explanation: The Synergetic Geometry of R. Buckminster Fuller* (Cambridge, MA: Birkhäuser Boston, 1987), clarifies Fuller's mathematical contributions for a nontechnical audience.

Her awards include the Accenture Award for significant contribution to improving the practice of management in 2004, and the Academy of Management's Cummings Award for midcareer achievement in 2006. In 2011, 2013, and 2015, she was selected for the biannual Thinkers50 list of the most influential thinkers in management, and in 2013 she was seventh on *HR Magazine*'s list of the 20 Most Influential International Thinkers in Human Resources. Amy received her PhD in organizational behavior, her AM in psychology, and her AB in engineering and design—all from Harvard University. She lives in Cambridge, Massachusetts, with her husband, George Daley, and their two teenage sons.

Susan Salter Reynolds

Ben DeFlorio Photography

Susan Salter Reynolds was a columnist and staff writer for the *Los Angeles Times* for 25 years, writing profiles of thought leaders, cultural figures, innovators, writers, and artists. She was also book critic for the *Los Angeles Times Book Review* and wrote a weekly column titled *Discoveries* and a biweekly feature titled *The Writing Life*. One of the writers she most enjoyed profiling was Tracy Kidder, author of *The Soul of a New Machine*. That book, which inspired so many innovators in her own generation, is one of the best examples of literary nonfiction, a form that combines human stories with primary data and deep insight into a particular corner of the universe.

The joy for readers of this form lies not only in the learning but also in the identification with the protagonists—their faults and talents. Books, with their insistence on separation from the cacophony of modern life and their relatively slow delivery of information, are ideal machines for percolating ideas. This is what fueled Susan's interest in teaming up on this book.

Susan received her BA in English from Middlebury College and did graduate studies in economics and political science at the University of California, Davis. She spent six years in New York City in the nonprofit world as the publications director for the Natural Resources Defense Council and at the Carnegie Council for Ethics in International Affairs, where she was publications director and editor of its quarterly journal, *Ethics & International Affairs*. After Carnegie she was an assistant editor at *The New York Review of Books*. She has edited several books, including Amy Edmondson's *Teaming to Innovate*.

She lives in New England with her husband, Douglas Harp, and has three children, Sam, Ellie, and Amelia, scattered around the globe, all of them destined for greatness and joy.

Amy and Susan have known each other since high school. Writing a book together was a true and long-awaited pleasure.

Berrett–Koehler
Publishers

Connecting people and ideas
to create a world that works for all

Dear Reader,

Thank you for picking up this book and joining our worldwide community of Berrett-Koehler readers. We share ideas that bring positive change into people's lives, organizations, and society.

To welcome you, we'd like to offer you a free e-book. You can pick from among twelve of our bestselling books by entering the promotional code **BKP92E** here: http://www.bkconnection.com/welcome.

When you claim your free e-book, we'll also send you a copy of our e-newsletter, the *BK Communiqué*. Although you're free to unsubscribe, there are many benefits to sticking around. In every issue of our newsletter you'll find

- A free e-book
- Tips from famous authors
- Discounts on spotlight titles
- Hilarious insider publishing news
- A chance to win a prize for answering a riddle

Best of all, our readers tell us, "Your newsletter is the only one I actually read." So claim your gift today, and please stay in touch!

Sincerely,

Charlotte Ashlock
Steward of the BK Website

Questions? Comments? Contact me at bkcommunity@bkpub.com.

Certified

Corporation
bcorporation.net